Public Management and Governance

Government is topical once again. After many years of speculation that the market could take over much of its role, strong and democratic government is now widely seen as critically important to society. Moreover, the quality of public services is a major electoral issue in most countries around the world.

This major textbook examines what it means to have efficient management and good quality services in the public sector and how public sector performance can be improved. Furthermore, it explores how the process of governing needs to be fundamentally altered if a government is to retain public trust and make better use of society's resources.

Key themes covered include:

- the challenges and pressures which governments experience in an international context;
- the changing functions of modern government in the global economy;
- the 'mixed economy' of public, voluntary and private service provision;
- the new concern with public governance issues such as public engagement, the equalities agenda and ethics.

Public Management and Governance is an exciting new textbook for students, featuring contributions from leading names in the field and covering the key topics in depth. The book includes discussion questions, group and individual exercises, case studies and further reading, making it essential reading for all students on specialist undergraduate and postgraduate courses in Public Services Management, Public Administration, Government and Public Policy.

Tony Bovaird is Professor of Strategy and Public Services Management at Bristol Business School. He has published widely in strategic management, public policy evaluation and performance management in the public sector. **Elke Löffler** is Chief Executive of Governance International, and Senior Research Associate at Bristol Business School. She has published widely in public governance and quality management in the public sector.

Public Management and Governance

Edited by Tony Bovaird
and Elke Löffler

Routledge
Taylor & Francis Group

LONDON AND NEW YORK

First published 2003
by Routledge
11 New Fetter Lane, London EC4P 4EE

Simultaneously published in the USA and Canada
by Routledge
29 West 35th Street, New York, NY 10001

Routledge is an imprint of the Taylor & Francis Group

Typeset in Pinched Crown by Florence Production Ltd, Stoodleigh, Devon
Printed and bound in Great Britain by TJ International Ltd, Padstow, Cornwall

British Library Cataloguing in Publication Data
A catalogue record for this book is available from the British Library

Library of Congress Cataloging in Publication Data
Public management and governance / edited by Tony Bovaird and Elke Löffler.
    p. cm.
Includes bibliographical references and index.
1. Public administration.   2. Government productivity.   3. Legitimacy of
governments.   4. Public administration–Citizen participation.   I. Title:
Public management and governance.   II. Bovaird, A. G.   III. Löffler, Elke.
JF1351.P824 2003
351–dc21   2003007032

ISBN 0–415–25245–8 (hbk)
ISBN 0–415–25246–6 (pbk)

Contents

Figures

Tables

Case examples

Contributors

Christine Bellamy is Professor of Public Administration and Head of the Social Sciences Graduate School at the Nottingham Trent University, UK. She has been a leading writer on e-government and e-democracy in Europe over the past ten years, and is a member of several European and international research networks. Her book *Governing in the Information Age* (Open University Press, 1998, co-authored with Professor John Taylor) is a standard text on the subject. Chris Bellamy is the immediate past Chair of the UK Joint University Council, which is the national association for Public Administration, Social Policy and Social Work Education.

Annette Boaz is a Senior Research Fellow in the UK ESRC Centre for Evidence Based Policy and Practice at Queen Mary, University of London, UK. She has carried out research for a wide range of organizations including the Cabinet Office, the Health Development Agency and the Inter-Ministerial Group for Older People. She worked previously at the Universities of Oxford and Warwick and was seconded recently to the Policy Research Programme at the UK Department of Health. She is currently working on issues relating to methodology development.

Geert Bouckaert is Professor of Public Management and Director of the Public Management Institute at the Faculty of Social Sciences at the Katholieke Universiteit Leuven in Leuven, Belgium. He is also the Co-ordinator of the Policy Research Centre for Governmental Organizations in Flanders. His main research interests are in performance management, public sector productivity measurement, quality management and financial management techniques in the public sector.

Tony Bovaird is Professor of Strategy and Public Services Management at Bristol Business School, University of the West of England, UK. He worked at the Department of the Environment, Birmingham University, and Aston University before joining UWE in 2000. He is director of the national research team which is undertaking a long-term meta-evaluation of the Local Government Modernisation Agenda in the UK on behalf of the Office of the Deputy Prime Minister. He recently authored reports for OECD on the evaluation of e-government and for the Cabinet Office on the evaluation of civil service reforms in the UK.

Mike Broussine is a Principal Lecturer at Bristol Business School, University of the West of England, UK and works with a range of organizations as a researcher and developer. He is Award Leader for UWE's MSc in Leadership and Organization of Public Services, a programme designed to promote learning across the public, private and voluntary sectors. His main research interests are emotions and power in organizations, leadership, gender issues, organizational research methods and public services management.

James L. Chan is Professor of Accounting at the University of Illinois at Chicago, USA, and Consulting Professor at Shanghai University of Finance and Economics and Xiamen University, China. He has written and consulted on public budgeting and accounting issues primarily from an international comparative perspective. He was a member of the US Comptroller General's Research and Education Advisory Panel (1990–2000). He has edited nine volumes of *Research in Governmental and Nonprofit Accounting*.

John Clarke is Professor of Social Policy at the Open University, UK. From a background in cultural studies he has developed a range of research interests around the ways in which welfare states are being transformed. These include: comparative studies, with a particular interest in the USA; the role of managerialism in reforming welfare states; and the significance of audit and evaluative practices in the management of public services. His publications include *The Managerial State: Power, Politics and Ideology in the Remaking of Social Welfare* with Janet Newman (Sage, 1997); and *New Managerialism, New Welfare?* co-edited with Sharon Gewirtz and Eugene McLaughlin (Sage, 2000). He is currently working on a book on the transformation of welfare states.

Howard Davis is Principal Research Fellow and Research Manager at the Local Government Centre, Warwick Business School, University of Warwick, UK. He has undertaken a wide range of local government projects in both Britain and the countries of Central and Eastern Europe. Current research interests include Best Value, the impact of inspection on local government, scrutiny and 'new' political management arrangements, ethics and standards in public life, and the 'freedoms and flexibilities' agenda.

Andrew Erridge is Professor of Public Policy and Management in the School of Policy Studies at the University of Ulster, UK. His main research interest is in public procurement. In recent years he has contributed to the Gershon Review of Civil Government Procurement, advised the National Audit Office on their study on Modernizing Procurement and carried out research for the NAO's Guide to the Audit of Procurement. In 2000 he completed a three-year ESRC-funded research project on UK Central Government Procurement. He has published three books, many book chapters and journal articles, and is a member of the editorial committees of the *European Journal of Purchasing and Supply Management* and the *Journal of Public Procurement*.

Peter M. Jackson is Dean of the University of Leicester Management Centre, UK, and has had a continuing interest in public finance and public sector management for over thirty years. Since starting out on his career as an economist with HM Treasury, he has made a major contribution to debates on public expenditure management and control and on approaches to measuring the performance of public sector organizations. His most recent work focuses on public private partnerships. In 2001 he was appointed as specialist adviser to the Finance Committee of the Scottish Parliament, assisting in its inquiry into the Private Finance Initiative.

Hae-Sang Kwon is currently Head of Division in the Korean Ministry of Planning and Budget whose main tasks are to make the national budget and to reform systems of public management and governance. He worked at the Public Management Service (PUMA) of the OECD as a project manager from 1999 to 2002. He studied economics and national security at the graduate schools of Birmingham University in the UK and Korean National Defense University.

Elke Löffler is Chief Executive of Governance International, a new nonprofit organization in the UK. She is also a Senior Research Associate at the Bristol Business School, University of the West of England, UK. Previously she was a staff member of the Public Management Service (PUMA) of OECD where she worked on performance and inter-governmental management. Prior to joining the OECD, she did international comparative research on administrative modernization while at the Research Institute for Public Administration (FÖV) in Speyer, Germany.

Steve Martin is Professor of Public Policy and Management and Director of the Local and Regional Government Research Unit at Cardiff University, UK. He is directing a series of major studies of current public sector reforms in the UK. He has written widely on public policy and local government management, focusing in particular on service improvement, public engagement and partnership working, and is an adviser to several national government departments and agencies and to many local authorities.

Alex Matheson has been Head of the Budgeting and Management Division of the Public Governance and Territorial Development Directorate of the OECD in Paris since the beginning of 2000, providing research, analysis and policy guidance on public expenditure and public sector management issues. His current work programme covers public sector modernization, performance measures and incentives in budgeting and management, 'distributed governance', leading-edge developments in public sector budgeting and accounting, management control and the prevention of corruption and the learning government. Before coming to the OECD, Alex was, for three years, a Special Adviser on Public Management for the Commonwealth Secretariat based in London, undertaking consultancy seminars in Africa, the Caribbean, South Asia, South East Asia and the South Pacific. Prior to his career in intergovernmental organizations, Alex worked for twenty-five years in the New Zealand Public Service, latterly with responsibility for the second-generation public sector reform agenda. He has published widely on public management issues in international journals and books.

Janet Newman is Professor of Social Policy at the Open University, UK. She has worked extensively with public service managers experiencing the changes introduced within the modernizing reforms of New Labour. She has also undertaken a range of research projects on these reforms, including projects on public service innovation, on partnership working and on public participation. She is the author of *Modernising Governance: New Labour, Policy and Society* (Sage, 2001) and the co-author, with John Clarke, of *The Managerial State: Power, Politics and Ideology in the Remaking of Social Welfare* (Sage, 1997).

Sandra Nutley is Professor of Public Policy and Management at the University of St Andrews, UK. Prior to becoming an academic she worked in local government. She is Co-director of the Centre for Public Policy and Management (CPPM) at St Andrews. She also heads up the ESRC-funded Research Unit for Research Utilization, part of the ESRC UK Network for Evidence-Based Policy and Practice. Her main research interests are in evidence-based policy and practice, the management of change, and performance management. She has published numerous articles and five books, including *What Works? Evidence-based Policy and Practice in Public Services* (with Huw Davies and Peter Smith, The Policy Press, 2000).

Wouter van Dooren is a Research Assistant at the Public Management Institute in the Faculty of Social Sciences at the Katholieke Universiteit Leuven in Leuven, Belgium. He is currently working on his doctoral thesis on supply and demand of performance information in the public sector and has published a number of articles on performance management and measurement in books and journals.

Acknowledgements

The editors and publisher would like to thank the following for permission to use copyright material:

Haufe Publishers for Banner, G. (2002), 'Zehn Jahre Kommunale Verwaltungsmodernisierung – was wurde erreicht und was kommt danach?', *Rechnungswesen und Controlling,* ed. E. Meurer and G. Stephan, Vol. 4, June 2002, pp. 7/313–7/342, Freiburg (Haufe Verlag).

OECD for Tables 3.1 to 3.6. Adapted from OECD *Economic Outlook* No. 68, Issue 2, December 2000; Table 3.1, General government outlays, by country (p. 42), Table 3.2, General government outlays, by economic category: consumption (p. 46), Table 3.3, General government outlays, by economic category: income transfers (p. 52), Table 3.4, General government outlays, by economic category: subsidies (p. 56), Table 3.5, General government outlays, by economic category: net capital outlays (p. 57) and Table 3.6, Gross total social expenditure, 1995, as a percentage of GDP (Atkinson, P. and van den Noord, P. (2001) and no.9220, *Managing Public Expenditure,* and no.8221, OECD Economics Working Paper.

Public Services Network for an extract from *Making or buying? The value of internal service providers in local government,* Entwistle, T., Martin, S. and Enticott, G. (2002); Cardiff University: Local and Regional Government Research Unit, for the Public Services Network.

Office of the Auditor General of Canada, *What we do,* http://www.oag-bvg.gc.ca/domino/other.nsf/html/bodye.html. 2002. Reproduced with the permission of the Minister of Public Works and Government Services, 2003.

Nomos Verlagsgesellschaft, *Developing local governance networks in Europe,* p. 10, Box 1, and pp. 35–36, 2002, Bovaird, T., Löffler, E. and Parrado Diez, S. Reprinted by Permission.

Sage Publications Ltd for Table 13.1, The move from local government to local governance, Bovaird and Löffler (2002), pp. 21–23 (Copyright © International Institute of Administrative Sciences, 2002), reprinted by permission of Sage Publications Ltd.

Blackwell Publishing for Table 13.2, The 'Rhodes typology' of policy networks, Rod Rhodes, (1997), *Understanding governance: policy networks, governance, reflexivity and accountability,* Teaching Politics, 8, 1996: 210–222.

Journal of the American Planning Association, 'The ladder of citizen participation', adapted from S.R. Arnstein (1971), *Journal of the Royal Town Planning Institute,* April, pp. 177–182. Reprinted by permission.

Blackwell Publishing, 'Modes of public participation', Martin, S.J, and Boaz, A. (2000), from Public participation and citizen centred local government: lessons from the best value and better government for older people pilot programmes, *Public Money and Management*, 20 (2), pp. 47–54.

A guide for the reader

AIM OF THE BOOK

This book has been written with the aim of giving readers a clear picture of the current state of play and the most important emerging issues in public management and governance. We intend that it will help students of public issues to be better informed and managers who work in the public domain (whether in public, voluntary or private sectors) to be more effective.

The book is also written to help readers to understand what it means to become better citizens and, as such, to help to change the current practice of public management and governance. In this way, we hope that the ideas in the book will help readers to make a greater contribution to their neighbourhoods, their local authorities, their regions and the countries in which they live – and perhaps even to the quality of life of citizens elsewhere in the world.

STRUCTURE OF THE BOOK

The book comprises three main parts:

1 An *introductory* part, setting out the role of the public sector, public management and public governance, and how these have evolved in recent years in different contexts.
2 A second part on *public management for public sector organizations*, exploring the main managerial functions which contribute to the running of public services.
3 A section on *governance* as an emerging theme in the public domain.

LEARNING OBJECTIVES, CHAPTER BY CHAPTER

Chapter   Learning objectives

This chapter is to help students:
1 ■ To be aware of the different meanings of 'public';
   ■ to understand the main differences between public management and public governance;

- to understand the motives for studying public management and public governance.

2
- To be aware of recent changes in the context of public policy;
- to understand the major paradigm shifts in public policy making in recent decades;
- to understand the changing role of politics in public policy.

3
- To understand the role and scope of government;
- to be aware of the trends in social spending and to understand the forces that shape them;
- to be aware of the changing composition of public spending;
- to understand the implications that these trends have for public sector management.

4
- To be aware of the objectives of the first generation of public sector reforms;
- to be aware of the results of the first generation of public sector reforms;
- to be aware of unresolved problems of the first generation of public sector reforms;
- to understand differences in public sector reform trajectories of OECD governments;
- to be able to undertake a more systemic analysis of public sector reforms.

5
- To understand what 'strategy', and 'strategic management' mean in a public sector context;
- to be able to prepare a corporate strategy and business plan for their service or organization;
- to understand the difference between strategic management and strategic planning;
- to understand how strategy making is different in a politically driven organization, as opposed to strategy making in a private firm;
- to understand how strategic management and innovation mutually reinforce each other.

6
- To understand the role of marketing in a public sector context;
- to be able to prepare a marketing strategy, and marketing plan for their service or organizational unit;
- to understand how marketing is different in a politically driven organization working on issues with wide-ranging public implications, as opposed to marketing in private firms;
- to understand the limitations of marketing in a public sector context.

7
- To understand the meaning of contracting;
- to understand why contracting for services has been increasing over the past twenty-five years;

- to be able to identify the pros and cons of contracting out of specific services;
- to understand the links between contracting, competition and collaboration;
- to understand how contracting could be used to pursue the wider socio-economic goals of government.

8
- To be aware of changes in governmental financial management systems and to understand their underlying conceptual models;
- to understand the context and content of each of the models discussed;
- to understand how each of the models is supported by its underlying disciplines.

9
- To be aware of the changing understanding of the significance of ICTs;
- to be aware of the implications of managerial and institutional change associated with ICTs;
- to understand the need for active policies to minimize the 'digital divide';
- to understand the critical importance of trustworthy processing of personal data.

10
- To be aware of the evolution of performance measurement and management in the public sector;
- to understand the key concepts in performance measurement;
- to understand the key concepts in performance management;
- to understand the main lessons learned in performance management;
- to be able to identify the main traps in performance management.

11
- To be aware of the differences of quality management in the public and private sectors;
- to understand the key issues associated with quality measurement in the public sector;
- to be aware of the major quality assessment instruments used in the public sector;
- to understand the key obstacles to and success factors in quality improvement in the public sector;
- to understand how the quality of public governance might be assessed.

12
- To be aware of the conditions leading to the recent 'audit explosion' in the public sector;
- to understand the new practices of audit;
- to understand the changing roles of scrutiny agencies;
- to understand the problems with and challenges to scrutiny of public sector organizations.

13
- To understand the key concepts of public governance;
- to be aware of how the role of governments is changing from policy making towards policy moderating;
- to be able to identify important stakeholders in public governance;
- to understand networks as a specific mode of public governance.

14
- To be aware of the current emphasis on leadership in public governance;
- to be aware of the history of the study of leadership;
- to understand the differences between leadership and management;
- to understand the interrelationships between leadership, power and politics;
- to be aware of the gender dimension in leadership;
- to understand the key issues in community leadership;
- to understand what leaders need to learn if they are to become effective.

15
- To be aware of the arguments in favour of engagement with service users and citizens;
- to be aware of the main forms of public engagement;
- to be aware of practical approaches to public engagement;
- to understand the obstacles to effective engagement and ways of overcoming these.

16
- To understand the politics of equality, and the different notions of justice that it draws on;
- to understand how far equality and diversity policies may be viewed as simply a matter of 'good business practice';
- to be able to identify the difficulties inherent in translating policy into practice;
- to understand how to rethink equality and diversity in the context of new forms of governance.

17
- To understand the reasons for the current emphasis on ethics and standards of conduct in the public sector;
- to understand the mechanisms by which corruption can operate in the public sector;
- to be aware of the rationale behind the recent move to strengthened codes of conduct in the United Kingdom and elsewhere;
- to understand the pros and cons of control-oriented and prevention-oriented mechanisms to ensure ethical behaviour;
- to understand the role of transparency as a mechanism for fighting unethical behaviour.

18
- To understand what counts as evidence for what purposes;
- to understand how evidence may be used to improve public services;
- to be aware of the obstacles to improved use of evidence;
- to understand how evidence-based learning can be encouraged.

CHAPTER MAP

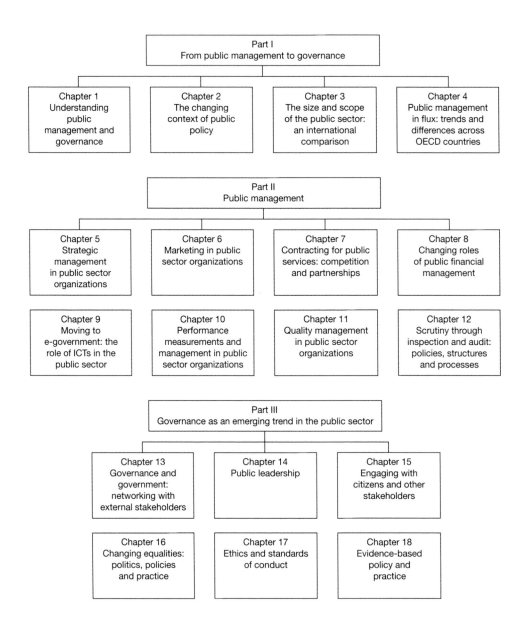

From public management to governance

Part I forms an introduction to the key themes of the book and locates the public sector in its political, social and economic context.

Chapter 1 examines what is 'public' about the public sector and about public services. It distinguishes public management from the wider issues of public governance.

Chapter 2 explores recent changes in the context of public policy, identifies the major paradigm shifts in public policy making in recent decades and examines the changing role of politics in public governance.

Chapter 3 examines the size and scope of the public sector. It compares trends in the size and composition of public expenditure across OECD countries and looks at some of the forces that shape these trends. It then considers the implications of these trends for public sector management.

Chapter 4 examines the objectives and results of the generation of public sector reforms in the 1980s and early 1990s, unresolved problems in these early reforms and the source of the new pressures for 'public governance' reform in OECD countries.

Chapter 1

Understanding public management and governance

Tony Bovaird, Bristol Business School, UK and *Elke Löffler*, Governance International, UK

INTRODUCTION

This book is about public management and public governance. We believe these concepts are fundamentally important to all citizens. Indeed, we shall argue that issues of public management and governance arise in most of the everyday activities which are important in people's lives.

For much of the past hundred years, these subjects were generally felt to be worthy but dull. We aim to show that these labels are no longer accurate.

Actually, issues of public management and public governance are often very surprising – and even exciting (see Box 1.1).

BOX 1.1 PUBLIC MANAGEMENT AND GOVERNANCE ARE EXCITING . . .

Londoners are shaking their heads in disbelief. Ken Livingston's congestion charge has delivered what it promised. Despite the deluge of scepticism and derision beforehand, London has suddenly become navigable; mobility is back. What was allegedly impossible – doing something about endemic traffic congestion – is, instead, with sufficient political will and daring, possible. Political action can change our world for the better. It says much about our impoverished times that I find it hard to think of a recent comparable action that has had such an obvious, instant and beneficial impact on our individual and collective lives, at least for those of us who live and work in London.

Source: Will Hutton, *Observer*, 2 March 2003

We also want to warn readers of this book that it can no longer be taken for granted that the activities of public management and governance are 'worthy' – sometimes they are conducted by 'sharks' rather than by 'suits' (see Box 1.2). Indeed, even when public services are managed by 'suits', the people wearing those suits may seek (and partially achieve) the lifestyle of 'fat cats' rather than 'public servants'.

BOX 1.2 . . . BUT NOT NECESSARILY 'WORTHY'

Congressional crook 'stole his own desk from office'

A former congressman recently jailed on ten charges of racketeering and bribery is now being investigated on suspicion of stealing his congressional office desk.

Just when Congress was adjusting to life without Jim Traficant – famed for his conical hairpiece, polyester flared suits, alleged Mafia connections and habit of ending speeches with the *Star Trek* catchphrase 'Beam me up' – officials are now examining how he comes to be selling a marble and walnut conference table, marked 'Property of the House of Representatives'.

Ex-Republican Traficant is serving eight years in jail for a two-decade career of crime, including demanding bribes, accepting illegal gifts, misusing public funds, tax fraud and forcing public employees to shovel horse manure on his farm.

Source: Extracts from David Rennie, *Daily Telegraph*, 28 November 2002, p. 21

Consequently, nowadays public managers have to earn our respect and gratitude, rather than simply assume it. And the players in the public policy arena have to earn the trust of those for whom they claim to be working, rather than claiming legitimacy simply on the grounds that they were elected or that they are part of a prestigious profession.

LEARNING OBJECTIVES

- To be aware of the different meanings of 'public'
- To understand the main differences between public management and public governance
- To understand the motives for studying public management and public governance

WHAT DO WE MEAN BY 'PUBLIC'?

Before we go any further, we should explore what we mean by 'public'. We start with a clear statement from Ranson and Stewart (1989, p. 10) – see box – as to what constitutes the public domain (they wrote in the context of local government, but their analysis applies quite generally).

This short passage explains how the public domain is the arena in which public choice is exercised in order to achieve a collective purpose. This is the arena which this book explores.

Ranson and Stewart also introduce another meaning of the word 'public' – the group (or groups) of people who inhabit the public domain. They clearly identify the political concept of 'a public which is able to enter into dialogue and decide about the needs of the

WHAT IS THE PUBLIC DOMAIN?

The essential task of the public domain can now be interpreted as enabling authoritative public choice about collective activity and purpose. In short, it is about clarifying, constituting and achieving a public purpose. It [local government] has the ultimate responsibility for constituting a society as a political community which has the capacity to make public choices. Producing a 'public' which is able to enter into dialogue and decide about the needs of the community . . . is the uniquely demanding challenge facing the public domain.

Source: Ranson and Stewart (1989, p. 10)

community', which we might contrast with the marketing concept of different 'publics', each of whom expects to be treated differently by public services and public managers.

Another common usage of 'public' is to distinguish between the 'public sector' and the 'private sector', which essentially revolves around differences of ownership (collective ownership, in the name of all citizens, versus individual ownership) and motive (social purpose versus profit). This meaning is particularly relevant when public managers try to claim that the public sector is different from the private sector, and therefore that private sector management methods would not work in their agency (see Allison (1997) on the concept that public and private management are alike in all unimportant respects!).

However, there are other, wider meanings to 'public'. For example, 'public services' are sometimes delivered by private utilities or contractors, rather than public agencies. Here, the concept of 'public' generally means that the providers have to observe and satisfy some form of 'public service obligation'. Again, 'public issues' are those which cannot simply be left to the decision making of private individuals – they typically necessitate mobilizing the resources of public and voluntary sector organizations or regulating the behaviour of private firms or individuals or groups in civil society.

We shall examine each of these dimensions of 'public' in this book. Consequently, we shall take the word 'public' to be part of the problematic, i.e. the set of issues to be explored in this book, rather than defining it unambiguously at the outset.

PUBLIC MANAGEMENT AND GOVERNANCE: SOME KEY ISSUES

So, what is public management? And what is public governance? While most people will immediately assume that they have a general grasp of what public management entails, fewer will have a feel for what is meant by public governance. Moreover, we want to argue that both concepts actually cover quite a complex set of ideas.

We shall take *public management* to be an approach which uses managerial techniques (often originating in the private sector) to increase the value for money achieved by public services. It therefore covers the set of activities undertaken by managers in two very different contexts:

1   in public sector organizations;
2   in public service organizations, whether in public, voluntary or private sectors.

5

This raises a number of issues which we will consider later:

- What distinguishes 'public management' from 'public administration'?
- What is 'public' about public services?
- Are 'public services' always in the 'public sector'?
- Is public management only about public services?

We take *public governance* to mean 'the way in which stakeholders interact with each other in order to influence the outcomes of public policies'. (You can see other approaches to defining 'governance' in Chapter 13).

The concept of *public governance* raises a different set of questions, such as:

- Who has the right to make and influence decisions in the public realm?
- What principles should be followed in making decisions in the public realm?
- How can we ensure that collective activities in the public realm result in improved welfare for those stakeholders to whom we accord the highest priority?

This chapter addresses these issues and sets the stage for the rest of the book.

Is 'public management' different from public administration?

In the mid-twentieth century, the study of the work of civil servants and other public officials (including their interface with politicians who were involved in legislation and setting public policy) was usually labelled 'public administration'. As such, there is no doubt that 'public administration' conjured up an image of bureaucracy, lifelong secure employment, 'muddling through' and lack of enterprise – dark suits, grey faces and dull day jobs.

From the 1980s onward, however, a new phrase began to be heard, and even achieved dominance in some circles – 'public management'. This was interpreted to mean different things by different authors, but it was almost always characterized by a different set of symbols from those associated with public administration (Clarke and Newman, 1997) – it was thought to be about budget management, not just budget holding (see Chapter 8), a contract culture, including contracts with private sector providers of services (see Chapter 7) and employment contracts for staff, which were for fixed periods and might well not be renewed, entrepreneurship and risk taking, and accountability for performance (see Chapter 10).

These differences can be (and often were) exaggerated. However, it appears that the expectations of many stakeholders in the public domain did alter – they began to expect behaviour more in keeping with the image of the public manager and less that of the public administrator.

What is 'public' about public services?

In everyday discussion, we often refer to 'public services' as though they were 'what the public sector does'. However, a moment's reflection shows that this tidy approach no longer makes sense in most countries nowadays (see Chapter 7).

 6

After all, we have for a long time become used to seeing private firms mending holes in our roads and repairing the council's housing stock. More recently it has become commonplace in many areas to see private firms collecting our bins and running our leisure centres. Moreover, there are very few services which are never run by the private sector in the UK – it is possible to find some places which have private provision of hospitals, schools, child protection, home helps for the elderly and disabled, housing benefit payments, and a local council's Director of Finance. (Indeed, in the UK we even had, for a while, provision of the post of Director-General of the BBC by a private company).

Furthermore, there are some things that are done by the public sector which may cause raised eyebrows if described as 'public services' – such as running a telecommunications company (as the city of Hull did until comparatively recently), or a city centre restaurant (as Coventry did up to the 1980s).

So what *is* public about public services? There is no single answer to this prize question – but neither is there a lack of contenders to win the prize. The answer you come up with is very likely to relate to the discipline in which you were trained and to your ideological position.

For welfare economists, the answer is quite subtle but nevertheless quite precise – public services are those which merit public intervention because of market failure (see Chapter 3). In other words, any good or service which would result in suboptimal social welfare if it were provided in a free market should be regulated in some way by the public sector, and in this way qualifies as a 'public service'.

This definition of 'public services' is attractively rigorous, but unfortunately very wide-ranging. Few services, under this definition, exhibit no degree of 'publicness', since the provision of most goods and services in the real world is subject to market failure for one or more of the common reasons – chronic disequilibrium, imperfect competition, assymetric information in supply or in consumption, externalities, discrimination based on criteria other than cost or technical ability to satisfy user requirements, uncertainty, non-rivalness in consumption, non-excludability in supply, or user ignorance of his or her own best interest. Consequently, this yields a definition of 'public services' which is useful only occasionally – for example, it suggests that all theatres and cinemas are worthy of public intervention (since they are at least partly non-rival in consumption), whereas anyone who has sat through a performance of many Broadway or West End musicals knows that there are real limits to the justifiable level of public subsidy to many theatrical events.

An alternative approach to defining the scope of 'public services' comes from politics. It suggests that 'public services' are those which are important for the re-election of politicians, or, more realistically, of political parties. Where a service is important in political decision making, then its 'publicness' must be respected and it should be subject to political influence. However, the attractive simplicity of this stance has again been bought at the expense of mind-numbing generalization of the sphere of 'public decisions'. There are very few goods or services which are never important electorally. However invisible is the widget in the sprocket in the camshaft in the car which is bought by customers who have no knowledge of or interest in the technical aspects of car manufacture, when it is proposed that a local widget factory should be closed and the widgets should be produced elsewhere (especially if it is 'abroad'), then that widget becomes a 'public good' under this definition.

7

DIFFERENCES BETWEEN THE CONCEPT OF A CITIZEN AND THE CLIENT/CUSTOMER/USER OF PUBLIC SERVICES

A citizen can be defined as a concentration of rights and duties in the person of an individual, within a constitutional state, under the rule of law, and within the hierarchy of laws and regulations.

A client is a concentration of needs and satisfactions of needs in an individual, within a market situation of supply and demands of goods and services, and within a hierarchy of needs, subject to the willingness to pay. A citizen is part of a social contract, whereas the client is part of the market contract.

Source: Pollitt and Bouckaert (1995, p. 6)

A third approach, which similarly sounds like common sense, focuses on all those goods where providers are placed under a 'public service obligation' when they are given the right to supply the service. This approach defines as a public service all those services in which Parliament has decreed a need for regulation. However, this approach probably results in a definition of 'public service' which is too narrow. For example, there is a legal public service obligation imposed on the providers of all electricity, gas and water utilities, and broadcasters, but not on the provision of leisure centres – yet the latter services may form a major part of the quality of life of certain groups, particularly young people and families with young children, and as such may be widely supported by politicians as important services to be provided by the local authority.

What is public governance?

Trying to define public governance seems to open Pandora's box. Even though there is a general acknowledgement that public governance is different from public management, the academic literature on governance (which increases exponentially each year) offers myriad definitions. Indeed, even the authors of different chapters in this volume offer different ideas of what is 'public governance'.

The definition of governance is not, in itself, of crucial importance, particularly because many practitioners are widely familiar with governance in practice, but find it difficult to recognize it in the forms discussed by academics (see Chapter 13). Nevertheless, we have given a definition above, because we believe it is useful in order to focus discussion.

Whereas in new public management a lot of attention was paid to the measurement of results (both individual and organizational) in terms of outputs, public governance pays a lot of attention to how different organizations interact in order to achieve a higher level of desired results – the outcomes achieved by citizens and stakeholders. Moreover, in public governance, the way in which decisions are reached – the processes by which different stakeholders interact – are also seen to have a major importance in themselves, whatever the outputs or outcomes achieved. In other words, the current public governance debate places a new emphasis on the old truths that 'what matters is not what we do, but how people feel about what we do' and that 'processes matter' or, put differently, 'the ends do not justify the means'. These two contrasting emphases make 'good public governance' exceptionally difficult – but they may well represent non-negotiable demands by the public in modern society.

The difference between a managerial and governance approach can be illustrated using the example of clean cities (Case Example 1.1).

CASE EXAMPLE 1.1 **DIFFERENCES BETWEEN MANAGERIAL AND GOVERNANCE APPROACHES**

Whereas public management-oriented change agents tend to focus their efforts on improving street cleaning and refuse collection services, a local governance approach emphasizes the role of citizens in respecting the communal desire that no one should throw litter on the streets in the first place, and that materials should be recycled, not simply thrown away. This involves education (not only in the schools, since 'litter-bugs' come in all sizes and ages), advertising campaigns, encouragement of people to show their disgust when dirty behaviour occurs, and the provision of proper waste facilities (including those for dog waste) which will help to prevent litter and dog-fouling problems from occurring in the first place.

The Cadbury Report defined corporate governance as follows:

Corporate governance is the system by which companies are directed and controlled.

Source: Committee on the Financial Aspects of Corporate Governance (1992), para 2.5

Whereas the governance discussion in the public sector is relatively recent (see Chapter 4), the term *governance* is much more common in the private sector where a debate about corporate governance has been going on for quite some time. *Corporate governance* refers to issues of control and decision-making powers within organizations (not just private companies). The 'corporate governance' debate has been triggered by the increase of the importance of transnational companies – today numbering more than 39,000 – which have experienced problems of unclear lines of accountability.

International organizations such as the OECD have issued guidelines as to how to improve corporate governance. Even though many reforms have been implemented recently in many OECD countries, the fall-out around the recent collapse of Enron in the US shows that corporate governance is not only a matter of drafting a stricter legal framework but also of respecting societal values.

Another long-standing governance debate comes from the field of international relations where the issue of *global governance* has become very topical. In a nutshell, global governance is about how to cope with problems which transcend the borders of nation states (such as air pollution, the sex tourism industry or the exploitation of child workers) given the lack of a world government. Pessimists suggest that globalization means that governments everywhere have become powerless and that managing globalization is an oxymoron, since globalization is shaped by markets, not by governments. Some have suggested that this powerlessness is reinforced by the coming of the Internet age – that there is no governance against the 'electronic herd' (Friedmann, 2000).

However, this pessimistic discourse on global governance was countered by a very different set of arguments put forward by the UN Secretary-General in his Millennium Report – he argued that globalization needs to be 'managed'. This was close to the language used by the Communiqué of the 2000 Ministerial Meeting of the OECD, headlined: 'Shaping Globalization'. Yet others have proposed to 'govern' globalization and 'make it work for the poor' (IMF's Deputy Director, Masood Ahmed) or simply to achieve 'globalization for all' (UNDP Administrator Mark Malloch Brown). The task of the times was 'to get globalizing processes within our control and focus them upon human needs' (Anthony Giddens, LSE). The events following 11 September in New York City have cast a further, more troubled, light on the idea that global activities (such as terrorism) can be 'fought' through collective international action.

Whereas governance is a positivistic concept, analysing 'what is', *good governance* is obviously a normative concept, analysing 'what ought to be'. Even though particular international organizations such as the United Nations and the OECD have excelled in providing rather abstract definitions of the characteristics of 'good governance', we believe that this concept is highly context-dependent. This means that instead of using a simple operational blueprint or definition, the meaning of 'good governance' must be negotiated and agreed upon by the various stakeholders in a geographical area or in a policy network.

'Good governance' raises such issues as:

- stakeholder engagement;
- transparency;
- the equalities agenda (gender, ethnic groups, age, religion, etc.);
- ethical and honest behaviour;
- accountability;
- sustainability.

More importantly, the implementation of all the governance principles agreed upon between stakeholders has to be evaluated – ideally, by those same stakeholders.

What is the role of public management within public governance?

The concepts of public management and public governance are not mutually incompatible with one another. Nevertheless, not all practices of public management are part of public governance, and not all aspects of public governance are part of public management (Bovaird, 2002).

For example, some practices of public management revolve around the best way to provide networks of computer workstations within the offices of a public agency (e.g. a personnel department). There are few public governance dimensions to this decision, which is a decision common to most organizations in all sectors. On the other side, there are issues of co-production of public service between family members and volunteers who come together to look after the welfare of an elderly person who wants to live an independent life in the community, but with enough support to ensure that no personal disasters occur. This is an issue in public governance but need not (and usually will not) involve intervention from any public manager.

Consequently, we suggest in this book that the realms of public management and public governance are separate but interconnected. One is not a precursor to the other, or superior to the other – they do and should co-exist, and should work together, through appropriate mechanisms, in order to raise the quality of life of people in the polity.

Of course, not all aspects of public management and public governance can co-exist. When taken to extremes, or interpreted from very contrasting standpoints, contradictions between public management and public governance can indeed be detected. For example, Rod Rhodes (1997, p. 55), writing from a governance perspective, characterizes NPM, or the 'New Public Management' (one branch of public management), as having four weaknesses: its intra-organizational focus; its obsession with objectives; its focus on results; and the contradiction between competition and steering at its heart. While each of these elements of NPM, if treated in a suitably wide framework, can be reconciled with a governance perspective, an extreme NPM proponent who insists that his or her view of the world is the only way to understand reform of the public sector is bound to antagonize a proponent of the governance perspective (and *vice versa*).

So why should you study public management and governance?

Finally, we want to make a claim for this book which we hope will encourage you to read it with more enthusiasm – and to read more of it – than you otherwise might. We want to claim that the study of public management and governance will not only make you a more informed student, and a more effective manager (whatever sector you work in), but that it will also make you a better citizen. You should be able to make a greater contribution to the neighbourhood, the local authority, the region and the country in which you live. You may even be able to make a contribution to the quality of life of many citizens elsewhere in the world. And if you decide you do *not* want to know more about public management and governance – just remember that you will be making it more difficult for all those people who will therefore have to work harder to substitute for the contribution you might have made.

But our greatest hope is that, however you use this book, it will help you to find out more about and care more about what it means to contribute to improving the decisions made in the public domain.

QUESTIONS FOR REVIEW AND DISCUSSION

1   How would you define public services? Show how this question would be answered by authors from different schools of thought and try to come up with your own definition.

2   In some UK cities, vandalism has become a serious problem. Think of a public management and a public governance solution to this problem. Why are they different?

READER EXERCISES

1   How do you think the image of the public sector has changed in the past five years? Have you personally experienced any improvements in public service delivery? If yes, what are these improvements and why did they happen? If no, why do think this was the case?
2   Does ownership matter – i.e. does the efficiency or effectiveness of a service depend on whether it is in the public or private sector? Why? How would you collect evidence to support your view – and how would you collect evidence to try to refute it?

CLASS EXERCISES

1   In groups, identify the main differences between 'public management' and 'private management', and between 'public governance' and 'corporate governance'. Thinking about the news over the past month, identify instances where these concepts might help in deciding who has been responsible for things which have been going wrong in your area or in your country. (Now try answering the question in terms of things which have been going right in your area or your country. If you find this difficult, what light does this throw on how the media shape debates on public management and public governance?)
2   In groups, identify some public services in your area which are provided by private sector firms. Each group should identify ways in which these services are less 'public' than those which are provided by the public sector. Then compare your answers in a plenary session.

FURTHER READING

Tony Bovaird (2002), 'Public administration: emerging trends and potential future directions' in Eran Vigoda (ed.), *Public administration: an interdisciplinary critical analysis*. New York: Marcel Dekker, pp. 345–376.

John Clarke and Janet Newman (1997), *The managerial state: power, politics and ideology in the remaking of social welfare*. London: Sage.

Stuart Ranson and John Stewart (1989), *Management for the public domain: enabling the learning society*. Basingstoke: Macmillan.

Chapter 2

The changing context of public policy

Tony Bovaird, Bristol Business School, UK and *Elke Löffler*, Governance International, UK

INTRODUCTION

In the early 1980s, budget deficits were a major motive for public sector reforms in many parts of the world – reforms which covered both the content of public policy and the way in which public policy was made. However, since that time, many governments, at least in the OECD countries, have achieved more favourable budget positions (see Chapter 3). Since then, other challenges have emerged to drive reforms in public policy. These new pressures on governments consist of a mixture of external factors (such as the ageing society, the information society and the tabloid society) and internal factors (including the consequences, both planned and unplanned, arising from the 'first generation' of public sector reforms, as outlined in Chapter 4). These new pressures have emphasized the quality of life implications of public policies and the governance aspects of public sector organizations. They have typically pushed the public sector in a different direction to the managerial reforms of the 1980s and early 1990s. In particular, they have re-emphasized the role of politicians in the public policy arena.

LEARNING OBJECTIVES

■ To be aware of recent changes in the context of public policy
■ To understand the major paradigm shifts in public policy making in recent decades
■ To understand the changing role of politics in public policy

RECENT CHANGES IN THE CONTEXT OF PUBLIC POLICY

Most policies have spending implications. If money becomes scarce, policy makers have less space to manoeuvre. However, financial crises also have an upside: they put pressure on public organizations to become more efficient. In particular, the fiscal crises in most OECD countries in the 1980s and 1990s was a key trigger for public sector reforms (see Chapter 4). As these crises receded in many OECD countries by the mid-1990s, the financial imperative for public sector reforms became weaker, although clearly it remained important that public services should be managed in an economic and efficient way.

From the early 1990s, other pressures on governments became more important, consisting of a mixture of external and internal factors. Many of the external factors have operated for several decades (see Box 2.1), but some have become significantly more important in recent years. A particularly powerful group of the external factors pushing for reform since the early 1990s has been associated with quality of life issues. The first of these to make a major impact were environmental factors, particularly since the Rio Summit in 1992. Since then, interest has grown in many countries around the world in the quality of health (not just healthcare), the quality of life of children, particularly the prevalence of child poverty (not just the quality of public services for children) and the quality of life of the elderly (not just the quality of social care).

BOX 2.1 EXTERNAL FACTORS DRIVING PUBLIC POLICY REFORMS

Political

- New political and social movements in many countries – and internationally – which contest the neo-liberal world view, especially in relation to world trade, the global environment and attitudes to civil liberties.
- Changing expectations, fuelled by globalization (particularly through tourism and the mass media) about the quality of services which governments should be able to deliver, given what is currently available in other countries.
- Changing expectations about the extent to which public services should be tailored to the needs of individual citizens.
- Increased insistence by key stakeholders (and particularly the media) that new levels of public accountability are necessary, with associated transparency of decision making and openness of information systems.
- Changing expectations that there will be widespread and intensive engagement with all relevant stakeholders during the policy making and policy implementation processes.
- Some long-established public service leadership elites have begun to lose popular legitimacy.
- But more market-oriented leadership-building alternatives have yet to prove themselves.

Economic/financial

- Decreasing proportions of the population within the 'economically active' category as conventionally defined, with knock-on effects to household income levels and government tax revenues.

- Economic boom of the 1990s in most OECD countries and many other parts of the world, generally producing rising tax revenues for governments.
- Increasing (or continuing) resistance by citizens to paying higher rates of tax to fund public services.
- Weakening roles of trade unions as labour markets become more flexible.

Social

- Traditional institutions such as the family and social class have changed their forms and their meanings in significant ways, so that old assumptions about family behaviour and class attitudes can no longer be taken for granted in policy making.
- Traditional sources of social authority and control – police, clergy, teachers and so on – are no longer as respected or influential as previously.
- Changing expectations about the core values in society – just as the 1980s saw traditional values such as public duty and individual responsibility being replaced by values of individual self-realization and rights, so in the 1990s there was a slow return to the understanding that caring and compassion are vital characteristics of a 'good society' and that 'social capital' is vital to a successful public sector.
- The ageing society, which means that much higher proportions of the population are in need of health and social care.
- Changing perceptions about the minimum quality of life for certain vulnerable groups which is acceptable in a well-ordered society – especially in relation to child poverty, minimum wages for the low paid, and the quality of life of elderly people (especially those living alone).
- A revolt against conceptions of 'difference', whether of gender, of race, of physical or mental (dis)abilities, as 'given' rather than socially constructed, with consequences that new political settlements are sought which suggest to disadvantaged groups that they should have rather higher expectations.
- Changing perceptions about which behaviours towards vulnerable people are socially acceptable in a well-ordered society – particularly in relation to child poverty, child abuse, domestic violence and levels of antisocial behaviour.
- The growing realization that public services not only alter the material conditions experienced by users and other citizens but also affect the emotional lives of users, citizens and staff, influencing their ability to form fulfilling social relationships within a more cohesive society.
- The growing desire by many citizens to realign the balance between paid work, domestic work and leisure time, particularly to tackle some of the gendered inequalities embedded within the current (im)balance of these activities.
- The new level of scrutiny which the 'tabloid society' provides of the decisions made by politicians and public officials (and also of their private lives), often concentrating more on the 'people story' side of these decisions rather than the logic of the arguments.

continued

continued

Technological

- Technological changes, particularly in ICT, which have meant that public policies can now take advantage of major innovations in ways of delivering services and also that the policy-making process itself can be much more interactive than before.
- The information society, in which a much higher proportion of the population can make use of new ICT technologies.
- Changing beliefs about the efficacy of 'hi-tech' solutions (e.g. renewed interest in 'alternative healthcare' and in 'alternative technologies').

Environmental

- Increasing concerns with global warming.
- Willingness to take some serious steps to reduce the level of usage of non-renewable energy sources and to recycle other materials
- Increasing pressure for governments to demonstrate the environmental impact of all new legislation, policies and major projects.

Legal/legislative

- Increasing influence of supra-national bodies (e.g. UN, World Bank, IMF, WTO, EU) in driving legislative or policy change at national level.
- Legal challenge in the courts to decisions made by government, citizens, businesses and by other levels of government.

Many of these external factors have tended to push most governments in rather similar directions – for example, the concern with child poverty has driven many governments towards 'workfare' programmes, the ageing society means that the pensions policies of most OECD countries are now under threat, the information society means that e-government is a major theme everywhere, and the tabloid society has driven governments in most countries to take public relations (now generally known as 'spin') much more seriously than (even) before.

However, the internal factors which are driving changes in public policy tend to be more context-specific. For example, in many countries governments are contracting out a high proportion of public services and also looking to the private sector for advice and consultancy on many policy-relevant issues. This is sometimes due to the superior access to capital finance enjoyed by the private sector, and sometimes due to the perception that the private sector has greater expertise in certain functions. This has had a number of important policy implications: for example, a new generation of public sector employees no longer expects to enjoy a 'job for life', which increases the flexibility of policy making (but probably also leads to higher salaries). Moreover, in those countries where governments have gone far down the road of contracting out public services to the private sector (see Chapter 7), there have emerged new and serious concerns about fraud and corruption in privately run public services (see Chapter 17). A different set of factors has meant that, whether or not public services remain in-house, the push for more holistic approaches and more inclusive value systems in relation to social policy have led to a reconceptualization of the roles both of service recipients and service providers. In particular, there is now much greater interest in exploring how service design and service delivery are shaped by – and should be more appropriately shaped by – a much wider agenda than simply the 'service needs' of the client and the 'professional needs' of the provider – social and public policy must make room for the emotions, the physical and bodily reactions, and the use of time of all stakeholders involved – including service users, service providers, citizens, politicians and so on (see Lewis, 2000a).

Again, the concerns about fragmented and disjointed public policies and governmental structures (often the consequence of 'agencification' or internal markets) have encouraged governments to find more mechanisms for co-ordination and integration, but in different ways in different countries. While it is widely agreed that today's 'wicked' problems can no longer be solved by a single policy or by a single actor, the emphasis on 'joined-up government' in UK central government contrasts significantly with the 'seamless services' agenda in the USA and the initiatives on 'one-stop shops' for citizens and investors in Spain and Germany.

CHANGING PARADIGMS OF PUBLIC POLICY

In the 1980s, the drivers of change, particularly financial pressures, pushed most Western countries towards a focus on making the public sector 'lean and more competitive while, at the same time, trying to make public administration more responsive to citizens' needs by offering value for money, choice flexibility, and transparency' (OECD, 1993, p. 9). This movement was referred to later by the academic community as 'new public management' or NPM (Hood, 1991) (see Box 2.2).

BOX 2.2 ELEMENTS OF NPM

- emphasis on performance management;
- more flexible and devolved financial management;
- more devolved personnel management with increasing use of performance-related pay and personalized contracts;
- more responsiveness to users and other customers in public services;
- greater decentralization of authority and responsibility from central to lower levels of government;
- greater recourse to the use of market-type mechanisms, such as internal markets, user charges, vouchers, franchising and contracting out;
- privatization of market-oriented public enterprises.

Source: OECD (1993, p.13)

Whereas some scholars considered this reform movement to be a global paradigm change (e.g. Osborne and Gaebler, 1992, pp. 325 and 328) others were more sceptical of the transferability of Westminster-type managerialism to Western Europe and other countries (e.g. Flynn and Strehl, 1996). Certainly, the credence given to the NPM paradigm by public sector practitioners in a major country such as Germany has remained rather low throughout the past two decades.

In the NPM, managers were given a much greater role in policy making than before, essentially at the expense of politicians and service professionals. While this clearly helped to redress the traditional balance in the many countries where management had been rather undervalued in the public sector, it quickly led many commentators to question whether this rebalancing had gone rather too far. In particular, it led to a vision of the public sector which often seemed peculiarly empty of political values and political debate.

As Chapter 4 shows, different countries responded to the challenges in different ways, depending on a whole variety of factors. However, one factor which ran through most of these responses was a concern with the governance dimension of public policy and the governance of public sector organizations (see Chapter 13). This governance-oriented response tended to emphasize:

- the importance of 'wicked problems' that cut across neat service lines, so that 'quality of life' improvements are more important than 'quality of service' improvements;
- the need for these 'wicked problems' to be tackled co-operatively, because they cannot be solved by only one agency – thus the need for multi-stakeholder networking;
- the need for agreed 'rules of the game' to which stakeholders will stick in their interactions with one another, so that they can trust each other in building new joint approaches to the problems they are tackling – extending 'corporate governance' principles into the sphere of 'public governance';
- the crucial importance of certain characteristics which should be embedded in all interactions which they have with each other, including transparency, integrity, honesty, fairness and respect for diversity.

Of course, the set of responses described above has developed gradually rather than overnight. Indeed, many of today's wicked problems are the emerging and unresolved problems from yesterday. In addition, in many cases, fiscal pressures have persisted and have been mixed with the new demands on governments. Which pressures are dominant and which are less relevant depends essentially on the setting (see Chapter 4). As public policy contexts become more differentiated in the future, the variety of governance reforms may well be greater than in the NPM era.

These challenges put public agencies under pressure to adapt. Whereas some agencies respond to the new environment quickly or even proactively, others change more slowly or not at all. As a result, old and new structures and management methods often exist side by side. This messy situation is multiplied by the many different kinds of reforms going on – some of which are described in Parts II and III of this book. Figure 2.1 shows the main directions of reform as a movement from law-driven ('*Rechtstaat*') to service-driven to

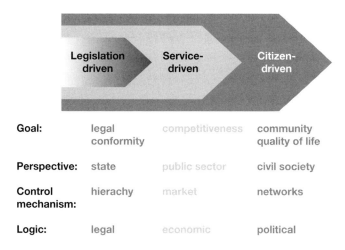

	Legislation driven	Service- driven	Citizen- driven
Goal:	legal conformity	competitiveness	community quality of life
Perspective:	state	public sector	civil society
Control mechanism:	hierachy	market	networks
Logic:	legal	economic	political

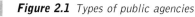

Figure 2.1 *Types of public agencies*

citizen-driven agencies, but with these co-existing with each other to some degree in any given agency.

Of course, it is not enough to diagnose what is happening in the public policy system; it is necessary also to decide what to do next. Pollitt and Bouckaert (2000, pp. 176–177) suggest that there are four strategic options (the '4Ms') for public sector reforms:

1 *Maintenance* of existing relationships between the political system, the system of public administration and law, and the market economy – usually involving tightening up traditional controls (e.g. restricting expenditure, squeezing staff numbers, running efficiency campaigns, rooting out corruption).
2 *Modernization of the system*, by bringing in faster, more flexible methods in all aspects of the administrative system (e.g. budgeting, accounting, staff management, service delivery), with some knock-on effects on the political system. This option has one variant which emphasizes the need for deregulation and 'empowerment' of lower levels of managers, while another variant emphasizes the need for citizen participation and stakeholder engagement.
3 *Marketization of the system*, by introducing as many market-type mechanisms as possible, while still keeping the general shape of the existing system of administration and law (e.g. through competition).
4 *Minimization of the administrative system*, by transferring to the market sector as many tasks as possible, through privatization and contracting out.

This latter option has been referred to by some academics as 'hollowing out the state', and they typically add other mechanisms such as the loss of national government powers to international organizations such as the WTO or the European Union. For much of the 1980s and early 1990s, this option haunted the public policy arena as a spectre threatening the extinction of the public sector as we know it. As Dunleavy (1994, p. 58) suggested:

> Current NPM thinking identifies government's optimal role, its core distinctive function, as being an 'intelligent customer' on behalf of citizens, purchasing privately supplied services so as to maximize the public welfare. But consuming without producing is new territory for liberal democratic governments, and we have no developed guidelines that could prevent loss of core competencies and the creation of 'hollow state' structures.

However, such fears have now abated. The debate is now rather about which (plural) roles the state should play, which (plural) reform modes it should adopt and in what context. As Pollitt and Bouckaert (2000, p. 178) suggest: 'Different regimes at different times appear to have leaned towards one or other of these strategies. The "4Ms" do not have to be taken in a particular order, but neither can they all be convincingly pursued simultaneously.' They go on to suggest that many reform programmes tend to opt for two of the strategies, in shifting combinations.

Consequently, we would argue that the dilemma outlined in the 'hollowing out of the state' debate misinterprets the issue at stake. The most important question is not whether the state will remain more powerful than other players but which set of formal (legal) and informal rules, structures and processes will be needed so that the state, the private and voluntary sector, citizens and other important stakeholders can exercise power over the decisions by other stakeholders so as to create win-win situations for all parties concerned. And if this is not possible, what changes are necessary to these political rules, structures and processes in order to ensure acceptable minimum outcomes (in terms both of quality of life and of quality of governance processes), especially for the most vulnerable groups in society.

THE POLITICS OF PUBLIC POLICY

The role of politics in the public sector, which in theory may seem to be central, has for long been under pressure from two other major sources: the professional groups who tend to believe that they are uniquely well informed about which policies are most likely to work and the managerial cadres who tend to believe that they are uniquely expert in getting the various professional groupings to work together effectively. More recently, a third set of actors has tried to push its way on to this already crowded stage: the groups of citizens and other stakeholders who have been told that they alone know best what they want, at least in terms of services which directly affect their quality of life. So is there still room for politicians to play a role upon this stage?

First, it is important to recognize that politicians play a number of roles – leadership of their polity (at a variety of levels), policy making for society, strategy making for the organization, partnership building with other organizations and with other stakeholders (including other countries or other communities), watch-dog over the decisions made within their polity, lobbyist in relation to decisions made in other polities, and last but not least, representation of their constituents. Not all of these roles are equally supported by the bureaucratic structures of the public sector – in particular, constituency roles tend to be rather poorly supported by officials, being regarded largely as 'political' and therefore for political parties to support.

How does this role differ in different contexts? Not only do the fundamental roles of politicians alter as we move from the global to the local stage, but so do the relative priorities between the roles and the dominant stakeholders with whom politicians have to interact. Furthermore, the political role varies depending on the balance in the polity between representational and participative democracy.

Starting at the global level, *global politics* is mainly about security, trade and environment, and is played out by heads of state and ministers. However, many of these decisions have major implications at national, regional, local and neighbourhood levels – for example, the 'peace dividend' can be a bonus for national social programme strategies (more funds are available from government budgets) but very bad for employment strategies in areas where army and naval bases are closed down. Again, global environmental strategy involves clashing national interests ('carbon guzzlers' vs. the rest?), while global environmental improvement often entails 'think global, act local' approaches. Thus national and local politicians cannot ignore the global level in their policy making, even though their role may often be essentially one of lobbying for their interests.

National politics is often the most ideologically driven, as it is the main forum for the debate about ideas which determine election results and subsequent government legislation programmes. Here, there are frequent clashes between ideological viewpoints, between national power groupings (which have variously been viewed through the lens of classes, 'fractions of capital', dominant coalitions of stakeholders, communities of interest and so on), and between the 'political' sensitivities of party politicians and the 'technical' recipes favoured by the 'technocracy'. Policy making at this level has a high emphasis on injecting political flavours into professionally designed strategies.

Regional politics is driven by different considerations in many countries. In Spain, there is a clear desire to allow expression within the *autonomias* to feelings of national identity as well as differing local priorities. This is clearly the case also with Scotland, Wales and Northern Ireland in the UK. In other cases, regional government has been formulated deliberately as a counterweight to central government (e.g. the role of the states in the US since 1776 and, nearly 200 years later, the role of the *Länder* in the post-1945 German constitution, largely fashioned in the US mould). In some cases, there is a mixture of motives – the slow movement towards some form of regional government in England may be seen as a partial recognition by central government of strong regional identities in some parts of the country, coupled with a desire to devolve some responsibility for unpopular transport and planning decisions away from Whitehall. At this regional level, politicians are in a halfway house between national and local politics. Where the region is strong (e.g. US states, some powerful Spanish *autonomias* such as Basque Country and Catalonia, some German *Länder* such as Bavaria and Baden-Württemberg), then regional politicians can have a national and even international significance. Where regions are weak (e.g. Spanish *autonomias* such as Murcia and Rioja, the regions in France and the regions created recently in Central and Eastern European countries), regional policies mainly play merely a 'gap-filling' role between policies set at the centre and in localities.

Local politics still usually has some ideological flavour but this is often idiosyncratic (local political parties often deviate quite far in their views from their national parties) and it is often less important than stances on local issues. Part of the role of the strategic politician in a local area is to lead the local community towards new goals, partly to help the local area compete against other areas (particularly in the same region) and partly to represent the community where policies (at all levels of government) are believed to have failed. Clearly, many local politicians are non-strategic, worried only about 'patch politics' and working on behalf of their constituents to improve the outcomes they experience from public services and from their dealings with other organizations. This means that many officials experience local politics as an irritant in the policy implementation process rather than a contribution to the policy-making process, which may explain why many have such a negative view of it.

Neighbourhood politics is usually far from the ideological level and is dominated by local issues – it therefore often pits individual politicians against their own party colleagues and leaders. Indeed, neighbourhood politics often involves the balancing of interests within and between neighbourhoods, producing coalitions on issues and across interest groups which have little parallel at any higher level of politics – NIMBYism (the 'Not In My Back Yard' syndrome) is the most obvious example of this. Consequently, highly rational strategies cooked up by well-informed professionals, and backed by top politicians in the local council and nationally, may still fail because they 'don't go down well on the street'.

Clearly, there is still a major role for political input into policy making, even in this era of highly professionalized 'new public management' and highly networked 'governance' partnerships. However, the autonomy of political decisions should not be exaggerated. There are many different pressure points by means of which politicians may be driven down roads which they do not personally like very much (see Chapter 5). For example, policy networks often contain strong voices from all the main stakeholders, and politicians, by becoming involved in them, magnify these voices (Bogason, 2000). Consequently, political platforms are usually designed to take on board the interests of a wide coalition of stake-holders. At worst, this can mean that politicians seek to 'please everyone, all the time'. In these circumstances, strategic policy making becomes next to impossible. Only if politicians are prepared to weather adverse comment when they follow strategic policies in which they believe can they claim to exercise political leadership and help their organizations and part-nerships to manage strategically.

SUMMARY

After the 1990s, fiscal pressures became less important as drivers of public policy change. A large number of major changes in the political, economic, social, technological, environ-mental and legislative fields have impacted on public policy making, the implications of many of which are not yet fully evident.

The paradigms of public policy making have changed significantly during the past two decades – the 'old public administration' was replaced partly by the 'new public manage-ment', which in turn has been supplanted partly by the 'public governance' movement. However, current public policy making in most countries still has strong elements of all three paradigms – and it is not clear how far or how fast the transition to a more 'unitary' approach will occur in the future.

Politics is integral to policy making but the role of politicians, which has never been as clear as the conventional model of democratic decision making has tried to suggest, is even more complex today, given the roles played in public decision making by professional groupings, managers, and engaged citizens and other stakeholders.

QUESTIONS FOR REVIEW AND DISCUSSION

1   Which of the main groups of factors driving changes in public policy (listed in Box 2.1) have been of most importance in the past five years? Is this likely to continue over the next five years?
2   What are the main paradigms of public policy making and what are the main differences between them?

READER EXERCISES

1   Get a copy of a serious newspaper, such as the *Guardian*, *Le Monde* or *Frankfurter Allgemeine Zeitung*. Try to find examples where factors listed in Box 2.1 are cited as influencing current government policy decisions.
2   In the same newspaper, identify ten politicians whose activities are being described in detail. Identify the roles they are playing. How many of these roles would you describe as 'policy-making' roles? And at what geographical level is this policy being decided?

CLASS EXERCISE

Divide into groups. Each group should identify the four major policy areas (at national or international level) where it believes current government policy needs to change. For each of these, the group should suggest how such changes might be initiated in the current political climate.

The groups should then come together and compare notes. Where there are communalities between the lists, suggesting that there is some consensus between the groups on the need for change, discuss why these policies have not yet been altered.

FURTHER READING

Gail Lewis (2000a), 'Introduction: expanding the social policy imaginary' in Gail Lewis, Sharon Gerwirtz and John Clarke (eds), *Rethinking social policy*. London: Open University in association with Sage Publications.

Christopher Pollitt and Geert Bouckaert (2000), *Public management reform. A comparative analysis*. Oxford: Oxford University Press.

Chapter 3

The size and scope of the public sector

An international comparison

Peter M. Jackson, Leicester University Management Centre, UK

INTRODUCTION

What is the appropriate scope and size of the public sector? The simple answer is, it all depends. It depends upon the vision of the state to which you subscribe and it depends upon your weighing up the costs and benefits of two highly imperfect social institutions: the market and the public sector.

The public sector is an ubiquitous social institution which has grown in size and complexity over the past fifty years. Nevertheless, this has not been a linear development. Whereas the development of the welfare state in the late 1960s and 1970s resulted in an unprecedented growth of the public sector in most OECD countries, the 1980s and 1990s were marked by concerns and attempts to reduce the size of the public sector, or, at least, to make it more efficient (see Chapter 4). In some cases this has meant privatization, in others devolving responsibilities to lower levels of government or simply the introduction of market-type instruments in the public sector (see Chapter 7).

Today, public expenditure in all developed countries accounts for between one-third and one-half of a country's gross domestic product (GDP). Given the fact that many OECD countries continue to suffer from budget deficits and high levels of debt, public expenditure management will remain high on the political agenda. Overall economic efficiency depends upon how well these public sector resources are managed not only because of the opportunity cost of wasted resources but because of the impact of taxation and public borrowing on private sector decisions.

LEARNING OBJECTIVES

- To understand the role and scope of government
- To be aware of the trends in social spending and to understand the forces that shape them
- To be aware of the changing composition of public spending
- To understand the implications these trends have for public sector management

25

THE ROLE AND SCOPE OF GOVERNMENT

Variations in public expenditure across time and space reflect differences in the vision of the role and scope of government (see Chapter 2). What then is the appropriate role, scope and size of government?

There is no simple or straightforward technically grounded answer to this question. Instead, there are conflicting perceptions of the proper scope of government. Nor is the question new. It has been the focus of an emotionally charged debate conducted by political philosophers and economists over several centuries. Central to the debate are the basic normative questions of 'what should governments do; how big should the share of public spending be in the national economy; and should governments engage in direct production activities?'

Recently, this debate has become more intense as those who advocate a minimalist state have sought to downsize, privatize, re-engineer or re-invent government. At the other end of the spectrum those who argue in favour of an active interventionist state emphasize the benefits of public policies and public spending programmes and the enlargement of the positive personal freedoms which accompany them. The position which any individual occupies on this spectrum reflects as much his or her preferences for what constitutes a 'good society' as any technical, philosophical or socio-economic arguments.

While this debate has been conducted for many years it has not been resolved. This is clearly demonstrated by the recent exchange between Buchanan and Musgrave (see Box 3.1) who each subscribe to significantly different answers to the fundamental question: what is the appropriate role of the state?

BOX 3.1 MUSGRAVE'S AND BUCHANAN'S VIEWS OF THE ROLE OF THE STATE

Musgrave is representative of a group of scholars who regard the public sector as having its own legitimacy and the public and private sectors to be complements (rather than competitors) working together to achieve maximum social welfare.

While Musgrave sees the state as 'an association of individuals engaged in a co-operative venture, formed to resolve problems of social co-existence and to do so in a democratic and fair fashion' (Buchanan and Musgrave, 1999, p. 31), Buchanan's view of the world is that majority politics results in the formation of coalitions between special interest groups that produce policies that best serve their own interests. For Buchanan the issue is to constrain these tendencies by the use of fiscal constitutions and rules. 'My concern and my primary motivation here in a normative sense is preventing the exploitation of man by man, or woman by woman, through the political process. That is what is driving my whole approach.'

Source: Buchanan and Musgrave (1999, p. 52)

THE ROLE OF THE STATE IS . . .

. . . *allocative*
- Correcting market failure through regulation, taxation, subsidies and providing public goods.

. . . *distributional*
- Achieving a just and fair society by regulation, the adjustment of rights, giving access to markets in the face of discrimination, progressive taxation and subsidies.

. . . *stabilization*
- Controlling economic growth, unemployment and inflation by demand and money management.

Source: Musgrave (1959)

Many years ago, Musgrave (1959) set out three distinct roles for an active state. This taxonomy provided a useful structure and fashioned the subsequent debate. For Musgrave a modern state transcends the primitive and minimal role of the 'nightwatchman' and embraces an allocative role, a distributional role and a stabilization role.

Within the allocative role the provision of public goods is seen as a means of overcoming various market failures that can arise from ill-defined property rights, externalities, incomplete information, high transactions costs or non-increasing returns to scale. These sources of market failure had long been acknowledged by, among others, Adam Smith and John Stuart Mill. Markets are said to 'fail' when they either do not exist, because transactions costs are so high, or when they produce an inefficient outcome. Correcting market failure gives rise to what Musgrave (1998) has referred to recently as the 'service state', i.e. an essential role which is to 'repair certain leaks in the efficient functioning of the market as a provider of goods' (p. 35).

The second role of government is concerned with distributional issues and forms the basis of the 'welfare state'. Given any initial distribution of rights, including property rights, the unfettered market system will grind out a distribution of welfares which may or may not be considered to be socially just and fair. The objective of the distributional role of the state is to adjust the market-determined distribution of welfare by bringing it closer to what 'society' regards to be just and fair. This is achieved through regulation, the adjustment of rights, giving access to markets in the face of discrimination, progressive taxation and subsidies.

The third role of government is represented by the stabilization role. Unconstrained market forces can result in a general equilibrium for an economy that is accompanied by unacceptably high levels of unemployment. Classical economists in the early twentieth century argued that if left alone market forces would adjust and unemployment would be eventually eliminated. However, Keynes pointed out that an economy can become stuck in a state of high unemployment for many years because the speed of economic adjustment is very slow – 'in the long run we are all dead'. In order to speed up the adjustment process Keynes advocated corrective action through changes in public spending and/or taxation, in order to manage 'effective demand', depending upon where the economy is on the business cycle. From the 1950s up to the 1980s the Keynesian consensus was dominant. Demand in the economy was 'managed' to achieve the twin objectives of low unemployment and price stability, while acknowledging that there was a trade-off between these objectives.

From the early 1980s, monetary economists (harking back to the classical school) regained the upper hand with their insistence that controlling the money supply was the only practical tool of stabilization policy. By the 1990s, both schools were represented in the governments of major OECD countries.

While writers such as Musgrave and Arrow had earlier emphasized market failures, they now also acknowledge 'government failure' and policy failure. Recently, Musgrave (1998) wrote about the 'flawed state'. Both markets and public bureaucracies are flawed institutions. Public sector failures arise for reasons that are similar to market failure – high transactions costs and incomplete and imperfect information – but in addition there are the inefficiencies that arise from inadequate incentive structures, severe principal/agent problems and inadequate demand revelation mechanisms as in the case of voting mechanisms. These failures result in both allocative and managerial inefficiencies within the public sector, reflected in inappropriate policies being implemented through wasteful bureaucracies.

THE CHANGING BOUNDARIES OF THE STATE

There is a great diversity in the size and scope of government across the various nation-states of the world. This in part reflects differences in preferences for the 'good society' but it also arises from variations in *per capita* real incomes and hence the capacity of countries to finance their public policies; differences in social factors such as population size and composition; and also differences in political institutions, for example, majoritarian compared to proportional electoral systems and presidential vs. parliamentary systems.

The absolute and relative sizes of the public sectors around the world have shown dramatic changes over the past 130 years. IMF data show that in 1870 the average relative size of the public sector around the world, as measured by the ratio of government spending to GDP, was 10.7 per cent. This increased to 19.6 per cent in 1920; 28 per cent in 1960; 41.9 per cent in 1980 and 45 per cent in 1996 (Tanzi and Schuknecht, 2000).

Up to 1950 there had been a lengthy period of *laissez-faire* during which public expenditures and the boundaries of the state changed modestly, only periodically being disrupted by major world wars. During the 1950s and the 1960s there were many Keynesian economists who advocated increases in public spending. Galbraith (1958) dramatically referred to public squalor amidst private affluence. Bator (1960) argued that society was 'dangerously short-changing (itself) on defence, foreign aid, education, urban renewal and medical services' (p. xiv). Increases in public spending on infrastructure and human capital (education and health) promotes economic growth but has to be paid for through increases in taxation. However, the growth in real *per capita* incomes is able to fund the increase in taxation.

Growth in public spending, however, is not inevitable. Some theories of public expenditure growth (see Brown and Jackson, 1990) such as *Wagner's law*, which relates public expenditure changes to real income growth, or *Baumol's cost disease model*, which relates it to changes in the terms of trade between the public and private sectors, are highly deterministic. These theories provide the means of carrying out an interpretation of historical trends but they ignore public choices. The demand for public spending comes from income growth, population growth, changes in the composition of the population, urbanization and the increasing complexity of society. The decision to spend is the outcome of public choices, which are shaped by changing perceptions about the role and legitimacy of government and hence where the boundaries of the state are drawn.

In examining trends in public expenditures and making international comparisons, we shall use two principal data sources – the IMF (as presented in Tanzi and Schuknecht (2000)) and the OECD. Their definitions and coverage differ somewhat from each other but both datasets give essentially the same qualitative picture of trends in public expenditure.

The rapid expansion in the absolute and relative size of the public sectors of the world took place during the period 1960 to 1980 as shown in Table 3.1. This was a period during which there were no world wars and when demographic trends were not placing signifi-cant pressures on public budgets. It was, however, a time when attitudes changed positively towards an interventionist role for government reflecting the advent of the welfare state and also Keynesian demand management policies. Public spending increased due to the introduction of new (especially welfare) policies along with expansion in the scope and coverage of existing programmes.

As one commentator has remarked, this was the 'golden age of public sector interven-tion'. It was also a period during which many had simplistic and romanticized views of how government worked and what government could achieve. These views played up market failure and were blind to the possibility of public sector failure – the costs of government intervention in terms of the distorting effects of taxation and public borrowing; the ineffi-ciencies of public bureaucracies; the self-interest politics of pressure groups and the possibility of corruption on a significant scale. This idealized view of government assumed that politicians and bureaucrats acted to promote maximum social welfare while ignoring the realities and consequences of 'rent-seeking' behaviour (i.e. the search for personal gain) (Tullock, 1967). Furthermore, it was implicitly assumed that policy makers possessed considerable knowledge; for example, that they knew with certainty which policy levers produced what effect.

Public choice theorists and libertarians mounted a series of challenges to the post-war consensus that public sector intervention was at all times beneficial. They pointed out the potential efficiency losses resulting from the distorting effects of high marginal rates of tax; the effect on interest rates of large public sector deficits (which also crowded out private investment) and the frequency of policy failures. Whether or not there was any convincing empirical evidence to support the anti-government rhetoric of the 1970s (and there was little) is of no significance; the point is that these arguments won the day, and ushered in the Thatcher and Reagan administrations and policies aimed at 'rolling back the frontiers of the state'. The 1980s and 1990s witnessed a series of initiatives that would change the balance between the public and private sectors – privatization; contracting out; reductions in public sector debt; balanced budget rules; fiscal constitutions; private finance initiatives and public private partnerships, and so on.

Were the frontiers of the state rolled back? Table 3.1 suggests not. The relative size of the public sector was in most cases greater in 2000 than it was in 1980. Even in countries such as the UK where the relative size of the public sector is smaller, this has more to do with the growth in GDP than the reduction in the absolute size of public spending. Nevertheless the rate of expansion of the boundaries of the public sector slowed down after 1980. The exception is Japan.

THE COMPOSITION OF PUBLIC EXPENDITURE

Real government spending on goods and services has been very modest in its growth. The main element of public expenditure growth over the past forty years has been transfer expenditures on income maintenance and subsidies, due to expansion in the welfare state. This increase in social spending has not been due primarily to demographic factors, such as the ageing of the population, as so many commentators have erroneously assumed. Of course, there has been some pressure from demographic factors but these have been modest when compared to the real factors, which have been increases in the scope of social programmes to embrace more individuals along with increases in the rates of benefits paid.

Table 3.1 *General government outlays, by country (% of GDP)*

	1965	1970	1975	1980	1985	1990	1995	2000[1]
Australia	24.6	25.2	31.3	32.3	37.8	33.0	35.4	31.4
Austria	36.6	38.0	44.4	47.2	50.1	48.5	52.4	48.8
Belgium	35.0	39.7	47.6	53.4	57.3	50.8	50.3	46.7
Canada	27.8	33.8	38.9	39.1	45.4	46.0	45.3	37.8
Denmark	31.8	40.1	47.1	55.0	58.0	53.6	56.6	51.3
Finland	30.3	29.7	37.0	37.1	42.3	44.4	54.3	44.8
France	37.6	37.6	42.3	45.4	51.9	49.6	53.6	51.2
Germany	35.3	37.2	47.1	46.5	45.6	43.8	46.3	43.0
Greece	22.0	23.3	27.1	29.6	42.3	47.8	46.6	43.7
Ireland	36.0	37.7	40.7	47.6	50.5	39.5	37.6	27.7
Italy	32.8	32.7	41.0	41.8	50.6	53.1	52.3	46.7
Japan	19.0	19.0	26.8	32.0	31.6	31.3	35.6	38.2
Korea	14.5	14.8	16.9	19.2	17.6	18.3	19.3	23.4
Mexico	–	–	–	–	–	–	21.4	–
Netherlands	34.7	37.0	45.7	50.9	51.9	49.4	47.7	41.5
Norway	29.1	34.9	39.8	43.9	41.5	49.7	47.6	40.6
Portugal	18.1	18.0	25.2	28.1	42.9	44.2	41.2	42.1
Spain	19.5	21.7	24.1	31.3	39.4	41.4	44.0	38.5
Sweden	33.5	41.7	47.3	56.9	59.9	55.8	62.1	53.9
United Kingdom	33.5	36.7	44.4	43.0	44.0	41.9	44.4	38.4
United States	25.6	29.6	32.3	31.3	33.8	33.6	32.9	29.3
Euro area	33.1	33.9	40.9	43.0	47.2	46.3	49.1	45.1
OECD	26.9	29.2	34.4	35.5	38.1	38.0	39.4	36.5

[1] Estimates

Source: OECD *Economic Outlook*, No. 68, Issue 2, December 2000, OECD National Accounts and OECD calculations, p. 42. Copyright © OECD, 2000

Furthermore, social spending programmes cover more and more situations and therefore bring more people into the benefit net. The full impact of an ageing population has yet to be experienced.

According to IMF data (Tanzi and Schuknecht, 2000), on average, total real spending around the world increased from 12.6 per cent of GDP in 1960 to 17.3 per cent in 1995. While this is a modest increase it is nevertheless overstated because it is not adjusted for the 'relative price effect', i.e. the fact that public sector costs tend to go up faster than private sector costs.

In Table 3.2, which shows public sector consumption expenditure (the amount of goods and services for end-users produced by means of public sector funding), there was only a modest increase and much of that was due to the reasons given above, i.e. that the growth

Table 3.2 General government outlays, by economic category: consumption (% of GDP)

	1965	1970	1975	1980	1985	1990	1995	2000
Australia	13.5	14.4	18.9	18.6	20.0	18.5	18.6	18.5
Austria	14.6	16.1	18.2	18.4	19.5	18.8	20.4	19.4
Belgium	16.7	17.6	21.4	23.0	23.0	20.3	21.5	21.0
Canada	15.6	20.5	21.8	21.3	21.9	22.4	21.4	18.4
Denmark	16.7	20.4	25.1	27.2	25.8	25.6	25.8	25.3
Finland	14.2	15.1	17.8	18.7	20.6	21.6	22.8	20.8
France	16.9	17.4	19.5	21.5	23.7	22.3	23.9	23.4
Germany	15.0	15.5	20.1	19.9	19.7	18.0	19.8	18.8
Greece	8.2	8.8	10.6	11.4	14.2	15.1	15.3	15.0
Ireland	13.3	14.3	18.2	19.4	18.1	15.1	14.9	11.8
Italy	16.2	14.9	16.1	16.8	18.6	20.2	17.9	17.9
Japan	8.2	7.4	10.0	9.8	9.6	9.0	9.8	10.1
Korea	9.5	9.7	11.3	11.9	10.4	10.5	9.7	9.7
Mexico	–	–	–	–	–	–	10.5	–
Netherlands	23.6	24.9	28.2	29.1	26.4	24.3	24.0	22.6
Norway	14.6	16.4	18.7	18.7	18.1	20.8	20.9	18.8
Portugal	11.5	13.3	14.4	14.0	15.0	16.4	18.6	21.0
Spain	9.1	10.2	11.3	14.3	15.9	16.9	18.1	16.9
Sweden	17.9	22.5	25.2	29.6	28.2	27.7	26.3	26.5
United Kingdom	17.2	18.0	22.4	21.6	20.9	19.9	19.8	18.3
United States	16.4	18.5	18.1	16.8	17.1	16.6	15.3	14.1
Euro area	15.4	15.8	18.5	19.5	20.3	19.7	20.4	19.7
OECD	14.6	15.7	17.3	17.0	17.3	16.8	16.6	15.7

Source: OECD Analytical Database. Figures underlying *OECD Economic Outlook*, No. 68, Issue 2, December 2000 and OECD National Accounts, p. 46. Copyright © OECD, 2000

in GDP slowed down. The significant increases in public spending for all countries have come from the absolute and relative growth in subsidies and transfers (see Tables 3.3 and 3.4). Part of the expansion in government's welfare role has been due, as mentioned above, to extending the coverage and benefit rates of these programmes. Another reason is the high levels of unemployment experienced, especially in European economies, during the 1980s and 1990s.

Capital expenditure is another element of public expenditure which has great economic significance, not only in terms of direct employment creation in the private sector but more generally in terms of the impact of public sector infrastructure on economic growth. Table 3.5 shows the net capital outlays of the public sector (i.e. net of depreciation). The data show wide variations. Because public sector capital programmes are easier to control than

Table 3.3 General government outlays, by economic category: income transfers (% of GDP)

	1965	1970	1975	1980	1985	1990	1995	2000
Australia	4.2	3.9	5.9	6.8	7.4	6.9	8.5	8.3
Austria	12.9	14.1	14.9	16.2	17.9	17.7	19.5	18.3
Belgium	11.9	11.0	14.5	16.1	17.2	15.1	15.5	14.4
Canada	5.2	6.5	8.6	8.3	10.5	11.2	12.6	10.9
Denmark	6.8	10.5	13.5	16.2	16.1	17.8	20.4	17.2
Finland	7.6	5.9	8.7	9.5	11.8	12.6	16.1	12.6
France	11.5	12.0	14.1	15.5	17.7	16.9	18.5	18.1
Germany	13.0	13.0	17.2	16.6	16.0	15.2	18.1	18.6
Greece	6.8	7.6	7.1	8.9	14.4	14.4	15.1	16.1
Ireland	10.0	10.0	10.0	10.7	12.9	11.9	12.6	9.7
Italy	11.9	11.8	14.4	14.2	17.1	18.1	16.7	17.3
Japan	4.7	4.6	7.7	10.1	10.9	11.4	13.4	15.7
Korea	0.9	0.6	0.7	1.3	1.5	2.0	2.1	3.3
Mexico	–	–	–	–	–	–	2.6	–
Netherlands	10.0	10.8	14.3	16.4	15.5	15.5	15.3	11.8
Norway	6.6	9.0	10.0	11.3	11.8	16.0	15.8	13.7
Portugal	2.3	2.1	5.2	7.0	7.8	8.5	11.8	12.5
Spain	4.5	5.9	7.4	10.9	12.7	12.7	13.9	12.4
Sweden	7.7	10.1	13.8	17.1	17.7	19.3	21.3	18.3
United Kingdom	6.9	8.0	10.2	11.6	13.7	11.9	15.4	13.1
United States	5.0	7.1	10.2	9.8	9.8	10.0	11.8	10.5
Euro area	10.9	11.2	14.0	14.7	15.8	15.5	17.0	16.7
OECD	6.5	7.5	10.2	10.7	11.4	11.5	13.2	12.8

Source: OECD Analytical Database figures underlying *OECD Economic Outlook*, No. 68, Issue 2, December 2000 and OECD National Accounts, p. 52. Copyright © OECD, 2000

public consumption spending they tend to be the first to be hit when public expenditure needs to be cut back. This is seen in the volatility of the ratio in Table 3.5.

As part of their welfare state role governments provide 'positive freedom goods', i.e. goods which expand individuals' freedoms to access markets that will then expand their opportunities. Examples of freedom goods are education, health services, pensions and unemployment benefits. Table 3.6 shows the variation in these different freedom goods across a number of countries. As expected there is a wide range which reflects prevailing local circumstances (e.g. population size and composition, *per capita* incomes) and local political preferences and institutions.

Data from the IMF reveal a steady increase in public sector education's share of GDP from (on average) 3.5 per cent of GDP in 1960 to 5.8 per cent in 1980 and 6.2 per cent in 1995.

Table 3.4 General government outlays, by economic category: subsidies (% of GDP)

	1965	1970	1975	1980	1985	1990	1995	2000
Australia	0.7	0.9	1.1	1.5	1.7	1.3	1.3	1.2
Austria	2.3	1.8	3.0	3.1	3.2	3.1	2.9	2.5
Belgium	2.3	2.3	2.6	2.8	2.4	1.7	1.5	1.5
Canada	0.9	0.9	2.5	2.7	2.5	1.5	1.1	1.1
Denmark	1.8	2.6	2.7	3.1	2.9	2.2	2.5	2.3
Finland	3.2	2.8	3.8	3.3	3.1	2.9	2.8	1.5
France	2.5	2.2	2.2	2.1	2.6	1.8	1.5	1.3
Germany	1.2	1.7	1.9	2.0	2.0	2.0	2.1	1.7
Greece	1.4	1.0	3.2	3.0	3.7	1.2	0.4	0.2
Ireland	2.7	3.4	2.5	2.6	2.3	1.1	1.0	0.7
Italy	1.7	1.9	2.8	2.9	2.6	2.0	1.5	1.2
Japan	0.7	1.1	1.5	1.5	1.1	1.1	0.8	0.6
Korea	0.3	0.3	1.4	0.9	0.6	0.6	0.7	0.3
Mexico	–	–	–	–	–	–	0.7	–
Netherlands	0.9	1.0	1.2	1.7	2.0	1.7	1.1	1.6
Norway	3.4	3.8	4.6	5.2	4.5	6.0	3.7	2.5
Portugal	1.0	1.3	1.7	6.0	4.2	1.8	1.4	1.2
Spain	0.5	0.5	0.7	1.1	1.3	1.1	1.1	1.0
Sweden	1.1	1.3	2.5	3.3	3.9	3.6	3.8	1.8
United Kingdom	1.6	1.7	3.6	2.5	2.0	0.9	0.7	0.5
United States	0.2	0.5	0.5	0.5	0.5	0.4	0.3	0.2
Euro area	1.6	1.7	2.0	2.1	2.2	1.8	1.7	1.4
OECD	0.8	1.0	1.4	1.4	1.4	1.1	0.9	0.8

Source: OECD Analytical Database figures underlying *OECD Economic Outlook*, No. 68, Issue 2, December 2000 and OECD National Accounts, p. 56. Copyright © OECD, 2000

This has been due to expanding the coverage of education programmes (e.g. raising the school-leaving age), but the main driver was demographic pressures arising from the post-1945 baby boom. An expansion in publicly funded university education, along with a general increase in entitlements at the tertiary level, has also contributed to the rise. While population increases have slowed down and will moderate the pressures on public education budgets, nevertheless there are new forces that will take their place (e.g. greater access to tertiary education and lifelong learning). Some of this demand may be met by greater private sector involvement.

Public spending on health services has also shown a substantial rise. Again, according to IMF data, public expenditure on healthcare increased from 2.4 per cent of GDP in 1960

Table 3.5 General government outlays, by economic category: net capital outlays[1] (% of GDP)

	1965	1970	1975	1980	1985	1990	1995	2000
Australia	3.8	3.6	3.1	2.3	3.8	2.4	2.8	1.4
Austria	6.0	4.8	7.0	7.0	6.1	4.9	5.3	5.1
Belgium	1.3	5.3	4.9	4.9	3.5	1.8	2.5	3.1
Canada	3.1	2.3	2.2	1.4	2.1	1.4	0.6	0.0
Denmark	5.4	5.4	4.7	4.6	3.6	0.7	1.5	2.0
Finland	4.3	4.9	6.1	4.7	5.0	5.8	8.6	6.7
France	6.7	5.0	5.3	4.9	5.1	5.7	6.0	5.1
Germany	5.4	6.0	6.4	6.1	4.9	6.1	2.6	0.4
Greece	5.1	5.1	5.1	4.3	5.5	8.3	4.6	5.2
Ireland	5.0	5.0	5.0	8.5	7.2	3.6	3.7	3.2
Italy	2.0	2.5	4.4	2.9	4.5	3.5	4.7	3.7
Japan	5.0	5.2	6.3	7.5	5.6	6.0	7.9	7.8
Korea	3.8	3.8	2.9	4.6	4.4	4.8	6.4	8.6
Mexico	–	–	–	–	–	–	2.7	–
Netherlands	−2.5	−2.7	−1.0	−0.1	1.8	1.9	1.4	1.5
Norway	3.2	4.1	4.9	5.6	4.2	4.9	4.4	4.1
Portugal	2.7	0.8	3.4	−1.2	9.3	10.9	4.3	4.2
Spain	5.0	4.7	4.6	4.6	7.6	6.9	5.7	4.6
Sweden	4.9	5.9	3.6	2.7	1.6	0.2	3.6	3.2
United Kingdom	4.1	5.1	4.4	2.6	2.4	5.9	4.9	3.8
United States	2.0	1.3	1.1	1.0	1.4	1.4	0.7	0.9
Euro area	4.3	3.9	4.6	4.1	4.3	4.4	4.2	3.0
OECD	3.5	3.2	3.4	3.3	3.3	3.8	3.8	3.4

[1] Net fixed investment plus net capital transfers.

Source: OECD Analytical Database figures underlying OECD Economic Outlook, No. 68, Issue 2, December 2000 and OECD National Accounts, p. 57. Copyright © OECD, 2000

to 5.8 per cent in 1980 and 6.5 per cent in 1995. Access to free healthcare at the point of consumption is regarded as a basic positive freedom right. Entitlements to healthcare have been expanded in many countries since 1950. At the same time technological changes in the form of new equipment, new surgical procedures and new drugs have expanded the scope and quality of treatment and greatly increased healthcare budgets. An ageing population also places pressures on health spending. There is a life cycle in the use of health services. When individuals are very young or very old they make the greatest use. Furthermore, it costs on average three times as much to care for someone over the age of 80 compared to someone who is 60 years old. Increases in life expectancy are due in part to improvements in healthcare but this then impacts on budgets.

As Table 3.6 shows, there is a wide variation in the private sector's role in the provision of services which have a social dimension. It remains to be seen whether or not those countries which have significant public sector involvement will turn to the private sector as the pressures on public spending become intolerable.

The biggest time bomb which is ticking away in every country is the ageing of populations and the impact that this will have on pensions. Public expenditures on pensions have increased on average from 1.2 per cent of GDP in 1920 to 4.5 per cent in 1960, 8.4 per cent in 1980 and 9.8 per cent in 1995. Not only has the coverage of entitlements increased but so too have benefit rates. In many countries pensions are indexed to inflation and in Germany they are indexed to net wage growth (i.e. net of taxes). It is estimated that by 2020 the share of the population who are above the age of 60 will, in most countries, have increased to 25 per cent, thereby increasing the dependency ratio. How countries will cope with this is currently an active topic of public policy debate. The retirement age could be increased. The age of 65 was introduced when life expectancy was lower. For example, in the UK the retirement age of women will be increased from 60 to 65 sometime between 2010 and 2020. In Italy the male retirement age of 60 was raised to 65 in 2001. Another means of dealing with the problem is to reduce the retirement benefits paid. In some countries (Japan, Germany, France and Italy) these are very generous. This does, however, break the implicit intergenerational social contract – a consequence of which would be that current generations would need sufficient warning in order to adjust their life cycle savings decisions. The role of private pensions is currently uncertain given the loss in their portfolio values following the puncturing of the bubble of 'irrational exuberance' in the world's equity markets in 2002. Public sector pension schemes are in many cases uncovered, which means that in order to cope with the future demographic time bomb tax rates will need to increase or radical changes to pension schemes will be introduced.

CONCLUSIONS

The public sectors in the developed economies are now significantly different compared to their size and composition in the mid-twentieth century. Over the next thirty to forty years further radical changes will take place. The future shape of the public sector will be influenced by the demographic time bomb of an ageing population and the complementary role played by the private sector. This places greater pressures on those who have to manage public services with the objective of providing value for money. At the same time, it offers

Table 3.6 *Gross total social expenditure, 1995, as a percentage of GDP*

	Australia	Belgium	Canada	Denmark	Finland	Germany	Ireland	Italy	NL	Norway	Sweden	UK	US
Gross public social expenditure[1]	17.8	28.8	18.2	32.2	31.9	27.1	19.4	23.7	26.8	27.6	33.0	22.4	15.8
Pension spending (old age & survivors)	4.7	10.3	4.8	7.7	9.1	10.9	4.6	13.6	7.8	6.2	9.0	7.3	6.3
▪ Unemployment	1.3	2.8	1.3	4.6	4.0	1.4	2.7	0.9	3.1	1.1	2.3	0.9	0.3
▪ Disability spending (incl. occupational injuries)	2.0	2.2	1.0	2.3	4.0	1.4	0.9	1.9	4.1	2.7	2.4	2.8	0.2
▪ Sickness benefits	0.1	0.5	0.1	0.7	0.5	0.5	0.9	0.1	1.0	1.2	1.2	0.2	0.2
▪ Public expenditure on health	5.7	6.9	6.6	5.3	5.7	8.1	5.2	5.4	6.7	6.6	5.9	5.7	6.3
▪ Other[2]	4.0	6.1	4.5	11.7	8.6	4.7	5.2	1.8	4.1	9.8	12.3	5.5	1.5
▪ Public cash benefits	10.7	19.7	11.4	21.4	22.9	17.3	13.2	18.0	19.7	15.6	21.4	15.4	8.7
▪ Public social services and health	7.1	9.1	6.8	10.8	9.1	9.8	6.2	5.7	8.1	12.0	11.6	7.0	7.1
Gross mandatory private social expenditure[1]	0.3	0.0	–	0.5	0.2	1.6	–	–	0.8	0.9	0.4	0.4	0.5
Gross voluntary private social expenditure	2.8	0.6	4.5	0.9	1.1	0.9	1.8	1.7	4.4	–	2.1	4.2	7.9
▪ Voluntary private social cash benefits[3]	1.9	0.2	3.5	0.7	1.0	0.7	1.2	1.4	3.1	–	2.0	3.9	2.8
▪ Voluntary private social health benefits[4]	0.9	0.5	0.9	0.1	0.1	0.1	0.6	0.2	1.2	–	0.1	0.3	5.0
Gross total social expenditure[5]	20.9	29.4	22.7	33.6	33.2	29.6	21.1	25.4	31.9	28.5	35.5	27.0	24.1

■ Total cash benefits	12.9	19.9	14.9	22.6	24.0	19.6	14.4	19.5	22.4	16.5	23.8	19.7	12.0
■ Total services	8.0	9.5	7.8	10.9	9.2	9.9	6.8	5.9	9.5	12.0	11.7	7.3	12.1
Public share in total social expenditure	85.0	97.9	80.4	95.9	96.2	91.6	91.7	93.3	84.0	96.9	93.1	83.2	65.3
Private share in total social expenditure	15.0	2.1	19.6	4.1	3.8	8.4	8.3	6.7	16.0	3.1	6.9	16.8	34.7
Services/cash ratio[6]													
■ Public social expenditure	66.7	46.0	59.8	50.7	39.6	56.6	47.1	31.6	44.9	76.5	54.2	45.3	81.9
■ Total social expenditure	62.3	47.9	51.9	48.4	38.1	50.6	47.3	30.5	42.6	72.4	49.2	37.1	101.0

[1] Source: OECD, 1999, *Social Expenditure Database*, Paris. Overall, compared to data on public social benefits the quality of data on private social benefits is relatively low. This is particularly so when central recording of private benefits is not stipulated. For example, employers do not have to report their actual spending on continued wage payments to their employees in case of sickness, and sometimes the aggregate value of such benefits can only be estimated by using information in labour costs surveys and surveys on sickness absenteeism.

[2] Includes public spending on groups across the following social policy areas: services for the elderly and disabled; family cash benefits; family services; active labour market policies (ALMP); and other contingencies (e.g. cash benefits to those on low income).

[3] Data provided by national authorities.

[4] Voluntary private social health benefits consist mainly of health benefits based on employer-provided plans (financed by employer and employee contributions). In general, estimates are based on information on private health expenditure (OECD, *Health Data 98*).

[5] For Norway, voluntary private social pensions are grouped under public benefits. As in the other Scandinavian countries, private social health benefits are likely to be very small in Norway.

[6] Expenditure on social services includes items grouped under the following social policy areas: services for the elderly and disabled, survivor benefits in-kind, family services, administration of public employment service, health and social services (e.g. rehabilitation for substance abusers).

Original Source: Atkinson and van den Noord (2001, p. 66). Copyright © OECD, 2001

opportunities to seek private sector solutions in a mixed economy model of public–private partnerships. While such partnerships may provide a macro solution, they will undoubtedly create micro-organizational problems that will provide significant challenges for public sector managers who will be required to control new boundaries and interfaces between the public and private sector.

SUMMARY

Public management and public finance explore a variety of management practices and techniques along with fiscal tools of the state in order to establish how best these may be used in order to achieve the meta-goals of public policy (see also Chapter 8).

The boundaries between the public and the private sectors obviously vary depending upon the vision of the 'good society' that is dominant at any particular time. Irrespective of where these boundaries are drawn there will still be relationships between the public and the private sectors which need to be established and managed effectively. The challenging question is how best these co-operative relationships can be managed (see Chapter 7).

Relationship management is central to public governance (Jackson and Stainsby, 2000). The idea of relationship management and the issue of where the boundaries of the state should be drawn results in a new role for government namely as a 'broker', i.e. brokering relationships in order to add value (Jackson, 2001).

Does the public sector have the capacity to design and deliver efficient and effective public services at a tax price which the electorate finds acceptable? This is the domain of public management and it is within this arena that much of government failure is found. Central to the achievement of value for money is knowledge, and yet there are significant knowledge deficits throughout the public sector (see Chapter 18). In many significant areas of public policy, the knowledge of the public sector is severely incomplete.

QUESTIONS FOR REVIEW AND DISCUSSION

1   What is the main cause of 'market failure' in your country at the present time? Which state interventions are most likely to correct it in a cost-effective way?

2   What is the main cause of 'government failure' in your country at the present time? Which market-based solutions are most likely to correct this government failure in a cost-effective way?

3   In what ways are politicians and public sector bureaucrats likely to behave which undermines the achievement of social or public welfare? How might this behaviour be controlled to minimize the damage it causes?

4   Is it possible for public expenditure to comprise more than 100 per cent of GDP? Demonstrate how this might occur and discuss what effects it might have on incentive effects in the macro economy.

5   If private sector firms provide public services, funded by public money, what effect

does this have on the public sector borrowing requirement and the level of efficiency in the macro economy?

READER EXERCISES

1   Choose a public service in your country in which you have a special interest. Find statistics on the level of expenditure on this public service, the level of employment in this service and the level of usage of this service over the past ten years.

■   Are the trends in spending change and employment change different? If so, why do you think this is? Can you find evidence to support your argument?

■   Are the trends in line with the change in the numbers of clients? What has been the biggest influence in the number of clients – the eligibility criteria for the service or the standards of service offered to eligible clients?

2   Pick out two different philosophies of the role of the public sector and highlight their contrasting views on the appropriate size of the public sector. What are the underlying assumptions about economic, social and political behaviour in these two philosophies which have led them to such different conclusions? How would you test which of these philosophies is most likely to be able to explain the decisions made recently by politicians in your country on the size of the public sector?

CLASS EXERCISE

What is the main economic role of the state? Is it the achievement of allocative efficiency, distributive justice or macro-economic stabilization? If these goals have to be traded off against one another, which should be given priority in your country at this period of time?

FURTHER READING

Charles V. Brown and Peter M. Jackson (1990), *Public sector economics*, 4th edn. Oxford: Blackwell.

James M. Buchanan and Richard A. Musgrave (1999), *Public finance and public choice: two contrasting visions of the state*. Cambridge: The MIT Press.

Peter M. Jackson (2001), 'Public sector added value: can bureaucracy deliver?' *Public Administration*, Vol. 79, No. 1, pp. 5–28.

Vito Tanzi and Ludger Schuknecht (2000), *Public spending in the 20th century*. Cambridge: Cambridge University Press.

Chapter 4

Public management in flux

Trends and differences across OECD countries

Alex Matheson, Public Management Service, OECD and *Hae-Sang Kwon*, Ministry of Planning and Budget, Korea

INTRODUCTION

The conditions under which OECD governments operate are changing fundamentally (see Chapter 2). With new challenges to the roles and functions of the public sector, a government's stance towards the nature of public service is increasingly becoming a major policy issue across the OECD (Barzelay, 2001). Ten years ago only a few countries were seriously involved in public sector reform. However, this now receives an unprecedented level of attention and there is no reason to expect that the pressures for change will ease off in the next ten years. The public sectors of all countries have to be reconfigured.

This chapter deals mainly with those aspects of public sector reform which have a significant impact on the dynamics of the governmental system as a whole. We call these results 'systemic and governance effects'. In particular, we consider here the variety of motives, drivers and methods with which countries have approached public sector reforms.

The chapter also suggests a new agenda for public management for the period ahead. We advance the proposition that there is no generic flaw in existing public administrative arrangements which can be tackled by a universal set of reforms. Indeed, public sectors almost everywhere are adapting and evolving before our eyes, but in different ways. Public governance and management are in a state of flux, and governments need a new capacity to understand and guide the adaptation process.

LEARNING OBJECTIVES

- To be aware of the objectives of the first generation of public sector reforms
- To be aware of the results of the first generation of public sector reforms
- To be aware of unresolved problems of the first generation of public sector reforms
- To understand differences in public sector reform trajectories of OECD governments
- To be able to undertake a more systemic analysis of public sector reforms

FIRST GENERATION OF REFORMS – EFFICIENT BUT INSUFFICIENT

> Objectives of the first generation of reforms:
> Many of these improvements are a matter of technical or operating efficiency – more outputs produced with fewer inputs. . . . But as important as it is, efficiency in producing outputs is not the whole of public management. It also is essential that government has the capacity to achieve its larger political and strategic objectives. . . . It will have to move from management issues to policy objectives, to fostering outcomes.
>
> *Source*: Schick (1996, p. 87)

There was a flowering of public sector reform efforts in some English-speaking and Scandinavian countries in the 1980s and 1990s which brought new thinking and processes into public services to make them more efficient and more responsive to clients.

The emphasis of such reforms differed from country to country and certainly the 'small government' ideology was far from universally accepted in those countries trying out reforms. However, a unifying factor was a perception that countries shared a common problem of centralized bureaucracy, and, even if it was not possible to see a common intellectual thread through the different reform approaches, they were united by the fact that they dealt with this common problem. Thus the US re-invention process, the Canadian 'La Relève', the UK Next Steps, the NZ and Australian versions of contractualization, the Irish Strategic Management Initiative, the German 'Lean State' reform programme and the Scandinavian reforms, despite huge differences, were seen as part of a unified new public management phenomenon.

A feature of these reforms was that they were directed at 'managerializing' the public sector. In the heat of rhetorical battles the well-established term *public administration* became non-politically correct. It became fashionable to refer to *public management* because *administration* was very much associated with rules, and part of the *managerialist* reform was to reduce the specificity of rules (see Chapter 1). In most cases the reformers were not setting out to change public governance – matters of constitutional arrangements and law were discussed only in terms of facilitating better management – but in some cases they did so.

RESULTS OF THE FIRST GENERATION OF REFORMS

Did reforms in OECD countries over the past fifteen years produce the desired results?

It is difficult to give a definite answer to this question. As Pollitt and Bouckaert (2000) point out, most scholars have been scared off by the methodological problems of comparative assessments at the

> Management efficiency as main result:
> Beyond the impressionistic evidence, there is strong reason to believe that restructuring public management has brought sizeable efficiency gains that are reflected in lower staffing levels and reductions in real operating expenditures.
>
> *Source*: Schick (1997, p. 10)

international level. Similarly, most OECD governments have not been very active in commissioning independent reform assessments – a clear exception to this is the comprehensive evaluation of the public sector reforms in New Zealand (Schick, 1996). This means that, at present, there is little hard evidence as to what kinds of results the first generation of reforms have produced.

Nevertheless, it is possible to make a number of observations regarding changes resulting from the first generation of public sector reforms. It is evident that many countries reduced their reliance on centralized regulation, giving managers autonomy in exchange for better accountability. A number of countries reduced the cost significantly of public services. Governmental processes moved away from the external control of cost, input and process to internal control and management by performance (OECD, 2002b). In many instances these changes have led managers and staff to take more active and flexible approaches to the management of public services, breaking down the compliance-dominated culture which characterized some parts of government. In a number of countries agencies have introduced private sector approaches to dealing with citizens as customers.

UNRESOLVED PROBLEMS OF THE FIRST GENERATION OF REFORMS

However, these changes, though necessary in those countries facing fiscal problems, have not turned out to be a sufficient condition for better government.

Even though the first generation of public sector reforms have produced positive results at the micro level, there have been some negative effects at a systemic level.

For example, Allan Schick's (1996) review together with a range of other reviews undertaken of New Zealand reforms (Petrie and Webber, 1999) suggest very strongly that the main weaknesses are largely concerns about the 'effectiveness' of the regime – see Case Example 4.1. They observed, for example, that the strong incentives on delivering 'outputs' meant insufficient attention to 'outcomes' and also that reinforced accountability for individual chief executives weakened the 'collectivity' of the senior management group.

A closely associated problem has been that some reforms had a perverse impact on matters of governance – who takes public decisions and how these arrangements are safeguarded.

For example:

- In the United Kingdom the creation of Next Steps agencies gave rise to public furores about the relative responsibilities of ministers and chief executives.
- In New Zealand the creation of arm's-length non-commercial public bodies under decision-making boards raised public concern about their accountability.
- In Canada the use of one arm's-length organizational form had the unforeseen effect of removing some aspects of public expenditure from scrutiny by the Auditor-General's office.

The 'first generation of reforms' has been characterized by insufficient attention to *systemic* and to *governance* effects. Systemic and governance effects of public sector reforms are results

CASE EXAMPLE 4.1 RESULTS FROM EVALUATION OF THE PUBLIC MANAGEMENT REFORMS IN NEW ZEALAND

New Zealand has been a front-runner in public sector reforms internationally. Certain deficiencies have emerged as reforms took hold, and New Zealand is making new efforts to make its system more dynamic and effective.

Perceived strengths

- More efficient production of outputs
- A more responsive, innovative public sector delivering better services
- Improved financial accountability
- Improved overall fiscal control

Perceived weaknesses

- The alignment of outputs with outcomes
- Weakness in the link between government strategy and budget spending
- The potential for conflict between purchase and ownership interests
- Problems in contracting for outputs
- Unforeseen consequences of the new regime
- Uneven performance of departments and agencies

Next steps

An advisory group reviewing the whole-of-government management arrangements ('The Review of the Centre') concludes that, although the New Zealand public management system provides a sound platform on which to build, it needs to meet the needs of ministers and citizens more effectively. It proposes improvements in three areas:

1 integrating service delivery across multiple agencies;
2 addressing fragmentation of the state sector and improving its alignment;
3 improving the systems by which state servants are trained and developed.

Source: Ministers of State Services and Finance (2002)

which concern public management as a total system. For example, there are many changes, such as from typewriters to word processors, or from paper systems to electronic systems, or the use of better software, or the use of new marketing techniques, or administrative simplifications or rationalizations, occurring across the range of services which governments provide but they do not change the distribution and safeguarding of power and authority in the public sector.

By 'systemic' we mean the impact on government as a single system: for example, a move to performance budgeting, related to the goals and results of government action, might be effective only if the audit office is able and willing to audit such results.

By 'governance' we mean the impact of changes on the deeper arrangements which determine who takes decisions within the governmental system – and how they are safeguarded over time. For example, the use of contracts for senior officials may impact adversely on the culture of apolitical professionalism which is important in some systems of government.

In our experience, there are three different conceptual problems which contributed to the insufficient attention to the *systemic* and to *governance* effects of what we might call the first generation of reforms:

1 *The first problem was the uptake of management ideas without sufficient attention to their inherent limitations.* There has been an overall tendency towards a reborn version of 'scientific management' with a strong emphasis on formal systems of tight specification and measurement. For complex activities, many of which are at the heart of what it is to be the public sector, a highly formalized approach to management has severe limitations. It is an approach to management which failed decades ago in the private sector, and in the public sector in command economies, because it could not address problems of complexity, change and bounded rationality.

2 *The second problem was a failure to understand that despite its size and complexity, government remains a single enterprise.* Governments operate in a unified constitutional setting and coherent body of administrative law. Their performance is determined by the interaction of a few crucial levers which work on the whole of government – levers such as the policy process, the budget process, the civil service management process and the accountability process, all of which operate within the ambient political/administrative culture (OECD, 2002a). Because of that, any reform aiming for systemic changes cannot hope to do so by concentrating on one lever alone.

Some of the early reform efforts misunderstood this interconnectedness either by changing a major lever of government (e.g. the civil service system) without thinking through the consequences on other parts of the system (e.g. the delegation of management responsibilities in New Zealand seriously weakened the central agency's capacity to develop future leaders), or by attempting to change attitudes and behaviour without addressing the underlying incentives under which people operate (e.g. by seeking to produce change by training and persuasion alone in a largely unaltered civil service system as in the case of Germany).

3 *The third problem was a failure to understand that public management is not only about delivering public services, but it also 'institutionalizes' deeper governance values and is therefore in some respects inseparable from the governance arrangements in which it is embedded.* For example, changing management contracts to give incentives to senior public servants to perform better in their own department may inadvertently undermine collective working in the civil service, which is a critical governance principle.

45

The first generation of reformers (with the notable exception of New Zealand) tended to treat the public management process in isolation from the political policy process and the legislative process. The Strategic Management Initiative (SMI) in Ireland, for example, sought to bring about major management change in the public sector, without addressing the role and accountability of ministers, Cabinet and Parliament in strategy and resource use. Because of that, the SMI succeeded in some micro reforms, but did not achieve its original strategic goals (Department of the Taoiseach, 2002).

WHY COUNTRIES RESPOND DIFFERENTLY TO CHANGING PUBLIC POLICY CONTEXTS

> We are all being lifted in the same tide – but our boats are very different.

The first-generation pioneers of public sector reform were a set of Westminster system and Scandinavian countries which faced some similar fiscal problems in adjusting to a changing world economy, and looked for solutions in reducing public expenditure, freeing up the public sector labour market and the greater use of market-like mechanisms in government.

The problems and solutions of the pioneers so dominated the early modernization agenda that the label 'New Public Management' was used initially to cover this category of changes (Hood, 1991). Some presented them as if they were a breakthrough in public management of universal application. When countries were said to be undertaking public sector reform, there was a degree of agreement as to what this might entail. Developing countries were (often mistakenly) encouraged to adopt NPM 'best practices' (Schick, 1998). There was a tendency in some quarters to see the public management world in terms of 'triage' – there were the heroes of reform, the moderates and the laggards. The x factor was something called 'political will' – the heroes had it and the others lacked it.

Many other OECD governments, however, were also feeling the pressure to change their historical way of operating, but considered that both the nature of the problem and the nature of the solutions might have to be found elsewhere than in the received wisdom of the pioneers.

On the basis of our examination of reform in OECD countries over the past two decades we have observed that responses to the pressures for change have been influenced by six major variables:

1 The state of the economy

Some countries which have been most radical were spurred by a fiscal crisis or by public perception of tax and expenditure levels dragging down national competitiveness. In these cases, a political mandate to reduce public expenditure sometimes became the catalyst for other deliberate public management changes. Economies are differently constituted and some countries where the public is currently prepared to accept high levels of taxation and public expenditure may yet experience the same pressures. In periods of growth and prosperity, governments will tend to buy off rather than confront politically contentious public management problems; however, this may simply defer a structural problem, if one exists, rather than resolve it.

2 Industrial relations

The power and influence of unions, including public sector unions, has profoundly influenced the kinds of adaptations made. Countries fall roughly into three camps:

- Those where labour–employer relations have been generally polarized and where government has confronted and reduced union power in that society. In these cases flexible personnel policies have been introduced in the public service which generally mirror those in the society at large.
- Those where government and unionized labour have managed to reach agreement which has allowed workable compromises between the governments' desire for change and the unions' desire to protect their members.
- Finally, those where dramatic public management changes have been avoided so far because of the political power of the unions and the adverse political consequences of challenging them. How sustainable this is will vary across countries, but in the event of a fiscal crisis, and/or a public perception of the public service as excessively favoured, the confront or compromise options may still have to be faced.

Which of these camps countries belong to is a matter less to do with current political will than it is to do with history and culture. It is important to note that countries do not fit neatly into these categories – reality is more complex – and, because these issues are rooted in politics, nor will they necessarily stay in a particular category over time.

3 Attitude to the role of government

Another variable on which OECD countries differ widely is in the attitude of their citizens in different countries to how big a role government, at whatever level, should play in their lives and in the degree to which they trust government to work in their interests (see Chapter 3). There is a spectrum of opinion ranging from those who believe that government should be kept as small as possible, to those who see a central and active role of government as a constitutive value of their society. There is a spectrum too, perhaps not identical, between societies that tend to trust government and those that do not. This context not only affects the acceptability of proposals to reduce or change the public sector, but also has an influence on how efficiently the state can operate.

4 Differing administrative cultures

Administrative cultures and traditions are another important variable determining how countries adapt to wider changes. OECD countries are yet again spread across a wide spectrum between those countries where formal changes may be expected to bring about predictable changes in behaviour and those where this is less certain. Given that reforms invariably involve rule changes, cultural differences around compliance with rules are clearly important in whether the new reform-driven rules make a difference.

5 Differing national priorities

What citizens want their governments to do in different countries is driven both by politics and the capacities of the other institutions in that society. Clearly a country such as the United States is richly endowed not only with a diverse commercial sector, but a wide range of non-governmental research and policy-oriented organizations that have capacities which can be drawn into the consideration of the public interest. However, many small countries are not so well endowed and their governments have to build more of those capacities themselves. Government priorities must reflect where that country is in terms of its economic and social investments and the popular perception of priorities.

6 Differing constitutional arrangements

The final determinant of how governments respond to the changes in their environment is the degree to which they are constrained by constitutional considerations. Important among these is how power is shared between the Executive and the Legislature and the relative roles of national and state governments in federal systems – or the powers of local government in unitary systems. In some countries, the subnational levels of government have been more responsive to taking up new approaches to public management than have their national counterparts. Constitutional considerations determine whether an Executive can push through major changes, or whether it must first win the consent of the Legislature or face challenges from the Judiciary.

THE NEW REFORM AGENDA: TOWARDS A SYSTEMIC UNDERSTANDING OF REFORM

The effort to improve the efficiency of service delivery has led to a reform discussion focused on *instrumental and technical* management tools. This 'instrument fixation' has meant that changes have been made without due consideration of their governance or systemic effects. A key challenge is now to consider the use of these tools from a *systemic perspective* in order to promote the public sector's overall capacity to adapt to challenges while keeping core values and public confidence. Traditionally, public sectors were designed to remain constant and stable while the world about them changed. In modern society, however, there is a heightened need for governments to be adaptive – to monitor changes in the international and domestic environment and to adapt government actions accordingly. The movement to 'performance' and attention to citizens as 'customers' introduces major pressures towards change. However, while such innovations may work well in a particular government service, attention must also be given to how they impact on deeper values – such as fairness – which are important to public confidence in government as a whole.

Table 4.1 shows the characteristics of the changing public sector reform agenda and the increasing importance of management tools with systemic impact. For the reasons touched on in this chapter, many instrumental reforms prove ineffective because they run counter to deeper incentives in the public management system. More importantly, some adversely affect how public management operates as a total system, and how certain governance values are institutionalized. Furthermore, these obstacles to successful reform differ from one society to another. It is these context-specific obstacles that justify academic caution, and which we believe will necessitate greater attention by governments in future.

The first generation of reformers opened up new possibilities for public management. The bulk of the instrumental innovations made during this very fertile period will find an enduring place in international public management practice. That some of those reforms had perverse consequences was an important reminder that public sectors have their own specificity, and governments need an endogenous capacity for systemic reflection. However, the spirit of innovation which gave rise to the reforms in the first place is also helping those countries deal with the attendant problems.

Fifteen years after the public reform movement began in earnest a number of important lessons may be drawn:

- The idea of there being a common generic problem – which might yield to a common generic set of best practice solutions – has fallen into disrepute.
- Some of the reforms conceived of as purely managerial have turned out to have an impact on public governance – how society arranges its decision making and keeps it safe over time.
- There is a stronger recognition that in many important respects the public administration arrangements of a particular country form an interdependent system in which the reform of one element has implications for the rest of the system.
- Some reforms turned out to be mainly rhetorical and to have made little behavioural change.
- We recognize that systems of public administration are becoming more porous as society as a whole changes so changes are occurring in the public sector independently of those encompassed by deliberate reforms. It is becoming increasingly important for public sectors to have an organizational learning capacity.

In the next phase of public sector reforms, the fostering of innovation should be under-pinned by more attention to the capacity of governments to diagnose the deeper characteristics of their public sectors; to understand the political economy of reform in that environment; to assess the risks and priorities within that context; to develop ways of deciding the point of intervention and sequence of action; and to pay active attention to their public service leadership and culture, especially in respect of governance values.

SUMMARY

The efficiency-oriented public sector reform movement which began in the 1980s has been overtaken by pressures on governmental adaptivity across a wider front. The first generation

Table 4.1 *A changing reform agenda*

	Instrumentalist approaches	Systemic approaches
Environment	Moderate uncertainty and risk	High uncertainty and risk
	Clear divisions of labour for actors	Partnership among government, business, civil society
	Pressure to reduce public expenditure	Globalization
	Pressure from market (transparency, anti-corruption)	Pressure for credibility and predictability
	Delivery structures	Governance arrangements
	Management focus	Policy focus
	Incentives for efficiency	Incentives for effectiveness
Main focus	Flexibility/autonomy	Joined-up, whole-of-government perspective
	Client/customer focus	Citizens' focus
	Specialization	
	Operational efficiency/accountability	Integration, coordination (horizontal, vertical)
	Output focus	Macro efficiency, impact/ accountability
	Short-term focus	Outcome focus
	Single-purpose agency	Longer term focus
	Differentiated issues/programmes	Multi-purpose ministry
	Efficiency and service improvements	Cross-cutting issues/programmes
		Risk management and fostering innovation
Challenges	Poor macro efficiency	How to balance different approaches/values
	Lack of coordination	Capacity building for adaptation to emerging challenges
	Weak in managing risk	
		Setting new partnerships among stakeholders

of reforms improved many services and processes. However, some of the more ambitious reforms failed because of unforeseen impacts on the whole of the government management system, and on underlying governance values and also because of the emergence of new problems.

QUESTIONS FOR REVIEW AND DISCUSSION

1   Explain why the public sector reform agenda in OECD countries has changed.
2   Compare the current reform agenda of your national government against the instrumentalist and systemic approaches to public sector reforms and try to identify to which type it corresponds more closely. Give reasons for your answer.

READER EXERCISES

1   Interview an official or an elected politician who is responsible for public sector reforms at national or local levels in your country. You might ask:
    ■ What do you perceive as the key challenges facing public agencies at present?
    ■ How do you respond to these changes?
    ■ What are the lessons to be learned from past reforms?
2   One of the most important achievements of the 'first-generation'-type public sector reforms has been efficiency gains. Examine an evaluation which has been undertaken of the public sector reforms of an agency or local authority and try to find statistical evidence for this hypothesis.
3   Check out the public sector reform programme of another OECD country on the OECD website (www.oecd.org/gov) and compare it with the reform agenda of your own country. Where do you see differences and commonalities?

CLASS EXERCISE

Mapping the reform paths of public sector reforms in your country

Work as a team with other students on this task:

1   Research sources in the library, on the Internet (in particular OECD) on the public sector reforms in your country and try to identify major reform themes.
2   Discuss what you have identified and try to agree on the three main reform themes in your country.
3   Divide up these three themes between three teams. Each team should identify the evolution of the reform process in respect of that theme. This involves:
    ■ identifying different phases of the reform process (with changing priorities);
    ■ description of the main reform objectives of each phase, what has been achieved and what the problems were.
4   Present this outline to your fellow students in the other teams and discuss whether or not the identified reform paths have been consistent.

FURTHER READING

Christopher Hood (1991), 'A public management for all seasons?', *Public Administration*, Vol. 69, No. 1, pp. 3–19.

OECD (2002a), *Distributed public governance: agencies, authorities and other autonomous Bodies*. Paris: OECD.

Allen Schick (1998), 'Why most developing countries should not try New Zealand's reforms', *The World Bank Research Observer*, Vol. 13, No. 1 (February), pp. 123–131.

Part II

Public management

The second part of this book explores the main managerial functions which contribute to the running of public services and the management of public sector organizations.

The main management functions considered are strategic management (Chapter 5), marketing (Chapter 6), procurement (Chapter 7), financial management (Chapter 8), information and communications technology (ICT) management (Chapter 9), performance measurement and management (Chapter 10), quality management (Chapter 11), and inspection and audit (Chapter 12).

While each of these management functions is shown to have acquired greater importance and to have developed increased momentum during the era of new public management, each chapter also maps the evolution of these functions in recent years, as they have been gradually reformulated to make a contribution within the rather different framework of public governance.

Chapter 5

Strategic management in public sector organizations

Tony Bovaird, Bristol Business School, UK

INTRODUCTION

Now everyone wants to have a strategy. To be without a strategy is to appear direction-less and incompetent – whether it be a strategy for the organization as a whole, for the corporate centre, for the service delivery units, for consultation with stakeholders, for staff remuneration, for introducing changes to front office opening hours, for office paper recycling. . . . Sadly, by the time a word means everything, it has come to mean nothing. So can we rescue any meaning for this much overused word 'strategy'?

Johnson and Scholes (2002) suggest that we can at least map out the characteristics which distinguish strategic from non-strategic decisions (Box 5.1). Thus strategic decisions help to determine what the organization does *not* do (its scope), how well it fits the requirements of its customers and adopts the technologies available to it in the marketplace, how much it focuses on what it does particularly well, how well it appeals to its stakeholders, how it balances long- and short-term considerations, and how it manages the potential knock-on effects of the narrow-minded and selfish decisions made in separate 'silos' of the organization. In this reading, a decision is strategic if it meets one of these criteria – if not, the decision may be characterized as *operational* or *tactical*, rather than *strategic*. However, 'strategic' should not be confused with 'important' – strategic and operational decisions are *both* important and will be effective only if aligned with each other. The key is to be able to distinguish between them.

BOX 5.1 STRATEGIC DECISIONS ARE CONCERNED WITH:

- scope of an organization's activities;
- matching the organization's activities to its environment;
- allocation and reallocation of major resources in an organization;
- values, expectations and objectives of those influencing strategy;
- the long-term direction for the organization;
- implications for operational change throughout the organization.

Source: Adapted from Johnson and Scholes (2002)

LEARNING OBJECTIVES

- To understand what 'strategy' and 'strategic management' mean in a public sector context
- To be able to prepare a corporate strategy and business plan for a service or organization
- To understand the difference between strategic management and strategic planning
- To understand how strategy making is different in a politically driven organization, as opposed to strategy making in a private firm
- To understand how strategic management and innovation mutually reinforce each other

THE BUILDING BLOCKS: 'STRATEGY', 'STRATEGIC PLANS', 'STRATEGIC MANAGEMENT' IN THE PUBLIC SECTOR

So what is 'strategy'? It is perhaps surprising, given how often the word is used, that it has no widely agreed definition. Perhaps we ought to start with an antidote to most definitions, after Karl Weick: 'A "strategy" is an after-the-event rationalization by top management of what they (often wrongly) believe their organization has recently been doing.' While this warns us not to believe everything we are told about strategy, we probably need to develop a more positive definition.

Mintzberg is helpful here. He suggests five different meanings which are often given to the word 'strategy' in management contexts (Box 5.2). These will each be appropriate in difference circumstances. Since they are already in wide currency, it would be unwise to insist that only one of these meanings makes sense.

BOX 5.2 WHAT IS A 'STRATEGY'?

- *Plan*: some sort of consciously intended course of action, a guideline to deal with a situation
- *Ploy*: a specific manoeuvre intended to outwit an opponent or competitor
- *Pattern*: a pattern in a stream of actions
- *Position*: a means of locating an organization in an 'environment' – the mediating force or 'match' between organization and environment
- *Perspective/paradigm*: an ingrained way of perceiving the world (what 'personality' is to the individual).

Source: Henry Mintzberg (1987)

However, when many people think of a 'strategy', they immediately think of a strategic plan (often contained in a written document). The idea of strategic planning is, of course, quite old. Its sources in the last two centuries included, first, the town and country planning movement (including the 'worker colonies' of Owen, Cadbury, Salt, Guell and so on, the 'garden cities' of Howard, and the 'machine for city living' of Le Corbusier), and second, industrial planning, starting in Soviet Russia in the late 1920s and spreading through the Comecon and many other countries since 1945. Ironically, these 'public sector' planning roots then gave rise, from the 1950s onwards, to private sector derivatives in Western countries, particularly budgetary and manpower planning, which in turn spread to many public sector organizations. Eventually, the idea of overall corporate plans for an organization, and separate business plans (or 'service plans') for units within the organization, became very strong both in private and public sectors.

However, it is clear that 'strategic management' is more than making and implementing strategic plans. It encompasses, at the very least, the other activities shown in Box 5.2 – the 'ploy making' of competitive organizations, the 'pattern making' of organizations which wish to give a sense of purpose and coherence to their different units and activities, the 'positioning' of the organization to achieve 'fit' between its activities and its environment, and the 'paradigm-changing' activities which try positively to influence the culture of the organization. To this list of alternative ways of perceiving strategy we might add strategy as 'pull' (or 'stretch') – the focus on improvement of the organization's core competences so that it can do better what it already does well.

Each of these perspectives on strategy has its own literature within the strategic management field, but several are also studied in other fields. 'Ploy making' clearly relates closely to games theory, studied in detail within mathematical economics. 'Paradigm changing' has been a major theme in organization studies. The definition of strategy as 'positioning' clearly indicates the close relationship between strategic management and marketing strategy.

PREPARING A CORPORATE STRATEGY AND BUSINESS PLANS

In this section, we will look at the conventional approach to strategic planning, covering the overall corporate plan and the business plans for individual units which typically are expected to spring from it.

We can see the corporate strategic plan of an organization as encompassing several constituent parts, which need to be aligned with each other:

- *the marketing strategy* (to respond to what the environment wants);
- *the service production and delivery strategy* (to make best use of internal capabilities);
- *the financial strategy* (to ensure that the necessary finance is available for all resources, including the right level of staffing, necessary for the service production and delivery strategy, and that these financial resources are allocated in the most efficient and effective way possible).

Moreover, each constituent unit of the organization can prepare a 'business plan' along similar lines for their part of the organization. In this way, business plans are nested within the overall corporate strategy and should be aligned with it.

This immediately suggests that the contents of the corporate plan may, in large measure, replicate the contents of the organization's portfolio of business plans. However, this would lead to a very cumbersome corporate plan, with little value added. Consequently, the corporate plan often focuses on laying down broad guidelines to which the departmental or divisional business plans should conform, with the greater level of detail being left in the business plans.

In this section, we look in particular at the preparation and implementation of corporate strategies and business plans, and their relationship to service production and delivery strategies. We leave the detailed consideration of marketing strategies to Chapter 6 and financial strategies to Chapter 8.

In order to prepare this suite of plans, three sets of analyses are necessary:

1   Analysis of the external environment of the organization.
2   Analysis of the internal environment of the organization.
3   Analysis of the strategic options available and their relative merits.

In Chapter 6, we discuss how the external environment can be analysed to help develop a marketing strategy. In this chapter, we will now look in turn at analysis of the internal environment and of the strategic options, before discussing how each of these three analyses can be used in formulating the corporate plan and business plans.

Analysing the internal environment

In analysing the internal environment of the organization, we seek to understand the factors influencing internal stakeholders and the consequent strengths and weaknesses of the organization, compared to other organizations working to serve the same needs and markets.

There are four main elements to this analysis:

1   Value chain analysis.
2   Core competence analysis.
3   Organizational culture analysis.
4   Competitor and collaborator analysis.

Value chain analysis explores the ways in which the organization creates value for its stakeholders and distributes this value between them. This requires a definition of 'value'. In the private sector, this normally refers to the set of benefits which are required by the firm's stakeholders (although now there are also pressures for 'corporate social responsibility' even in the private sector). Typically, in the public sector 'value added' has rather more dimensions:

- *user value;*
- *value to wider groups* (such as family or friends of service users);

- *political value* (support to democratic process, e.g. through co-planning of services with users and other stakeholders);
- *social value* (creation of social cohesion or supporting social interaction);
- *environmental value* (ensuring sustainability of all service provision).

Taking this multi-level concept of value, we need to understand how a public sector organization can create value. The model which has been used typically to do this is the value chain, again derived from work in the 1970s by Michael Porter. Since Porter's version of the value chain was developed essentially for manufacturing firms, it needs to be altered significantly when applying it in the public sector (Figure 5.1).

The primary activities are the 'front-line' activities or the basic 'production function' of a service organization, with an extra step for 'needs assessment' to allow for the fact that not all those who want the service will meet the eligibility or priority criteria set by a public sector organization. The support activities are the 'back-room' processes which support the 'front line'. For an organization to be excellent, it must be good at each of these primary and support activities, and, in addition, it must be good at combining them.

It is possible for each organization to attempt to benchmark these processes – indeed, value chain analysis is valuable only when used for comparisons. In activities where the organization is not very good, it might either try to improve them or to outsource them to other organizations apparently able to do them better. In this way, the value chain suggests how the organization might focus on those links in the chain where it is uniquely able to add value. However, Porter also recognized that an effective organization should also be able to integrate all the activities of the value chain. Consequently, outsourcing is not unambiguously the right answer, even when some value activities are done better by someone else, if the organization is less able to integrate externally sourced activities. This argument has often been seized upon, perhaps sometimes too readily, to claim that 'the in-house team

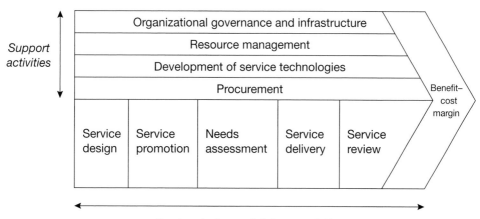

Figure 5.1 *Public sector value chain*
Source: Adapted by the author from an original concept by Porter (1985)

may not do some things well, but we are used to working with them'. Clearly, this could lead to complacency in the face of unfortunate levels of inefficiency.

Core competence analysis also explores the strategic capabilities of the organization, as does the value chain, but it focuses on the underlying competences which make the organization particularly useful to its customers. A core competence resides in the organization, not in individuals or in the technology alone (Box 5.3).

BOX 5.3 A CORE COMPETENCE IS . . .

. . . a bundle of skills and technologies that enables an organization to provide a particular benefit to customers.

. . . Because core competences are the highest level, longest-lasting units for strategy making, they must be the central subject of corporate strategy.

Source: Hamel and Prahalad (1994), pp. 199 and 220

There are many different ways in which core competences can be developed. Some examples of common core competences are illustrated in Box 5.4.

As in the value chain, a key lesson from the analysis is meant to be that an organization should focus only on those activities for which it has a core competence. Other activities should either be abandoned, or (if they are necessary to deliver value to customers) outsourced.

Hamel and Prahalad suggest that an organization should seek to have many core competences. However, it is possible that organizations in the public sector cannot focus so ruthlessly on activities for which they have a core competence and abandon those activities for which their core competences do not fit them. Consequently, it may be difficult for a public sector organization to develop more than a few core competences – and some may struggle even to achieve that.

BOX 5.4 SOME EXAMPLES OF CORE COMPETENCES

Speed. The ability to respond quickly to customer or market demands, and to incorporate new ideas and technologies quickly into products.

Consistency. The ability to produce a product that unfailingly satisfied customers' expectations.

Acuity. The ability to see the competitive environment clearly, and thus to anticipate and respond to customers' evolving needs and wants.

Agility. The ability to adapt simultaneously to many different business environments.

Innovativeness. The ability to generate new ideas and to combine existing elements to create new sources of value.

Source: Hamel and Prahalad (1994)

Organizational culture analysis explores the underlying taken-for-granted assumptions and norms in the organization. There are two well-established ways of exploring organizational cultures – one is the 'four cultures' approach of Charles Handy (Box 5.5) and the other is the 'cultural web' of Johnson and Scholes.

The 'four cultures' approach is a valuable way of distinguishing between very different types of organizational culture. However, as Handy himself recognizes, most organizations are likely to have all four cultures simultaneously; for example, the role culture is likely to predominate in 'steady state' parts of the organization (such as payroll), the task culture is likely to predominate in the innovative parts of the organization (such as new service development), while the power culture is likely to predominate in those parts of the organization which deal with frequent crises, where a strong and consistent 'hand on the tiller' is needed (e.g. in public relations or at the very top of the organization).

BOX 5.5 THE 'FOUR CULTURES'

The *power culture*: all power rests with one individual at the centre of the organization (the spider at the centre of the web, pulling all the skeins) – this is typical of family firms and those small businesses where the founder is still running the organization.

The *role culture*: all individuals play a clear, standardized role within their own 'silo' of the organization, reporting to a line manager and managing the staff below them in the hierarchy, but they do not exercise initiative and do not communicate with anyone outside of the line management structure – this is typical of large bureaucracies (in both public and private sectors).

The *task culture*: individuals undertake tasks in multidisciplinary, multi-departmental groups, in addition to working within a line management structure – this tends to be the culture aspired to by professional staff working within large organizations

The *person culture*: individuals tend to work alone, with only passing reference to line management responsibilities and only working in teams where it suits them – this tends to be typical of the academic community, of small consultancies, and of the research and development function of technically and scientifically oriented firms.

Source: Adapted from Handy (1993)

A more action-oriented approach to the understanding and change of organizational culture is given by the 'cultural web', which suggests the mapping of six different aspects:

1   The *stories* within the organization. (Who are the heroes? Who are the villains? What does 'success' look like?)
2   The *routines and rituals* within the organization. (How seriously is staff appraisal taken? How fair is the annual promotion round? Whose work gets special mention in the Annual Report or Improvement Plan?)

3   The *symbols* of the organization. (Whose room has a carpet/bookcase/sofa or has three windows? Do people use first names or family names when talking to each other? How do people dress?)

4   The *power base* in the organization. (Who has the greatest power in practice? Who controls access to those with power?)

5   The *structure* of the organization. (Hierarchical? Many-layered or de-layered?)

6   The *control* system of the organization. (How does the organization stop things happening – formally and informally? How much initiative and innovation is encouraged?)

In summary, the cultural web seeks to establish what is the *paradigm* of the organization – the 'set of assumptions held relatively in common and taken for granted' in the organization (Johnson and Scholes, 2002). Mapping of the cultural web is, of course, only the beginning. It is necessary for the leaders of an organization to take active steps to change those aspects of the culture which are not appropriate. Typically, they start with the more visible parts of the culture – the structures and control system. However, this is not enough – for culture change to take root it is necessary to ensure that the stories, rituals and routines and the symbols are altered as well. This is clearly a much harder (and longer) task – it entails winning the 'hearts and minds' in the organization.

Before engaging in such a difficult process, leaders need to be confident that they know what a better culture would look like. Kotter and Heskett (1992) have produced strong evidence (although admittedly mainly from the private sector) that high-performing organizations tend to have highly adaptable cultures, which not only respond positively to change but actually value change and seek out innovation. Most studies of the public sector indicate that such attitudes are rare in people and even rarer in organizations as a whole. This possibly remains the single greatest challenge to strategic management in the public sector.

Competitor and collaborator analysis allows us to build on these analyses of the internal environment. Essentially, we need to ask 'How do we compare in terms of value chain and core competences with those rivals we wish to outdo and those collaborators with whom we wish to work?' This allows us to do a 'Strengths and Weaknesses' analysis of our organization *vis-à-vis* other organizations in our sector. Once again, as with all elements of an analysis of the internal environment, this leads to a questioning of how to balance in-house production with outsourcing. Where our competitors are better than us, we have the choice of improving, outsourcing or of working with the competitors in 'strategic service delivery partnerships' (which can allow us to use their strengths to make our service offering better). This latter option is often unwelcome in the public sector, especially among staff and politicians. However, if the alternative is to continue to do a worse job, then strategic partnering may become seen as desirable. Once again, the most difficult part of the analysis is to ask 'How well will the two organizations gel together in practice – will they achieve synergies working with each other, or will they cause difficulties for each other so that the partnership is less than the sum of the parts?' As always, this is hard to analyse a priori – sometimes the only way to answer this question is to 'suck it and see'.

Developing and evaluating strategic options

Taken together, the analyses of external and internal factors allow a SWOT (strengths, weaknesses, opportunities and threats) analysis to be compiled for the organization. (It may seem a little cruel that we have taken so long to reach a point which many people feel they can sketch out in five minutes on the back of an envelope, but academic analysis can always make the simple appear much more complex – sometimes fruitfully so!)

The SWOT analysis needs to be turned into a series of strategic options for doing things better in the future – building on strengths, reducing weaknesses, seizing opportunities, countering threats.

The notion of a 'strategic option' is not very clear from the literature – it is often seen as any change which might be made in the existing elements of a strategy. However, a more rigorous approach suggests that a strategic option should be a coherent alternative strategy in itself (Box 5.6).

BOX 5.6 A STRATEGIC OPTION

This is a connected series of decisions on:

- strategic basis of the organization – ownership, mission, values, scope
- 'generic strategy' – cost leadership or quality leadership
- relation of corporate HQ to service units
- 'strategic direction' – consolidation, new services, new markets, or both
- growth strategy – 'grow own timber', acquire, buy new, form alliances or partnerships
- competitive tactics
- a new organizational culture

Source: Adapted from Johnson and Scholes (2002)

For an organization to be successful it must be imaginative at devising a full range of strategic options, so that they can be evaluated and the most appropriate strategic option chosen. Of course, this requires imaginative and creative people who are able to play a role in mapping out these alternative 'futures' for the organization – and such people are not always easy to find, nor do organizations (especially bureaucracies) always allow 'creatives' to play such important roles.

Once a full range of strategic options has been mapped out, they need to be evaluated (unless top management has already decided that it prefers one of them, in which case the evaluation will be more of a 'show trial' for the undesired options). The evaluation process can use three sets of criteria – feasibility, suitability and acceptability – to test out the strategic options before selecting one of them (Johnson and Scholes, 2002).

The *suitability* of the options is screened typically by use of a number of portfolio analyses, which test if the proposed portfolio of services (for specific target groups) will offer a coherent set of activities, which will provide a good fit between what the external environment requires and the strengths and weaknesses identified in the organization. We will look briefly at two such portfolios. The first is the 'Boston Matrix', which comes from the perspective of the provider side in a public sector organization (Figure 5.2). Here services are ranked by their growth in demand (or need) and by their 'net social value' (which might, for example, be their contribution to meeting the needs of high-priority users, or meeting high-level organizational objectives). Clearly, the services in the 'dead ducks' box are likely candidates for closure, so that more resources are available to grow the 'star' services, repackage and relaunch the 'bread and butter' services, and pilot the 'question mark' services appropriately (so that they either become star services or can be dropped altogether as failed experiments).

The second suitability test is the 'Need and Provision Matrix', from the perspective of commissioning organizations in the public sector (Figure 5.3). This suggests that an organization should make extensive in-house provision only where need is high and is not being met by other agencies. This essentially starts from the viewpoint that a commissioning organization must make the most of its scarce resources to encourage the widest possible provision from all agencies in the field, only using its resources for direct provision when all other avenues have been explored.

The *acceptability* of the options needs to be tested against stakeholder objectives, which therefore have to be understood by the organization. In the private sector this would include rate of return on investment, shareholder value added and so on. In the public sector these objectives are likely to be much more complex – and there are usually many more stakeholders as well. In order to understand the objectives, it is necessary to show the cause-and-effect chain linking high-level 'impact objectives' to the lower level 'service objectives' whose achievement it is believed will contribute to the impact objectives (i.e. a 'hierarchy of objectives').

Figure 5.4 illustrates how this might be done in the case of community safety initiatives. The overall map of objectives might belong to the police force, but a more restricted set of objectives (those inset in the smaller box) might apply to a community safety unit in a local

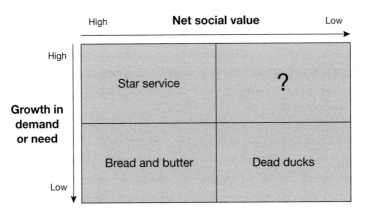

Figure 5.2 *Public sector Boston matrix*

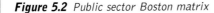

authority. If there are unproven or disputed links in the logic of these 'cause-and-effect' chains between different levels of objectives, then there is a need for a more evidence-based approach to setting strategy in this area (see Chapter 12).

The *feasibility* of the options includes financial, technological, staffing and managerial feasibility. However, when an otherwise highly desirable option appears to be unfeasible, this should not be accepted without a fight. Most feasibility constraints can be removed or circumvented through the use of energy – or money. Only when the constraint itself has been tested and found to be binding can a feasibility test be accepted as final.

The performance of each of the strategic options can be reported in a *Balanced Scorecard* (Kaplan and Norton, 1996), in order that their relative merits may be assessed. This sets out

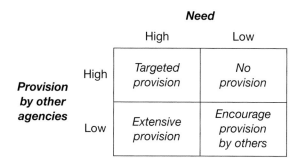

Figure 5.3 *Need and provision matrix*
Source: Walsh (1989)

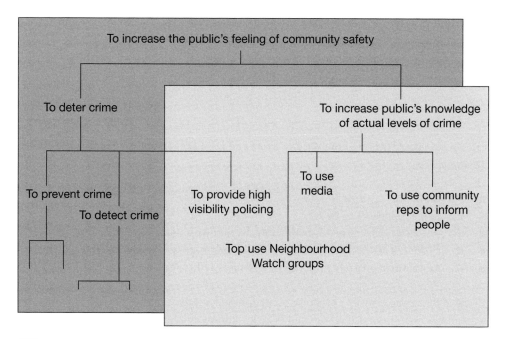

Figure 5.4 *Maps from two stakeholders*

performance indicators for each of the main organizational objectives, usually grouped under such headings as 'citizen and user results', 'process improvement results', 'organizational learning and development results' and 'financial results'. While this technique was originated for reporting in the private sector, it has now also become popular in public sector organizations in the UK and USA. (Issues in the use of performance indicators in the public sector are dealt with more fully in Chapter 10.)

Selecting a strategic option

The analysis and evaluation of strategic options should help a public sector organization to select its preferred strategic option. This option should spell out three major components:

1   A marketing strategy (and associated marketing plans).
2   A service production strategy (and associated service delivery plans).
3   A resource mobilization and utilization strategy (and associated resource plans).

The components of the marketing strategy are considered in Chapter 6, and the components of the resource mobilization and utilization strategy are considered in Chapter 8.

The key elements of the service production strategy which emerge from the corporate and business planning exercises will be:

■   a decision on which core competences to maintain and to develop;
■   a portfolio of services which will be provided in-house;
■   a portfolio of services which will be outsourced;
■   a procurement process and protocols, which will ensure that the choice of suppliers and partners is transparently fair and that all external providers sign up to the achievement of the objectives of the organization;
■   a set of objectives and targets which can be monitored to show whether the services have been efficiently delivered to the quality level specified.

How can this service production strategy be put into practice? Typically, service delivery plans are prepared which allow the key issues to be considered and co-ordinated in detail. These include:

■   the quality standards to be set;
■   the staffing standards to be set;
■   the communications process, both internally and with other suppliers;
■   the logistics of service delivery, including staffing rotas and transport arrangements;
■   the maintenance of assets (particularly premises and transport).

Clearly, the separation of corporate strategies and business plans into the elements of marketing strategy, service production strategy and resources strategy is artificial and these strategies will often overlap considerably. Similarly, the marketing plans and service delivery plans will often overlap (e.g. making sure that proper transport arrangements are in place is part of the 'place' factor in the marketing plan, but also part of the 'logistics' factor in the service delivery plan).

JOINING UP STRATEGIES AND 'SEAMLESS SERVICES'

So far we have essentially been discussing the strategy of one public sector organization. In practice, no public sector organization can expect to be successful without close interaction with many other agencies. Most public sector organizations need to work with others:

- to ensure, through their supply chain, that they have high-quality inputs, of which the most important in the public sector is staff (highlighting the importance of relationships with staff training and development organizations, for example);
- to ensure that their services are well designed to meet the needs of service users and other affected stakeholders (highlighting the importance of market research organizations and co-planning with prospective service users);
- to ensure that the holistic needs of service users are met, and not just those needs in which each organization specializes (highlighting the importance of partnership planning and the delivery of 'seamless services');
- to ensure that the impact of services on the client is as high as possible (so that advice to service users, particularly that given by current or past users of the service – 'expert clients' or 'expert patients' – can be very valuable).

The complexity of the interactions in the public service supply chain are illustrated in Figure 5.5. This demonstrates how, in the case of one client group, the elderly, there are typically many public agencies which do or potentially could contribute services. It may or may not be the case that one is prepared to take the lead in co-ordinating this overall service provision. Further back in the supply chain, of course, all of these organizations have their own suppliers (of equipment, of transport, sometimes of agency staff and so on).

Figure 5.5 also highlights a facet of supply chains that is usually much more important in the public sector than in the private sector – the fact that the service user is not the sole beneficiary of the service (and in some cases may not even consider her or himself to be a beneficiary at all). In addition to benefits to the service users, there are also benefits to families, carers and so on who will often be relieved of some responsibilities because of the services given. Furthermore, there are often benefits to other customers – for example, the experience of 'expert patients' or of enthusiastic day centre attendees may be used to encourage reluctant clients. Finally, there may be significant benefits to other citizens, either because they altruistically wish to see people in need being well looked after, or because they may feel reassured that they themselves, in turn, will be well looked after in future when they too need such services. Of course, a supply chain is only as strong as its weakest link. The public sector must ensure that the links between *all* these value chains are managed, although it may be able to convince others (e.g. voluntary groups) to take on responsibility for managing some of these links.

67

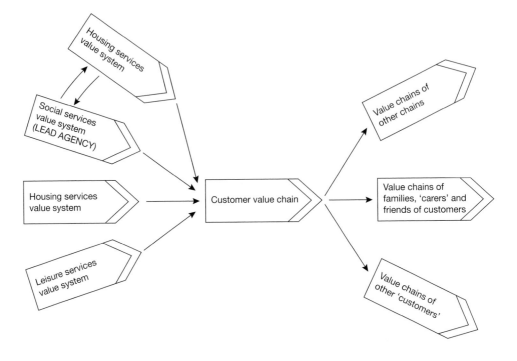

Figure 5.5 *The public service supply chain*

STRATEGIC MANAGEMENT, STRATEGIC PLANNING AND STRATEGIC THINKING

In the above sections, we have concentrated on strategy as 'plan'. This clearly can be a very productive approach. However, it belongs to the view that strategy making is a 'linear' process, based on rational planning – a 'determination of the long-term goals of an enterprise and the adoption of courses of action and the allocation of resources necessary for carrying out these goals' (Chandler, 1962).

In the 1980s, a very different view of strategic management began to emerge, influenced particularly by the work of Henry Mintzberg. He suggested that very few planned, intended strategies are actually implemented in the end – most of them end up in the rubbish bin. Moreover, many strategies which do get realized were never planned – they might, for example, have been imposed on the organization by a dominant political leader or chief executive, or have been the result of seizing an opportunity which was too good to turn down. Mintzberg then suggested one other type of strategy which has had enormous influence on the field in the subsequent period – 'emergent strategies'. Emergent strategies are those which are grounded in the practice of staff, rather than planned by top managers. They are adopted implicitly, often unseen, because they work better than the official 'planned strategies'.

Of course, not all the emergent strategies which creep out of the woodwork are desirable – it depends on which stakeholder they help. So, for example, public sector staff have often been accused in the past of taking a 'job's worth' approach. This is often an emergent strategy, flatly contradicting the explicit customer-oriented strategies of their organization – but it works for such staff while they can get away with it. More sinisterly, corrupt practices sometimes originate as emergent strategies – for example, when officials give a licence to a local business more quickly than normal by short-circuiting proper procedures and are then offered a small payment as a mark of thanks. This can quickly develop into an expectation (on both sides) that a faster route exists if a 'backhander' is given.

Nevertheless, emergent strategies have the potentially desirable characteristic that they are particularly likely to correspond to the needs of the environment in which they emerge. This is because they tend to be developed by the front-line staff and lower level managers who are especially close to service users – the people whom Michael Lipsky labelled 'street-level bureaucrats'. Experience in many public service redesign initiatives (e.g. the 'business process re-engineering' vogue of the 1990s in the USA and the recent Best Value reviews in UK local government) suggests that it can be extremely difficult to get staff to take part formally in service improvement programmes – thus emergent strategies which are developed naturally at this level of the organization may be all the more valuable.

What are the organizational implications of emergent strategies? Mintzberg suggests that they alter the balance in the creation of strategy, moving it from 'planners' to managers:

> Strategies are not things that are written down periodically, although people do try to write them down. Strategies are things that exist in people's heads; strategic visions cannot easily be written down. So I think managers create the strategy; planners might formalize it.
>
> (Mintzberg, 1992)

Of course, this formalization role is important – it allows an organization to test emergent strategies once they become noticed. Those which are not in the best interests of the organization can then be stamped out, while those which are valuable can be incorporated into the planned intended strategy and rolled out through the organization.

However, Mintzberg's critique throws serious doubt on the 'plan fetishism' which has long been a characteristic of the public sector and which has perhaps been brought to its apogée by the current UK government, in which not only must every government agency have a strategic plan, but so also must each of its organizational units – and all of these must be either externally inspected or clearly tied to a performance target, so that its achievement may be monitored.

STRATEGIC MANAGEMENT IN A POLITICAL ENVIRONMENT

Many of the analytical frameworks used earlier in this chapter are also used in the private sector (although some, such as the concept of planning, actually originated in the public sector). It is important that we do not fall into the trap of believing that there is no difference between strategic management in public, private and voluntary sectors. The key differences which spring from the political context in which public sector organizations work include:

- the role of politicians, who often clash openly on major strategic issues;
- the interaction between politicians and other stakeholder groups;
- the pressure for 'short-termist' decision making arising from regular elections.

Strategic management involves difficult decision making. It normally means selectivity – *not* doing some things – and this usually annoys some stakeholders. Only if the organization is prepared to weather the adverse comment which selectivity normally brings about can it hope to manage strategically. In the private and voluntary sector, selective decisions are often internally controversial but, when the strategy has been selected, it is expected that all groups will abide by it and support it in public.

However, the public sector can rarely hope to enjoy the luxury of such public consensus. Opposition politicians often see it as their role to contest publicly, and very vocally, almost all strategic decisions made by the ruling group. Indeed, they often seek to mobilize opposition from any groups which have been disadvantaged by a decision.

For a strategic direction to be maintained, the ruling group needs to be able to be steadfast in defending its main strategic decisions. However, there are many pressure points by means of which politicians may be driven to make inconsistent decisions or to reverse strategic decisions already taken. These pressures may come from:

- political parties;
- policy networks;
- the civil service or managerial systems;
- professional groups;
- charities or voluntary organizations (at national or local level);
- community groups;
- sponsors who provide funding for a party or an individual.

Political platforms are usually designed to take on board the interests of a wide coalition of stakeholders. At worst, this can mean that politicians seek to 'please everyone, all the time'. In these circumstances, strategic management becomes next to impossible. However, even where politicians start out by plotting a clear and principled course, relatively minor changes in the balance of their coalition of stakeholders can demand that they revise their strategies.

The need to maintain political coalitions also helps to explain why highly rational strategies, cooked up by well-informed professionals and backed by top politicians in the local council and nationally, may still fail because they 'don't go down well on the street'. Since politicians are subjected regularly to this street test in the form of elections, their strategies are likely to be over-influenced by the short-term and narrow factors which sway voters at a given time (Joyce, 1999).

STRATEGIC MANAGEMENT AND INNOVATION

Finally, it is important to consider the interaction of strategic management and innovation. We stressed above that a healthy organizational culture is, above all, one which is adaptable and which seeks out innovation and change. On the other hand, innovation can be disruptive and even destabilizing to an organization, and, as McKevitt (1998) says, 'it is hardly feasible to expect large, rule-bound organizations to be responsive and alert to client needs' (p. 118). What is the role of strategic management in embedding innovative attitudes, balancing their potentially damaging effects and overcoming bureaucratic inertia?

There are many ways in which a public sector organization can innovate, including:

- new services;
- new customers (target groups);
- new service production processes;
- new procurement processes;
- new partnership arrangements with the rest of the public sector, with the voluntary sector and with the private sector;
- new decision-making processes ('addressing the democratic deficit');
- new governance structures and processes;
- new goals and ambitions for the organization;
- new organizational culture.

Given the importance of many of these, 'no change' is clearly not an option in strategic management in the public sector. However, it is almost certainly also true that here, as always, being strategic means being selective and focused. Not all of these innovative directions can be pursued effectively at once – this way madness lies. The UK public sector has often been accused of 'initiativitis' in recent years because it has not accepted this lesson. So perhaps public sector strategy makers will have to accept that, just as 'no change' is not an option, similarly 'all change' is not an option either.

SUMMARY

This chapter has argued that strategic planning and strategic management are distinctively different. While both are important, strategic management is essential, whereas strategic planning may be desirable only in more limited circumstances. The chapter has considered a range of techniques for understanding the internal environment of organizations and for identifying and evaluating strategic options.

The chapter has emphasized that public sector organizations need to work together with other organizations, in all sectors, if their work is to be effective. They also need to co-plan and co-produce most services with the service users and other citizens, to make the most of the resources in the community.

Political processes are intrinsic to good strategic management in the public sector but some aspects of political decision making can make it difficult to develop and maintain appropriate strategies in the public sector.

Finally, the chapter has argued that innovation is the lifeblood of good strategic management – and that strategic management must therefore ensure that innovation is embedded within public sector organizations. 'No change' is not an option (but neither is 'all change').

QUESTIONS FOR REVIEW AND DISCUSSION

1   How do you think strategic plans in the public sector would differ if they were initially drawn up by politicians and then considered for approval by professionals and managers in the public sector?

2   In what circumstances do you think that realized strategies would be more likely to stem from planned intended strategies than from emergent processes? Why?

READER EXERCISES

1   Find a strategic plan for a public sector organization with which you are familiar. How well has it analysed its external and internal environments? Does it give an indication of the strategic options it considered before it chose its preferred strategy? Does it make clear the evaluation criteria on the basis of which its preferred strategy was chosen?

2   Look through a recent copy of a serious national newspaper (such as the *Guardian*, *Le Monde* or *Frankfurter Allgemeine Zeitung*). Identify all the references to the 'strategies' of public sector organizations. How many of them meet the criteria outlined in Box 5.1? Do you think that any of the 'strategies' which do *not* meet the criteria in Box 5.1 are nevertheless genuinely dealing with 'strategic' decisions? If so, how would you amend or add to the criteria in Box 5.1 to allow for this?

CLASS EXERCISES

1   Divide into four groups. Each group should prepare a ten-minute presentation to argue for *one* of the following propositions:
    ■ Public sector organizations should prepare and publish detailed strategic plans for all of their activities.
    ■ Public sector organizations should prepare and publish strategic plans only for their most important activities.
    ■ Public sector organizations should prepare and publish strategic plans only for those activities which are highly controversial.
    ■ Public sector organizations should not bother to prepare and publish detailed strategic plans at all, but rather should consult widely on their detailed proposals for changes to their activities.

2   In groups, identify some organizations you know, in public, voluntary and private sectors, which have the core competences listed in Box 5.4. Compare your results, paying special attention to what sector differences appear to emerge.

FURTHER READING

Paul Joyce (1999), *Strategic management for the public services*. Buckingham: Open University Press.

Gerry Johnson and Kevan Scholes (eds) (2001), *Exploring public sector strategy*. Harlow, Essex: Financial Times/Prentice Hall.

David McKevitt (1998), *Managing core public services*. Oxford: Blackwell.

Chapter 6

Marketing in public sector organizations

Tony Bovaird, Bristol Business School, UK

INTRODUCTION

For many years in the 1970s and 1980s, lectures on marketing in the public sector began apologetically with an explanation of why marketing might be important – and generally they adopted a rather defensive standpoint, assuming that many in the audience would be predisposed to be hostile to the concept. This is no longer the case, as the growing literature on public sector marketing attests. However, the suspicion remains that public sector marketing has to demonstrate its role carefully and has to demarcate itself clearly from private sector marketing. This chapter looks at how marketing can contribute to the more efficient and effective operation of public sector organizations and services.

LEARNING OBJECTIVES

- To understand the role of marketing in a public sector context
- To be able to prepare a marketing strategy, and marketing plan for a service or organizational unit
- To understand how marketing is different in a politically driven organization working on issues with wide-ranging public implications, as opposed to marketing in private firms
- To understand the limitations of marketing in a public sector context

THE ROLE OF MARKETING IN A PUBLIC SECTOR CONTEXT

Marketing is often thought of as essentially commercial – that is, oriented towards making profits. This clearly is not relevant to most aspects of public services and public sector organizations.

Again, marketing often has rather negative connotations associated with selling, even 'high-pressure selling'; or of promotion of goods or services, perhaps through 'hype'; or of advertising, perhaps through subliminal influencing. Clearly, if marketing is to play a valuable role in a public sector context, these negative aspects will have to be transcended.

Fortunately there is no reason to believe that marketing must be viewed only in these pejorative terms. It is quite possible to define marketing in ways which suggest that it could be highly valuable to public sector organizations (Box 6.1). After all, 'markets' are only the contexts in which those needing a service are able to use alternative providers, either in the public, private or voluntary sectors. Using markets is therefore not inherently contrary to the public interest. The role of marketing, then, is to mediate between those needing the service and the organization hoping to provide the service. Clearly this can be done either efficiently or inefficiently, fairly or unfairly, ethically or unethically, respectfully or insultingly to the potential service user. In all these respects, marketing is no different from other service functions such as production, HR management or financial management, in terms of the potential for abuse of stakeholders involved in the activity. Perhaps the sensitivity about the potential for abuse of the marketing role comes from the widespread belief that marketing is the most dishonest and unethical of business functions in the private sector. Whether or not this belief is soundly based need not concern us here (although we might say in passing that private sector marketing has a number of competitors for this distinction – including tricky lawyers, creative accountants and captured auditors, all of whom are regularly in the public eye as a result of major corporate scandals).

BOX 6.1 DEFINITIONS OF MARKETING

- 'The role of marketing is to make selling superfluous' (Michael Baker).
- 'Marketing means making products that don't come back for customers who do' (Peter Drucker).
- 'Identifying the needs of your target audience and satisfying them according to your organizational objectives' (Institute of Marketing).

To make this clearer, we can contrast the two polar extremes – a *product orientation*, as might typically be evidenced by professionals working in the field who are convinced that they know better than anyone else what service should be provided, and a *market orientation*, such as would be advocated by marketing specialists (Box 6.2).

Clearly, 'customers' in a public sector context include many different stakeholders, all of whose needs require to be considered in public sector marketing. Here we need to refer back to the types of value added in the public sector which were identified in Chapter 5 – value added for users, for wider social groups, for society as a whole ('social value added), for the polity ('political value added') and for the environment. Marketing can be employed to explore how to increase value added for all the stakeholders involved in each of these ways.

However, there are a number of very different modes in which marketing may be used (Box 6.3). Some of these modes seek fundamentally to serve the user's interest (positive marketing, and some variants of anti-marketing), while some seek to serve society's interest (social marketing) and some seek to serve the interests of target users at the expense of non-target users (de-marketing).

BOX 6.2 PRODUCT ORIENTATION VS. MARKET ORIENTATION

Product orientation

- Emphasis on getting the 'product' right in professional terms.
- Product is developed first, then there is an attempt to attract customers.
- Organization is inward-looking, its production needs come first.
- Success is measured primarily in terms of professional esteem, with a secondary emphasis on the number of customers attracted.
- And if the service fails? 'We did our best, we produced a really good service – but the market didn't appreciate it.'

Market orientation

- Emphasis on doing what the customer wants.
- Services are developed to meet expressed wants *and potential wants* in a co-ordinated way.
- Organization is outward-looking – the customers' needs come first.
- Success is measured primarily both by the number and satisfaction level of customers (i.e. 'quality' as well as quantity).
- Customers are central to everything the organization does (i.e. there is a culture of 'customer obsession').

BOX 6.3 MODES OF MARKETING

- *Positive marketing*: encouraging target groups to use particular goods, services or organizations because it will meet their needs.
- *Social marketing*: advancing a social, environmental or political viewpoint or cause because it will meet society's needs.
- *Anti-marketing*: encouraging target groups to cease using particular goods, services or organizations, either because it is against their interest or because it is against society's interest.
- *De-marketing*: deterring non-target groups from service uptake.

Source: Adapted from Sheaff (1991)

One of the key issues which emerges from this discussion is 'Who is the customer?' There are many potential customers for the public sector, including:

- people currently receiving the service;
- people waiting for the service;
- people needing the service but not seeking it actively;
- people who may need the service in the future;
- people refused the service;
- carers of people needing the service (both those receiving it and those not receiving it);
- taxpayers;
- citizens;
- referrers of potential clients of the service.

In the rest of this chapter, we speak of all of these as 'customers' but a proper marketing strategy and marketing plan will normally try to identify the particular needs of each of these different customers and tailor the service to those needs.

PREPARING A MARKETING STRATEGY AND MARKETING PLANS

In this section, we will consider how marketing strategies and marketing plans can be constructed in public sector organizations.

There is clearly a very strong connection between strategic management and marketing strategy. Indeed, a marketing strategy will always be an integral part of the overall strategy for any organization (or organizational unit such as a service department). The *corporate marketing strategy* will consist of that part of the strategy in which the organization decides:

- which sectors to work in;
- which portfolio of services to provide;
- which target groups to provide with these services;
- what objectives and targets may be set to show whether the target groups have received the benefits expected from the services.

Clearly, this relates very closely to Mintzberg's concept of 'strategy as positioning'. The corporate marketing strategy responds to what the environment wants. It will complement the service production and delivery strategy (to make best use of internal capabilities) (considered in Chapter 5) and the financial strategy (to make best use of all resources) (considered in Chapter 8).

Typically, each constituent unit of the organization is expected to prepare a 'business plan' for its part of the overall organization, nested within and aligned to the corporate strategy. Similarly, each business unit is likely to prepare a marketing strategy, which starts from the decisions in the corporate marketing strategy on which markets that business is expected to serve and goes into greater detail on which services it should produce and what are the target markets for those services. Finally, the marketing strategy at business unit level needs to be developed into a marketing plan, considering the detailed elements of the 'marketing mix'.

78

In order to prepare this suite of plans, three sets of analyses are necessary:

1   Analysis of the external environment of the organization.
2   Analysis of the market segments which the organization might serve.
3   Analysis of the market options available and their relative merits.

We will now look at each of these in turn, before discussing how these analyses may be used in formulating the corporate marketing strategy and business marketing plans.

Analysing the external environment

In analysing the external environment, we seek to understand the factors influencing external stakeholders and the consequent opportunities and threats which face the organization.
There are three main elements to this analysis:

- stakeholder mapping;
- PESTEL analysis and risk assessment;
- 'Five Forces' analysis.

Stakeholder mapping involves identifying the most important stakeholders in the organization and prioritizing them. This is typically done by drawing up a 'stakeholder power/interest matrix' (see Table 6.1). Stakeholders with high power over the organization and high interest in it are clearly crucially important – they should be given central roles in the organization's decision making and activities. At the other extreme, organizations with neither power over nor interest in the organization can be largely neglected (subject to giving them the level of information which is required by law – and perhaps rather more than that, just to be on the safe side).
However, the lesson from Table 6.1 is clear – not all stakeholder groups are equal and a public sector organization must decide how to allocate its resources to work most closely with those stakeholder groups which it considers to have priority. Other forms of mapping may be used to help in setting these priorities – but the need for some set of priorities is unavoidable.
PESTEL analysis sets out a statement of the main factors which are likely to impact on external stakeholders in the future, separated out into:

- political factors;
- economic factors;
- social factors;
- technological factors;
- environmental and ecological factors;
- legal and legislative factors.

This analysis is notoriously simple to do, to the extent that one can very easily end up with a document which is ludicrously large, detailing all potentially relevant factors. This is

79

Table 6.1 *Stakeholder power/interest matrix*

		Stakeholder interest	
		Low	*High*
Stakeholder power	*Low*	Low priority	Keep informed
	High	Keep satisfied	Work together to achieve common goals

Source: Adapted from Mendelow (1991)

clearly of no practical use, so some sort of filter must be applied to ensure that only the most relevant factors are included in any final document. (However, this still implies that the organization must attempt a very wide and imaginative search for all potentially relevant factors, so that the filter can be applied to them. Of course, in practice we must expect that organizations – and individuals within them – will display 'blind spots', prejudices and plain ignorance in making this search, so that PESTEL analysis cannot ever pretend to be fully comprehensive.) *Risk assessment*, the filter applied to the factors, is clearly a crucially important part of PESTEL analysis. There are many different ways of doing this, but typically factors are more likely to be included in the PESTEL statement if they score highly on at least one of the following criteria:

- Is the factor high impact at the moment?
- Will the factor have increasing impact over time?
- Is the factor likely to have a positive or negative effect on external stakeholders? (This takes account of the fact that many stakeholders are risk averse, placing more importance on potential costs and losses than on potential benefits and gains.)
- Is there a high probability that the factor will indeed occur as forecast?
- Will the factor affect our organization more than other similar organizations which are involved in the same type of activity? (This takes account of the fact that an organization will typically be sensitive to changes in its potential competitive advantage in relation to its stakeholders.)

The final piece in the external environment jigsaw is the '*Five Forces*' *analysis* of Michael Porter, whereby an organization can consider how attractive are the prospects in a specific sector – and which sectors are therefore unattractive. The Five Forces are:

1 The *threat of new entrants* which would compete away profit margins.
2 The *threat of substitutes* which puts a ceiling on the prices which can be charged.
3 The *bargaining power of suppliers* (including the distribution channels) which puts pressure on costs.
4 The *bargaining power of customers* which puts a ceiling on prices.
5 The *level of competitive rivalry* which drives down prices.

This approach was originally applied by Porter to analyse which sectors would be regarded by a private firm as the most competitive – with the implication that these would be the least attractive. Such a model may be relevant for some service-providing organizations in the public sector, where they are driven by the need to make target levels of profit (or not to exceed target levels of subsidy). However, it needs to be adapted to a public sector context. In particular, we need to take account of the fact that:

- public sector organizations do not always have a choice of which sector they work in (so that this analysis is irrelevant for some organizations, which can only work in certain named sectors, and cannot be applied to some sectors where a particular public sector organization is prohibited from working – and the model is clearly not relevant to service-commissioning organizations);
- public sector organizations are not always competitive in their intent, and there are other stakeholders impacting on their choice of sector (particularly government).

Consequently, the Five Forces analysis has a different role in the external environmental analysis undertaken by public sector organizations. First, it helps providing organizations to highlight the sectors in which they are likely to meet strong competitive rivalry. As with private organizations, this is likely to be interpreted as a danger signal: sectors where competitive rivalry is weak will be more attractive.

Second, public sector organizations also need to consider the bargaining power of other stakeholders (which might either increase costs or lower revenue) and the likelihood of interference by other levels of government (which again might affect costs or prices, or might even rule out any work in the sector). Both of these extra forces may make a sector less attractive. (*Note*: these two factors now mean working with a 'Seven Forces' model, but it is highly unlikely that it will become known as anything other than the 'Five Forces' model.)

Third – and rather differently from many private sector providers – public sector providers need to consider the collaborative potential of the sector. Since so much of their success will depend on working closely with other bodies – groups representing customers, voluntary organizations filling in gaps in public provision, universities evaluating the cost-effectiveness of alternative service designs – it is important that these different bodies are collaborative in nature and prepared to form effective partnerships (Kooiman, 2003). We will consider this in more depth in the next section, but for the moment it is important to note that public sector use of the Five Forces can – and should – reject using it purely to explore the competitive rivalry of the sector. It is important to ask, in relation to each of the Five Forces: How does it affect the sector's ability to work in collaboration?

Analysing market segments

Different market segments will normally prefer different services or different designs of a given service. The most typical criteria for drawing up market segments in the public sector are:

- demographic (e.g. age, household composition);
- socio-economic (e.g. class, socio-economic group, income);

81

- membership of economically or socially disadvantaged group (e.g. pensioners, unemployed, low income, disability groups, women, ethnic minorities, isolated people);
- geographic (e.g. neighbourhood, ward, town, region).

However, more recently there has been greater interest in using such criteria as lifestyle and tastes (often using psychographics). Each of these approaches naturally tends to miss some of the important differences between individuals, while trying to allow a move away from treating all customers as a mass market. Another form of market segmentation looks at the customer's attitude to the service being provided (unaware, hostile, aware, interested, wavering towards action, trialing, occasional user, loyal). Each of these approaches is useful for a particular form of marketing initiative but the crucially important issue is to prioritize between these market segments in order to determine which segments should form the target or priority groups for the public agency. This is one of the fundamental political tasks in any public sector organization.

Analysing market options

The analyses of external factors allow an OT (opportunities and threats) analysis to be compiled for the organization, which can help to identify future market options, and can in turn be combined with internal analysis of the organization to feed into a full SWOT analysis (see Chapter 5), which may be used to produce a series of integrated strategic options for the organization. These strategic market options should form coherent statements of a market position – a market to be served, a service to be provided and a target market segment for that service. However, it may well be unproductive to try to evaluate these market options on their own. The evaluation of strategy is most likely to make sense when it considers full strategic options, which combine market options with internal capabilities and financial/resource options. Otherwise, the evaluation is likely to come up with a ranking of market options which is blind to the organization's strengths and weaknesses and resource constraints – this is very likely to lead to the choice of a suboptimal strategy.

Evaluation of market options need not simply be a cognitive exercise, based on a desk study. It is also possible to do market testing of options, either by conducting trials or by analysing the offers made by alternative suppliers. This is considered further in Chapter 7.

From marketing strategy to marketing plans

The analysis and evaluation of strategic options should help a public sector organization to select its preferred strategic option, including its marketing strategy, with the following key elements:

- a decision on which sectors to work in;
- a portfolio of services which will be provided to users;
- a description of the target groups for whom these services will be provided;
- a set of objectives and targets which can be monitored to show whether the target groups have received the benefits expected from the services.

How can this marketing strategy be put into practice? Typically, a marketing plan is prepared which allows the key issues (the 'marketing mix') to be considered and co-ordinated in detail (Figure 6.1).

These elements of the marketing mix are closely interrelated and therefore need to be planned together, so that they are aligned with each other and support the chosen strategy:

- The *product* (or *service*) needs to be designed with the needs of the customer in mind. Design features need to include not only the core features of the service itself but also the way in which it is delivered, including such 'customer care' aspects as the availability of the service (e.g. opening hours), reliability (e.g. how often is the service defective?), responsiveness to customers' needs (e.g. does the service take account of differences in gender, age, ethnicity, (dis)ability, etc?), and the empathy with which staff treat service users. A key element of service design is market research, which is becoming much more central to public services management, whether conducted by surveys, focus groups or other methods.
- The *promotion* of the service has to be suitable for the target group, so that over time the users become aware of the service, interested in it, keen to use it and then take action to try it out. The mix of promotional methods needs to be thought out carefully, including advertising, special sales promotions, sponsorship deals and public relations campaigns.
- The *place* in which the service is available has to be suitable for the target service user (so that it is comfortable to use, and appropriate transport is available) or services can be made available in e-government initiatives, (e.g. over the Internet or through a call centre).

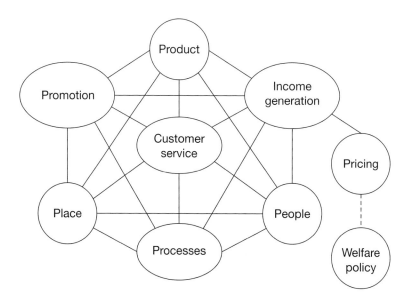

Figure 6.1 *The expanded marketing mix for public services*
Source: Adapted from Christopher et al. (1991)

- The *processes* which are used to assess eligibility and to provide the service have to be clear and understandable to the target group (which includes clear and easy-to-use forms, with availability of translation if required) and should be designed to minimize time taken and hassle.
- The *people* who supply the service have to be welcoming and sympathetic to the target group and well trained in giving the service.
- The *income generation* activities of the organization have to be consistent with its principles and organized efficiently so that the net income is maximized. Sources of income might include fund-raising by volunteers, donations, sponsorship, sales of associated services (e.g. from a charity shop), merchandising, sales of advertising space or pricing.
- The *prices* which are charged have to be appropriate to the target group's means (which will be determined partly by the overall national welfare policy to which the organization must conform and to which it contributes), proportionate to the benefits given and consistent with the organization's income generation plan. This will sometimes entail a concessions system (which may require income assessment procedures, with the consequent problems of stigma, deterrence of potential users and high transaction costs).

Clearly, there will be considerable overlap between marketing strategies and marketing plans – for example, the decision on the portfolio of services to be offered figures in both, although it is handled at a finer level of detail in marketing plans. Again, promotion is just one branch of marketing communications, by means of which the organization seeks to keep in touch with its various customers. (Stakeholder engagement is considered in more detail in Chapter 15.) Moreover, marketing plans and service delivery plans will often overlap (e.g. making sure that proper transport arrangements are in place is part of the 'place' factor in the marketing plan, but also part of the 'logistics' factor in the service delivery plan).

MARKETING IN A POLITICALLY-DRIVEN ORGANIZATION

Marketing is never easy in any context but it assumes extra dimensions of complexity in a political environment. There are three particular areas in which thorny political issues tend to arise:

- Strategic marketing, like strategic management in general, requires clear statements of priorities, particularly about which target groups are priorities for each policy. This means telling many groups that they are *not* priorities – which is politically embarrassing.
- Promotion of policies and services generally tries to attract customers to use them – but this can be interpreted as 'selling' the ruling group's achievements to the population. Consequently, promotion can often take on a strong 'political' resonance. Furthermore, the political opposition often feels unconstrained in attacking policies and services, which can undermine marketing efforts to improve take-up and perceptions of quality – not something with which private companies normally have to deal.

■ Pricing of services is usually highly controversial and changes of prices tend to be made relatively infrequently, removing for significant periods the use of one potentially valuable tool in the marketing mix.

The first of these issues is by far the most important. We might expect, given the rhetoric of the public sector over recent decades, that it has particularly targeted and helped the most disadvantaged groups in society. However, as Le Grand pointed out twenty years ago, 'Almost all public expenditure in social services in Britain benefits the better off to a greater degree than the poor . . . [even in] services whose aims are at least in part egalitarian, such as the NHS, higher education, public transport, and the aggregate complex of housing policies' (Le Grand, 1982). He went on to suggest that substantial inequalities persist in public expenditure per user, in use (standardized by level of need), in opportunity, in access (including cost of access and time taken to gain access), and in outcomes. He also suggested that, in many policy areas, public policies have probably even failed significantly to reduce inequality. These conclusions are likely to have been reinforced by the events of the past twenty years (Percy-Smith, 2000). If politicians cannot or will not address the need to target public expenditure and public services at the most disadvantaged, while claiming to take disadvantage seriously, then it seems likely that marketing will remain a relatively weak tool for achieving the purposes of public sector organizations – and those purposes will be much harder to achieve.

LIMITATIONS OF MARKETING

While marketing can help public sector organizations to work more effectively to please their customers, there remain significant limitations to its use in the public sector.

First, it is clear that it is often artificial to regard all those who come into contact with the public sector as its customers – certainly prisoners and parents who abuse their children do not fit this description easily. In some cases, the relationship between the state and its subjects is – and is likely to remain – characterized by relations of dominance and punishment rather than exchange and mutual reward. Marketing is less relevant in these circumstances.

Second, the manipulation of public tastes and preferences to make the public sector's services more desirable is questionable in the public sector. This largely rules out some of the approaches of private sector marketing, such as the encouragement of the 'conspicuous consumption of the leisure classes' (Veblen), or the use of 'the Hidden Persuaders' which create demand for unnecessary services and encourage motives based on 'base desires' such as power, greed and sex (Packard, 1957), or the resort to built-in obsolescence and emphasis on style rather than performance (Ralph Nader).

Third, there are areas where individuals making their own choice will not contribute to the highest good of the society in which they live – whether because of spill-over effects of their decisions, the poor quality of information on which they act, their lack of understanding of their own (long-term) best interest, or for other reasons. Where this is the case – and it seems likely that there are significant areas of such decision making in human behaviour – then collective decisions based on political processes will remain superior to individual decisions aided by marketing processes.

85

In general, then, the balance between marketing as a way of mediating between service users, citizens and service producers is one which will always be hard to find and is likely to shift over time. While marketing may have played too small a role in traditional public administration up to the 1980s, it has perhaps been in danger of encroaching too far in some areas of public policy in the past two decades.

SUMMARY

This chapter has considered a range of techniques for understanding the external environment of organizations and for identifying and evaluating strategic market options. It has also linked these strategies to the marketing plans needed to ensure that they are implemented. It has argued that marketing in a political environment can help to force political decision making to be more open about its underlying purposes, especially in relation to priority target groups, but marketing also has to be sensitive to its limitations when applied in the public domain.

QUESTIONS FOR REVIEW AND DISCUSSION

1   What does 'marketing' mean? What relationship does it have to 'markets'? Why does the term 'marketing' often appear to have a pejorative meaning? Is this justified?
2   What is the relationship between marketing strategy and the marketing mix? When would changes in the marketing mix be so significant that they would amount to changes in the marketing strategy?

READER EXERCISES

1   Consider a public sector organization which you know. Try to identify the main elements of its marketing strategy. Consider one of its services: try to identify the main elements of the marketing mix. Can you suggest some changes to the marketing strategy or the marketing mix which would make this organization more accessible to vulnerable groups?
2   What are the main pros and cons of using an income assessment approach to giving lower prices to disadvantaged groups? How might the net gains from an income assessment system be maximized?

CLASS EXERCISES

1   Divide into groups. Each group should identify the main elements of the marketing mix in the higher education system and proposed changes which would help to increase the enrolment of students into this system. Compare notes and identify the reasons behind the main differences in each of the proposals.
2   What are the main limitations of marketing in the public sector? Give examples of these limitations in practice. How might they be best overcome?

FURTHER READING

Alan Andreason and Philip Kotler (2002), *Strategic marketing for nonprofit organizations*, 6th edn. Upper Saddle River, NJ: Prentice Hall.

Adrian Sargeant (1999), *Marketing management for nonprofit organizations*. Oxford: Oxford University Press.

Rod Sheaff (2002), *Responsive healthcare: marketing for a public service*. Buckingham: Open University Press.

Kieron Walsh (1995), *Marketing in local government*. London: Financial Times Prentice Hall.

Chapter 7

Contracting for public services

Competition and partnership

Andrew Erridge, University of Ulster, UK

INTRODUCTION

This chapter examines the debate surrounding contracting for services and empirical evidence on the effectiveness of UK Conservative and Labour government policies since 1979. These followed initiatives of the Reagan administration in the USA, and subsequently similar policies have been introduced in countries throughout the world (see Chapter 4).

In general, there has been a shift from competing for contracted services through compulsory competitive tendering (CCT) towards more complex contractual arrangements managing multiple contracts and supplier relationships, building and maintaining accountable partnerships with users, communities and other organizations where appropriate ('co-production of services'). This chapter will examine the merits of competition and more collaborative 'partnership' relationships as mechanisms for managing the delivery of contracted services.

LEARNING OBJECTIVES

- To understand the meaning of contracting
- To understand why contracting for services has been increasing over the past twenty-five years
- To be able to identify the pros and cons of contracting out of specific services
- To understand the links between contracting, competition and collaboration
- To understand how contracting could be used to pursue the wider socio-economic goals of government

THE RISE OF CONTRACTING FOR SERVICES: FROM COMPETITION TO PARTNERSHIP?

Competition

We have seen in chapters 2, 3 and 4 that in the 1980s and 1990s, many OECD governments, but most notably Mrs Thatcher's incoming government of 1979, were committed to reducing the size and role of the public sector, believing that it was less efficient than the private sector in delivering public services. This led to a fundamental shift away from direct service provision through the hierarchy of public sector organizations towards market-based competition and contractual relationships between public sector organizations and private or nonprofit organizations. The ideas of the New Right were successful partly because they succeeded in linking with other influential strands of thought, in particular the growing critique of bureaucracy in the management and organization literature (see Chapter 3).

The ideas of cost reduction (economy) and efficiency (see Box 7.1) were central to the argument in favour of competitive tendering, and a number of subsequent studies (e.g. Walsh, 1991a) described the cost-saving potential of contracting.

BOX 7.1 INCREASING EFFICIENCY MAY REFER TO . . .

Productive efficiency – increasing the level of output (e.g. patients treated, lessons taught, dustbins collected for the same or a lower level of inputs (staff, money, equipment)).

Allocative efficiency – providing that distribution of public services which most closely satisfies the preferences of all citizens.

In practice allocative efficiency is value laden and almost impossible to assess, and productive efficiency tends to be what service performance is measured against.

Government guidance states that 'goods and services should be acquired by competition unless there are convincing reasons to the contrary' (HM Treasury, 1988), and that 'competition is the best guarantee of quality and value for money' (Chancellor of the Exchequer, 1991). Through this policy, it is argued, government can avoid accusations of favouritism and fraud, and the openness of the system will encourage more suppliers to participate, thus increasing competition which will in turn reduce prices, improve quality and lead to greater competitiveness among suppliers.

One important policy of the UK government leading to an increase in the contracting out of public services was compulsory competitive tendering (CCT). CCT required local authorities and to a lesser extent the National Health Service and other public bodies to invite tenders for the provision of public services from private companies. Usually these services were previously delivered by staff of the organization (the 'in-house' provider), and these service providers were now required to compete against outside bidders. This involved setting up a direct service organization (DSO) separate from the client (usually the previous management of the service) which was responsible for the competitive tendering process. As Box 7.2 illustrates, CCT was extended to a progressively wider range of services up to 1992, and rules on the tendering process were tightened. This was mainly because in-house providers won a very high proportion of bids, and the government felt that they had an unfair advantage due to having access to information not available to outside bidders, as well as not being charged in full for common services which were provided centrally by the local authority.

Box 7.2 presents the policies of the UK government for central, local and NHS services in the UK between 1979 and 1992.

BOX 7.2 COMPULSORY COMPETITIVE TENDERING (CCT) IN LOCAL GOVERNMENT: SERVICES COVERED AND OTHER MAIN POLICY CHANGES

1980: construction, buildings, highways;

1988: building and street cleaning, catering, grounds maintenance, vehicle repair;

1989: maintenance of sport and leisure facilities;

1992: (1) direct (e.g. theatres and libraries); construction related (e.g. architecture, engineering); corporate (e.g. administrative, legal, financial, personnel and computing); manual (e.g. police support)

(2) client–contractor split reinforced

(3) specified time periods for each stage in tendering process

(4) restriction on costs allowed to be offset against in-house bids.

Partnership

While competition was the hallmark of Conservative governments in the UK up until the early 1990s, partnership relations with suppliers were identified as a key element in the 1995 White Paper *Setting New Standards*. This initiative sought to develop a new approach to supply relations which had been characterized previously by short-term competitive tendering procedures. The White Paper (HM Treasury, 1995, p. 13), for example, states that:

> Departments will work together with suppliers to secure improvements in the performance of both parties. Although they will press suppliers to reduce cost and improve quality, they will recognise that mutually satisfactory relationships are in the interests of both sides and will avoid an unnecessarily adversarial approach.

By emphasizing co-operation and collaboration, UK policy initiatives set out to change the nature of the procurement function and of the relationship between government departments and suppliers. By moving away from the competitive market model represented by compulsory competitive tendering (CCT), partnership arrangements with suppliers can build social capital, which means that partnership working can lead to reduced transaction costs, increased outputs and improved outcomes (e.g. greater social cohesion). Social

91

capital, according to Woolcock (1998), is a complex resource which encompasses the 'norms and networks facilitating collective action for mutual benefit' (p.155). Social capital research (see Erridge and Greer, 2002, pp. 504–507) suggests that:

- increased interaction and exchange leads to the development of trust and the creation of norms and sanctions which reduce transaction costs;
- it can improve access to resources among network members;
- it can create identity resources which build a sense of 'belonging' and shared action;
- it can have positive ripple effects within society by encouraging participation and creating greater social cohesion.

Since 1997 Labour government policies in the UK have reflected a more participative, collaborative approach, with CCT replaced by Best Value, the expansion of the private finance initiative (PFI) through public private partnerships (PPP), and an approach to contracting which facilitated the effective delivery of more complex services.

In relation to issues such as the environment or quality of life for disadvantaged groups, network relationships have provided an opportunity for interested stakeholders to work together more closely and set out common and clear objectives to address community problems. For example, collaborative supply relations have facilitated close engagement between the Department of the Environment (DoE), registered charities, and local schools and communities in the implementation of local environmental projects. Under this arrangement, partnership stakeholders collaborate to share information, set up performance measures, report on the progress of environmental projects and disseminate good practice in an effort to improve the environment in local communities. Similarly, the DoE's home energy efficiency scheme has established interdependent working relationships between Buying Solutions (part of the Office of Government Commerce), Department of Social Services, local councils and the charity Help the Aged to improve the quality of life for disadvantaged groups in society. By addressing such complex and diverse issues, trusting relationships have encouraged the sharing and co-ordination of information regarding performance and quality standards, facilitated common strategies between stakeholders, and encouraged co-operative action in working towards a collective goal (Erridge and Greer, 2002, p. 517).

The scope and nature of service contracting

While based upon different methods of measurement, recent estimates of procurement spend in central government, the NHS and local government are (Byatt 2001, Annex C):

- central government departments and agencies: £20 billion including £7 billion military equipment (HM Treasury, 1998);
- NHS: £11 billion (Coote, 2002);
- local government: £31.5 billion (England only).

The most significant change has been a substantial increase in spend on services, primarily as a result of the Conservative governments' privatization policy. Results of a questionnaire survey of procurement directors in central government departments and agencies (Erridge, 2000) showed that average percentage procurement spend by central government departments and agencies in 1996/7 was 34 per cent on goods, 41 per cent on services and 13 per cent on capital. 'Other' spend accounted for 12 per cent, including research, property rental and telecommunications.

Over half of respondents stated that their procurement spend had increased over the past three years, with the principal reason being growth in large service contracts. The most commonly cited area of spend is information technology, both in terms of computer equipment and consumables, and also associated support and logistics. Other services frequently identified include consultancy, transport, training, security, insurances, telecommunications, catering, cleaning, maintenance and travel. With private finance initiative (PFI) projects, for example, for the construction, equipping and facilities management of hospitals, schools or colleges, or for the provision of all information technology processing requirements for the Department of Social Security over a twenty-five-year period, such disparate goods and services are being grouped increasingly into larger, longer term packages, in the process changing the nature of public procurement.

In the NHS, drugs and medical supplies account for the largest areas of procurement spend. Ancillary services accounted for 24 per cent of spend. The main local government ancillary services subject to CCT were cleaning, refuse collection, vehicle maintenance, catering, ground maintenance, and sport and leisure management.

CHOOSING BETWEEN THE PUBLIC/VOLUNTARY OR PRIVATE SECTORS

The above evidence demonstrates that there has been a considerable increase in contracting for services which were previously delivered directly by public sector organizations. This reflects a move away from the predominant form of service delivery before 1979 through the internal bureaucracy to alternative forms of delivery, or 'governance structures'. The outcomes of market testing for a central government department or agency service, or of a CCT exercise for a local authority or NHS service, could be as follows:

- retain the service in-house;
- contract out to a private sector contractor;
- contract out to a voluntary sector provider;
- a 'mixed economy' of provision involving in-house, voluntary and private sector providers.

In a recent report on behalf of the Public Service Network, Entwistle and colleagues of Cardiff Business School summarized the arguments for and against internal service provision as shown in Box 7.3.

93

BOX 7.3 THEORIES ON INTERNAL AND EXTERNAL SERVICE PROVISION

Transaction cost economics

In an extensive body of work, Williamson and Ouchi (1983: 18) has argued that the make-or-buy decision should be determined by the comparison of the transaction costs of internal versus external provision. He argues that it is cheaper to buy one-off services – such as building a school – than it is to maintain all of the labour and plant in-house. However: 'Internal organisation is well-suited to transactions that involve recurrent exchange in the face of a non-trivial degree of uncertainty and that incur transaction-specific investments.'

Principal–agent theory

Donahue (1989) analyses make-or-buy decisions through the lens of principal–agent theory. Successful contracting requires that the agents tasked with performing a particular function can be readily controlled by their principal (the client). Contracting will be successful where exact specifications can be drawn up, outputs easily measured and inadequate suppliers quickly replaced. It is the logic of principal–agent theory that informed CCT. Donahue cites waste collection as a case study of the benefits of contracting, concluding that: 'Contractors chosen by fair and honest bid contests typically out-perform public monopolies' (p. 68).

Contestable markets

Many of the criticisms of public providers hinge upon the absence of competitive forces. Public providers are seen as inefficient because they are monopoly suppliers. The remedy, it is argued, is clear. Local authorities should, where possible, create competitive pressures by giving service users as wide a choice as possible from a broad range of alternative providers. The cure for the ills of public provision is not externalization per se, since it is not clear that private monopolies would be in any sense preferable to public monopolies, but a mixed and vibrant economy of provision. This is the reasoning that underpins the Blair government's objective of encouraging local authorities to 'create the conditions under which there is likely to be greater interest from the private and voluntary sectors in working with local government to deliver quality services at a competitive price' (DETR, 1998a, clause 7:30).

Functional matching

The fourth perspective suggests that the make-or-buy decision can be made on the basis of an understanding of the functional attributes of different sectors. Simply stated, the public, private and voluntary sectors are good at doing different things. In the words of one of the managers of our case study authorities, 'some things the public sector will do better, some the private sector will do better'. With a clear understanding of the different strengths of the different sectors, local authorities can allocate functions to their most suited sectors. Similarly, Billis and Glennerster (1998, p. 95) suggest that the voluntary sector may have 'a comparative advantage over other sector agencies in areas where their distinctive ambiguous and hybrid structures enable them to overcome problems of principal–agent gap, median voter reluctance, weak messages from politicians to staff and lack of market interest'.

Source: Entwistle *et al.* (2002, pp. 10–11)

The above theoretical considerations suggest that internal providers have an advantage in the provision of 'high-discretion responsive services' where:

- future needs and priorities cannot be predicted with certainty;
- outputs are diffuse and difficult to measure;
- flexibility and responsiveness, local knowledge and the exercise of political judgement are required.

In such circumstances it is difficult to specify what is required in contractual clauses, monitoring becomes more difficult and expensive, and costly variations are likely to be necessary.

> Where there is a high level of trust between contractor and client it may be possible to alleviate some of these problems. In many cases, however, local authorities and private contractors are likely to start from a relatively low base of trust and mutual understanding. Although there has been much talk of new relational approaches to partnership neither side seem eager to forgo the security of tightly specified contracts.
>
> (Entwistle *et al.* 2001, p.11)

CHOOSING BETWEEN CO-OPERATION AND COMPETITION

Even though traditionally UK public procurement policy has reflected the competitive approach, the keyword in the current UK approach to public procurement is 'value', which involves making taxpayers' money go further in meeting user requirements (HM Treasury, 1998). In the public sector, the definition of 'value' is far from straightforward since the relationship between user requirements and how taxpayers' money is to be spent will vary depending on the nature of the contract and the political ideology of policy makers.

As Box 7.4 points out, value can be broken down further into three popular ideas of public procurement goals: economy, efficiency and effectiveness (see also chapters 10 and 11).

These three criteria are useful in studying value but on a general level it is impossible to provide concrete specifications of desired levels of efficiency, economy and effectiveness which apply to all contracts. For example, with simple purchases, traditional performance

BOX 7.4 ECONOMY, EFFICIENCY AND EFFECTIVENESS

- *Economy* means acquiring resources of a given quality at least cost.
- *Efficiency* means producing outputs (of a given quality) with the least possible amount of inputs (of a given quality).
- *Effectiveness* means achieving the organization's objectives, not only in terms of quantity but also quality.

indicators such as price can be appropriate although issues such as quality, total cost and after-sales service must also be taken into account. For more complex purchases involving service to citizens, especially healthcare, these performance criteria change to more subjective notions with value relating to service quality (user requirements) rather than to cost (taxpayers' money). Therefore value is often seen as a balancing act between cost and quality, and can only be properly determined on a case-by-case basis taking into account the nature of the contract, stakeholder aspirations and resources available.

The means by which value is to be achieved is also a source of much debate. Domberger and Jensen (1997) found that a conventional approach which emphasizes economic efficiency through competition can reduce cost and improve quality. However, Walsh (1991a) suggests that this is mainly because increased attention is being paid to quality through monitoring, explicit inspection and emphasis on standards.

The dilemma for policy makers is that they are now influenced by the reported success of the private sector models while they are also looking for ways to reconcile strategic approaches with traditional practices. The 1995 White Paper *Setting New Standards* advocates a strategy for government procurement based on continuous improvement and world-class purchasing, proposes the use of pro-active contract management, whole-life costing and a more collaborative approach to suppliers, and states that the strategy should: 'combine competition and co-operation in an optimum way' (HM Treasury, 1995, p. 37). The European Commission is also interested in adopting a more strategic approach – it now suggests that there should be greater flexibility as regards dialogue between purchasers and suppliers. This change in public procurement thinking has led to an interest in improving supply networks and changed perceptions on the performance of procurement. In this context it is assumed that a more professional approach can reduce costs by working with suppliers to identify inefficiencies in the supply chain, while improved supply market intelligence and a better use of resources can lead to commercial gains without competition.

The policies of the incoming Labour government since 1997, while retaining of necessity the element of competition to comply with regulatory requirements, have reflected this increased emphasis on collaboration through partnership with the private and voluntary sectors. The NHS internal market was abolished to be replaced by a more collaborative process of commissioning for services between primary care consortia, trusts, private and voluntary providers. Best Value was announced as the replacement to CCT and requires a process of service review, consultation with stakeholders and competition on a voluntary rather than compulsory basis. Partnering with the private sector was pursued more vigorously, especially through public private partnerships, to fund infrastructure capital projects (e.g. London Underground) and service delivery (e.g. the provision of administrative services to the Office of National Savings by Siemens plc).

CONTRACTING FOR WIDER SOCIO-ECONOMIC GOALS OF GOVERNMENT

At present, policy on contracting, through the structures and procedures mentioned above, partly reflects the market model supported by public choice theorists but also new arrangements of co-production between public, private and nonprofit sectors. Self (1993) argues that the market model is inconsistent with the public interest, which he defines as the normative standards and practices which guide the political life of society based upon widely shared moral principles or beliefs, on three grounds:

1   Public choice encourages the individual to maximize economic opportunities and personal wealth, whereas public interest requires identification or sympathy with others' needs.
2   Political liberty cannot be treated as the dependent variable of a strong, autonomous market system; rather a balancing of the roles of the state and the market is required.
3   The market system makes no distinction between individuals' 'wants', and common 'needs' essential for a tolerable life.

Of course, there is always a danger that the dominant voices heard in supply chain debates will be commercial interests, usually large, powerful corporations which ignore other issues, such as environmental damage created, unfair employment conditions or the exploitation of poorer producers. This suggests that public sector organizations should provide moral leadership by incorporating this broader social dimension into contracting decisions.

The socio-economic dimension of public procurement involves 'any purposeful action intended to improve the social welfare of the whole or part of the same population' (Fernandez Martin, 1996, p. 39). Policy areas which tend to be considered include unemployment, social exclusion, protection of minorities, income distribution, economic development, particularly in relation to small firms, and environmental policy (Bovis, 1997; HM Treasury, 1995).

There are a number of methods through which the objectives of these policies could be achieved. Contractual clauses may be included requiring contractors to comply with wider government goals such as combating discrimination on grounds of sex, race, religion or disability. Set-asides overcome market inequalities by allowing only certain sections of the economy (e.g. small firms) to tender for contracts and thus increase competitiveness. Prompt payment policy protects smaller firms and subcontractors in particular against larger customers' opportunistic behaviour by providing that payment be made within thirty days. 'Green' sourcing protects natural resources and the environment in which citizens live. Coote (2002) argues that the purchasing policy of the NHS could influence health and sustainable development by encouraging local suppliers and helping to regenerate and support the economies of disadvantaged neighbourhoods. It could also choose goods and methods of production and distribution that are likely to safeguard health and the environment.

97

Opponents of the use of procurement for socio-economic purposes have argued that the outcome is likely to be extra or hidden costs and therefore policy should remain market based. However, as we have already discussed, given that the market model is flawed there is a moral imperative for governments to ensure that the public interest is served.

SUMMARY

This chapter has found that, for all of the radicalism of Mrs Thatcher's governments, policy on contracting did not result in a massive transfer of service provision from the public to the private sector. Where services were delivered by the private sector, there is some evidence of financial savings and improved quality, but these must be weighed against higher transaction costs, incidences of contractor failure and inequality effects on public sector employees.

The Labour government has pursued partnership with the private sector, adopting a more collaborative approach but backed by an increase in inspection and audit. While there is therefore a common recognition of the necessity of using private sector expertise and finance, the difference perhaps lies in the Labour government's greater respect for a public sector ethos, and recognizing the distinctive contribution that public sector employees can make. However, this attitude does not persist where these employees are felt to be resistant, or where the services they provide are deemed to have failed (whether schools, hospitals or local authorities). In these cases, the Labour administration has proved equally, if not more, prepared to intervene than its predecessors, based upon ever more prescriptive performance targets.

A good example of this in respect of local government is seen in the recent local public service agreements and arrangements for intervention where targets are not met. This suggests that the core problem that recent governments in the UK and elsewhere have sought to address through contracting is the perceived failure of public agencies to manage the delivery of public services efficiently and effectively. Increasingly, the solution is being found in a mixed economy of public, private and voluntary provision.

There are some key areas where we cannot yet be sure of the lessons emerging on contracting out and partnership working, and where, therefore, further research is needed. These include, in particular:

- Can a more collaborative approach be developed through amending the European Directives and UK rules and regulations on procurement policy?
- How can socio-economic goals be pursued through contracting while retaining the focus on best value for money and collaboration with the private sector?

QUESTIONS FOR REVIEW AND DISCUSSION

1   Should social and employment rights be protected through the contracting process by the insertion of relevant clauses in contracts? What are the benefits and risks of allowing such concerns to be embedded in contracts?

2   Why is it easier to operate market-based contracting approaches for simple repetitive services than for complex, professionally based activities? Discuss which services fall into these categories in (1) a major metropolitan local authority in your country, and (2) an executive agency of central or regional government in your country.

3   What are the main factors which make local authorities reluctant to contract out services to the private sector? What steps do you consider central or higher levels of government might take to encourage local government to make more use of effective opportunities for contracting out?

READER EXERCISE

Select at least three articles on using private sector contractors or private finance to provide public services from quality daily or Sunday newspapers. What arguments and/or evidence do they provide in relation to the issues discussed in this chapter?

CLASS EXERCISE

Identify in class some public services which have been contracted out, whether through a process of CCT/market testing/Best Value. In groups, discuss the extent to which the contracting out of these services has more successfully met the needs of:

- those for whom the service is provided;
- the providers (i.e. the managers and employees);
- the government's political and managerial goals.

FURTHER READING

Nicholas Deakin and Kieron Walsh (1996), 'The enabling state: the role of markets and contracts', *Public Administration*, Vol. 74, No. 1 (Spring), pp. 33–48.

Simon Domberger and Paul Jensen (1997), 'Contracting out by the public sector: theory, evidence and prospects', *Oxford Review of Economic Policy*, Vol. 13, No. 4, pp. 67–79.

Peter Self (1993), *Government by the market?* London: Macmillan.

Chapter 8

Changing roles of public financial management

James L. Chan, University of Illinois, Chicago, USA

INTRODUCTION

The importance of money to government may be obvious, but good public financial management is often taken for granted. This chapter will discuss how the changing roles of public management alter government's financial management systems. These systems are analysed in terms of their underlying conceptual models. It will be argued that, as government has evolved from a hierarchical bureaucracy to an organization with multiple stakeholders and eventually to a node in an institutional network, the tasks of public managers have been transformed from direct control to balancing the interests of stakeholders (see also Chapter 1). Corresponding to these stages of evolution are the classical model, the NPM (new public management) model and the governance model based on the original insights of Barnard (1968, originally 1938) and Simon (1945). These models are described and compared, along with the key issues faced by practice and research.

Public financial management (PFM) faces several identity issues. First, governments are urged to adopt best practices, but there are few guidelines for assessing PFM quality. Since PFM is a service function, what is its value to clients, and who are these clients? Furthermore, how much resource should be spent on quality improvement? The second issue is whether it is appropriate for government to uncritically emulate private sector practices. Third, what is the proper boundary of PFM? Does 'public' include only core governmental agencies? Or does it encompass government-owned nonprofit institutions and business enterprises? Finally, finance often involves the creative search for financing alternatives; this may be antithetical to prudent and routine management. Therefore, how much weight should be given to the 'finance' and 'management' aspects of PFM? These issues are resolved differently in various PFM systems, which are analysed in terms of three conceptual models below.

LEARNING OBJECTIVES

- To be aware of changes in governmental financial management systems and to understand their underlying conceptual models
- To understand the context and content of each of the models discussed
- To understand how each of the models is supported by its underlying disciplines

THE THREE MODELS

The classical model

There are two cardinal rules in the classical PFM model: (1) a government should balance its budget, and (2) a government unit should not overspend its appropriations. These rules are codified in laws and regulations. In the United States, most state and local governments operate under balanced budget laws. Even though the federal constitution does not require a balanced budget, it does stipulate that 'No money shall be drawn from the Treasury, but in consequence of Appropriations made by Law, and a regular Statement and Account of the Receipts and Expenditures of all public Money shall be published from time to time' (Constitution of the United States, Article I, Section IX, Clause 7). In conformity with this provision, there are statutes and regulations on budget preparation, approval and execution, and eventual cash disbursement by the Treasury. Financial management makes budgetary resources available to officials to carry out authorized purposes.

PFM is often described in terms of revenue collection and spending. There is, however, no general agreement about the scope of financial management. The revenue side is often slighted, with more attention paid to public expenditure management. Here, budget specialists believe that financial management starts after a government agency receives appropriations – legal authorization to enter into contracts or make cash outlays. As such, financial management is an invisible bureaucratic function uninvolved in policy decision making and largely unaffected by budgeting approaches. As PPBS, ZBB and mission budgeting come and go, financial management ensures organizational stability and continuity by following standard operating procedures (see Box 8.1).

BOX 8.1 BUDGETING APPROACHES

- *PPBS* (planning, programming budgeting system): favoured in the 1960s to stress longer time horizon and detailed specification of activities.
- *ZBB* (zero base budgeting): a 1970s antidote to incremental budgeting, requiring the justification of every dollar requested.
- *Mission budgeting*: a 1990s reincarnation of PPBS, relating resource requests to goals.

These procedures dictate how transactions are handled. Whereas the budget embodies substantive decisions – who gets what, how much and when – financial management dutifully carries out spending policies. While specific procedures differ from one jurisdiction to another, they generally entail some or all of the following steps: (1) annual appropriations are divided into quarterly allocations; (2) contractual commitments are approved and made; (3) goods and services are received; and (4) payments are made. These transactions are recorded in the budgetary accounting system in terms of the use of appropriations, and in the financial accounting system in terms of effects on assets (economic resources), liabilities (obligations for goods/services received), and revenues and expenditures/expenses (increases and decreases in net resources, respectively).

In addition, there are some specialized functions such as investment management and debt administration. Interested readers are referred to textbooks (e.g. Mikesell, 1995; Coombs and Jenkins, 2001) and manuals for practitioners (e.g. Allen and Tommasi, 2001).

Sound financial management is easier said than done. This is the case anywhere, but especially so in developing countries. The situation is abysmal in the poorest nations:

> What is budgeted is often not disbursed, and what is disbursed often does not arrive. Salaries go unpaid for months, operating funds do not materialize, and government debts remain unsettled. At the same time, the executive branch makes unbudgeted expenditures throughout the year. These loose practices make public spending data extremely spotty – and the data that does exist is often inaccurate or even falsified.
>
> (Thomas, 2001, p. 39)

For all its contributions to the smooth functioning of government, the classical PFM model cannot solve two problems: intentional budget deficits and operational inefficiency. Governments can run deficits by deliberately pursuing fiscal policies that cause spending to exceed revenues. They do so in order to achieve macro-economic objectives (e.g. stimulating production and employment) or for political reasons (e.g. placating interest groups). In that case, even the most competent financial management cannot hope to raise enough revenue or reduce sufficient expenditure to compensate for such 'deficits by design'. Nor can the faithful execution of the law necessarily achieve economy and efficiency. Finance-related laws do not usually deal with performance issues. Furthermore, a mentality of legal compliance is not conducive to creative thinking or actions to lower cost and increase efficiency. The NPM model of financial management arose to deal with these inadequacies of the classical model.

The 'new public management' (NPM) model

In the idealized NPM model, the distinction between public management (as distinguished from administration) and business management is blurred to the point that private sector practices are urged upon government. Government bureaucracies turn into strategic business units competing with each other, and citizens become customers. The budget-maximizing bureau chiefs are reformed into cost-conscious and revenue-hungry entrepreneurs. Performance and results – not inputs – are stressed. Government officials follow not the laws of specific jurisdictions but the universal rules of the marketplace: economy and efficiency. A businesslike government naturally uses private sector management techniques.

Accounting-based tools figure prominently in 'new public financial management' (NPFM), a term coined by Olson et al. (1998). NPFM takes a number of strong normative positions. It insists that accounting principles, set preferably by professional groups independent of government, should be used in budgeting. Double-entry recording should replace the single-entry system. Accrual accounting is offered as an alternative to the cash

103

budget (see Case Example 8.1). The government's financial picture should be presented as a whole to the public. The full costs of government services should be calculated as a basis for setting prices both for public and internal services. Outputs and outcomes should be measured, compared with benchmarks and verified by value-for-money audits.

CASE EXAMPLE 8.1 **THE USE OF ACCRUAL ACCOUNTING IN THE UK**

In business (including state-owned enterprises), accrual accounting requires recognition of revenue only after delivery of goods and services and expenses – costs of resources used and debts incurred – are matched against the revenue to arrive at a period's income. Applying this method to the core public sector, where taxes are levied to finance collective goods jointly consumed by the public, is highly problematic. Accrual accounting also refers to the recognition and reporting of various rights (assets) and obligations (liabilities).

In the UK since 2000, all financial planning in central government has been done on the basis of accrual accounting (or 'resource accounting', as it is called). Instead of departments having separate cash budgets for 'current' and for 'capital' expenditure, they have a consolidated expenditure limit, calculated by making estimates of the likely current costs and capital costs over the budget period (now typically three years). All assets which are used by the department are charged for, to exert pressure on their economical usage. Departments have much more freedom to decide the balance between capital and current expenditure (but this is still constrained, as capital expenditure usually has to be financed through public–private partnerships, such as the private finance initiative). This system also allows the clear separation of the 'programme budgets' which are used to provide goods and services to customers (e.g. the levels of benefits payments made to claimants), and the 'running costs' which are the managerial costs of administering the programmes.

Source: HM Treasury (2000a)

That is the rosy scenario NPFM offers to government. Yet, despite extensive experimentation in half a dozen countries over two decades, a 'globally standardized NPFM system' still does not exist, as there is 'no one way of understanding NPFM' (Olson *et al.*, 1998, p. 437). Although billed as a global movement, the above practices have made the most headway only in the English-speaking developed countries. There the accounting profession, led by chartered accountants or certified public accountants, enjoys a high degree of independence and wields considerable power as arbiter of what constitutes full disclosure to the public. Either directly or in alliance with others, accountants and auditors formulate or heavily influence auditing and accounting principles for corporations, nonprofit organizations and the public sector. These principles encourage (indeed, mandate) transparency of financial matters to the public gaze. Internally, cost-cutting and revenue-enhancement opportunities are identified (see Case Example 8.2).

CASE EXAMPLE 8.2 **TURNING COST CENTRES INTO REVENUE CENTRES**

Osborne and Gaebler, the champions of 're-inventing government', encouraged governments to be entrepreneurial. For example:

- The Milwaukee Metropolitan Sewerage District turned 60,000 tons of sewage sludge into fertilizer every year and sold it for $7.5 million.
- Phoenix earns $750,000 a year by selling methane gas from a large wastewater treatment plant to another city for home heating and cooking.
- The St Louis County Police, after developing a system for officers to telephone in their reports, licensed the software to a private company and earned US$25,000 for every new user.
- The Washington State ferry system in the early 1980s earned $1 million new revenue a year through re-tendering its food service contracts; more than US$150,000 a year by selling advertising spaces in its terminal building; and another US$150,000 a year by allowing duty-free shops on its two international boats.
- Paulding County, Georgia rented extra beds in its gaol to other jurisdictions for US$35 a night to handle their overflow, generating US$1.4 million in fees with US$200,000 in profit.
- Some Californian police departments reserved motel rooms to serve as weekend gaol cells for convicted drunken drivers at US$75 a night.

Source: Adapted from Osborne and Gaebler (1992, p. 197)

The above stories illustrate the way 'new public managers' deal with financial problems. They act like entrepreneurial businessmen, turning cost centres into revenue or profit centres. They master the concept of opportunity costs and eagerly make use of otherwise idle resources. They think 'outside the box' by defying conventions and offering creative solutions. Instead of following the rules, they make the rules.

NPFM has the potential to energize an ossified bureaucracy, but there are several problems with it. First, it does not address the core issue in government. In the final analysis, government exists to take care of the consequences of market failure, doing those things for which business lacks incentives or is not equipped to handle. Besides its peripheral agencies and activities (which can be and have been privatized), the government promotes general welfare by providing collective goods and financing them through general taxation. Equity rather than efficiency, economy or even effectiveness is the ultimate criterion in public or political decision making in a democracy. Second, the worst bureaucracies are often pitted against the best-run corporations, thus creating a distorted comparison. As the collapse of Enron (the giant American energy-trading company) and Andersen (one of the former Big Five international auditing/consulting firms) and subsequent corporate scandal shows, all is not well in the business world and the auditing profession. Indeed, the principles of democratic government – separation of powers, checks and balances – might well help to reform corporate governance. Third, in its extreme form, NPFM may be as unsustainable as previous radical reforms. It elevates administrative discretion at the expense of legislature power. It promotes the ethos of the business-minded accountants against the politically savvy policy analysts. It does not appreciate the primacy and resiliency of budget rules in government. It fails to recognize that cost-cutting could only go so far: below the fat lie the bones – the core government institutions to which the public turns in time of crisis and turmoil. What is needed is a governance model that recognizes the respective roles, competences and advantage of government, civic society and businesses.

The Barnard–Simon governance model

The roots of governance may be traced to an organization theory pioneered by Chester Barnard and Herbert Simon. Instead of profit maximization for stockholders, Barnard (1968, originally 1938) argued that the manager's function was to motivate the contribution of everyone who holds resources needed to carry on the business. Simon (1945) applied Barnard's insight to government in his landmark *Administrative Behavior*. He views an organization – government or business – as being in equilibrium when its managers succeed in balancing the contributions from, and the inducements given to, its stakeholders (see Table 8.1 for examples). Given their knowledge of input–output relationships, managers are keenly aware of the complementarity and substitutability of the resources held by different stakeholders. Their essential task is to maintain a critical mass of the inputs which will be necessary to assure the organization's ability to deliver services. In this regard, what makes financial management crucial is that it controls money – the currency for acquiring a wide variety of other resources. The organizational role of the financial manager is to keep the score of finance-related exchanges, advise management on the terms of those exchanges, and monitor financial performance of all the parties concerned.

Barnard and Simon focused on individual organizations. However, the solution of many complex societal problems requires the co-operation of a network of public and private institutions (see Chapter 13). For example, in the 1999 fiscal year, the federal government in the United States spent only 5.2 per cent of its total expenditures itself in direct provision of goods and services; over 70 per cent was spent through 'indirect government' or 'third-party government' (Salamon, 2002). In such a situation, to be effective, government has to empower others, rather than exercising direct control (see Kickert *et al.* (1997) for elaboration). In addition to minding the government's own finances, public financial managers keep a watchful eye on the viability of the institutional network and its participants. Such a role is not unlike that of an organization's financial managers, who monitor its creditors and debtors alike. This similarity has led me to name the governance model of public financial management after Barnard and Simon.

Working through others provides government with more tools (Table 8.2). Besides direct provision of goods and services, government could enter into contracts with, or give grants to, business and nonprofit organizations. It could provide loans, loan guarantees or insurance coverage. Even less directly, it issues regulations to influence others' behaviour.

Table 8.1 *Government as a coalition of stakeholders*

Stakeholders	Contributions (benefits to the organization)	Inducements (costs to the organization)
Voters	Legitimacy	Public services to individuals and for general welfare
Taxpayers	Tax dollars	Public services to individuals and for general welfare
Customers	Fees	Specific goods and services for personal use
Grant givers	Financial resources, mandates[1]	Services to target or general population
Bond holders	Financing (for fixed periods)	Interest payments, principal repayment
Vendors	Goods and services	Payments or promises of payments
Employees	Services, skills, ideas	Compensation and benefits (current and future), non-financial benefits
Governing boards, oversight bodies	Authority, policy guidance, monitoring of performance	Power, prestige, services to constituency, likelihood of re-election, achievement of personal agenda
Managers	Skills in negotiation, persuasion and implementation	Salary, promotion, career advancement

[1] From higher levels of government, to allow grants to be used in specific ways, and policies as conditions of the grant.

Source: Adapted from Chan (1981)

Compared with taxation and spending, these are more complex contractual arrangements. They all have financial implications. Grants, loans, guarantees and insurance are financial transactions. Regulations may seem relatively inexpensive to government (other than administrative costs), but they do impose compliance costs on the regulated. In all these relationships, there exist a set of claims and obligations that bind the government and its network partners. An important function of government financial managers is to help structure contracts with network participants and monitor their contractual performance.

COMPARATIVE APPRAISAL OF THE MODELS

After discussing the models underlying public financial management individually, it is time to bring them together for comparison and appraisal in terms of their context, content and supporting analytical disciplines.

As a service function, the role of financial management is influenced heavily by its environment. Specifically, the nature of the entity being managed and the higher level manager tend to affect what financial managers do (Table 8.3). In a bureaucracy headed by directors bent on strong control, the financial manager follows rules and carries out orders. The same approach will not work if the financial manager works for a business-minded taskmaster who is constantly looking out for cost-cutting opportunities. Furthermore, a manager

Table 8.2 Tools of government

Tools	Product/activity	Producer or provider	Recipient
Direct provision	Both public and private goods and services	Public agency by government employees	Service recipients, both individuals and organizations
Contracting	Goods and services with attributes of private goods	Contractors (business and nonprofit organizations)	Service recipients, mostly individuals, could be organizations
Grants	Goods and services: public or private goods	Grantee: lower level of government, nonprofit organizations	The public or specific individuals
Direct loans	Credit facility, loan, borrowed money, financing	Public agency approving the loans	Individuals, businesses, other governments, nonprofit organizations
Loan guarantees	Promise to make principal and interest payments in case of default of borrower	Public agency making the promise	Individuals, businesses, other governments, nonprofit organizations
Insurance	Promise to pay for losses incurred	Public agency	Individuals or businesses
Regulation	Rules and regulations	Public agency	Individuals and organization subject to jurisdiction

Source: Adapted from Tables 1–5 of Salamon (2002, p. 21)

in the self-centred mode of NPM has to change his or her mind-set when confronted with the need to weave together a network of similarly self-interested institutions. The new environment calls for the ability to see others' perspective, an essential skill in successful negotiations.

Its different roles in altered contexts have serious implications for the content of public financial management (Table 8.4). Financial managers are rewarded for their contributions to conformity (classical model), short-term efficiency and economy (NPM model), and long-term effectiveness and equity (governance model). Consequently, they think of what is managed differently, and monitor different aspects of financial performance.

Public financial management – in the broad sense – is aided by budgeting, accounting and auditing (Table 8.5). The input and control orientation in the classical model gives way to the mission-driven output budgets favoured by the NPM model. The macro perspective of the governance model requires a more encompassing (i.e. global) budget to see how resources are allocated to various service providers. Similarly, rule-based budgetary and financial accounting would not be appropriate for the NPM model; what is needed is the

Table 8.3 *Context of public financial management*

	Classical model	NPM model	Governance model
Entity	A hierarchical bureaucracy in a government with separate powers and checks and balances	A mission-driven and cost-conscious strategic business unit	An organization interacting with others in a network of public, civic and business institutions
Image of the general manager	A budget-maximizing civil servant obsessed with legal compliance and financial control	A public entrepreneur focusing on customer satisfaction, raising revenues and cutting costs	A savvy executive knitting together and maintaining an institutional network to deliver services
Primary role of financial management	Implementing fiscal policies on revenue, expenditure, borrowing and investment	Searching for potential revenues and least-cost method of service delivery	Securing financing in order to keep intact the organizational and network coalitions

Table 8.4 *Contents of public financial management*

	Classical model	NPM model	Governance model
Goals and performance criteria	Legal and contractual conformity	Efficiency, economy	Effectiveness and equity
Object of management	Organizational units and sub-units	Services, activities	Multilateral institutional relations
Key financial variables and tools	Revenues, expenditures, investments and debts	Full cost recovery, cost savings and incremental revenues	Revenues, expenditures, grants, contracts, loans, loan guarantees, insurance, regulations

ability to analyse costs in support of management decisions. The multiple contractual arrangements in the governance model require keeping track of many claims and obligations. By the same token, the scope of auditing is broadened to encompass non-financial aspects of performance.

SUMMARY

Scholars of public management have over time changed their views of what a good government is. A good government used to be an efficient bureaucracy that faithfully executed public policy. More recently, advocates of 'new public management' endow a good government with an entrepreneurial spirit that treats citizens as customers (who care more about

Table 8.5 Supporting information services

	Classical model	NPM model	Governance model
Budget	Departmental, line-item input budgets	Mission-oriented budgets with output/outcome orientation	Global budgets
Accounting	Budgetary accounting, financial accounting	Product/service costing, differential costs and benefits	Accounting for claims and obligations
Auditing	Compliance and financial audits	Operational audits: economy, efficiency	Audits focusing on outputs, outcomes, effectiveness and equity

outputs and outcomes than inputs). Now a good government plays its part in a larger institutional network. These shifting perspectives have in turn redefined the ideal public administrator/manager. She used to fight to enlarge her agency's share of the budget pie; now she cuts costs and searches for new revenues, and builds strategic alliances. In service of the new public manager, the financial staff person has to acquire new skills. It is not enough for him to know how to keep the books correctly; he has to spot opportunities for cost savings and revenue enhancements. Better still is a financial wizard who can leverage others' strengths and defeat competitors. In order to integrate the diverse finance functions, governments have appointed chief financial officers (CFOs) with expanded authority and responsibility. If the rise – and occasional spectacular fall – of corporate CFOs is any guide, public financial management will be anything but dull as governments seek to tackle their fiscal problems with rigour and creativity.

QUESTIONS FOR REVIEW AND DISCUSSION

- What are the salient features of the three models of public financial management and what factors gave rise to their development?
- In what ways can the adoption of the NPM and Barnard–Simon governance models be regarded as changes for the better, as compared to the classical model?

READER EXERCISES

1   Write the job descriptions which you think should apply to the following government officials: chief finance officer, budget director, comptroller, treasurer, internal auditor.
2   Find a copy of the annual report and accounts of your local authority or state government. Try to find within it the following data:

- the overall level of borrowing of the agency;
- the overall value of assets of the agency;
- the proportion of costs of leisure and cultural services which are recovered by fees and charges;
- the proportion of costs of social care services which are recovered by fees and charges;
- the level of locally raised taxes as a proportion of total local expenditure.

What do the answers tell you (1) about potential changes in local financial policy, and (2) about the level of transparency in local financial management?

CLASS EXERCISES

1   Should governments in poor countries be exempted from the financial management requirements discussed in this chapter? Which of the models discussed in this chapter is more appropriate for developing countries? Why?

2   A local government health department operates a community mental health centre. The centre's basic occupancy costs (e.g. rents, utilities) are paid by the local government. However, its services are financed by grants. Currently, there are two programmes. The Clinic is financed by a multi-year state grant, and the Community Outreach programme is paid for by a federal grant. Today the centre's executive director received three letters. The health department wants to reduce the centre's budget by 20 per cent. The state is cutting its grant by 30 per cent, and the federal grant programme is being phased out in two years. Advise the executive director what to do and how to go about it.

FURTHER READING

Richard Allen and Daniel Tommasi (eds) (2001), *Managing public expenditures: a reference book for transition countries*. Paris: OECD.

Robert D. Behn (2001), *Rethinking democratic accountability*. Washington, DC: The Brookings Institution.

Hugh Coombs and David Jenkins (2001), *Public sector financial management*. London: Thomson Learning.

John L. Mikesell (1995), *Fiscal administration*. Belmont, CA: Wadsworth.

Chapter 9

Moving to e-government

The role of ICTs in the public sector

Christine Bellamy, Nottingham Trent University, UK

INTRODUCTION

It was in the early years of the 1990s that governments throughout the developed world first became interested in the potential contribution of information and communications technologies (ICTs) to transforming public services and governance (Bellamy and Taylor, 1998). Since then, we have seen huge changes in these technologies and in the way they are used. ICTs are no longer elite technologies, available only to those with special training and know-how. Innovations such as:

- the extraordinary growth of the Internet and World Wide Web;
- widening public acceptance of plastic card technology and online shopping;
- the imminent advent of third generation (3G) mobile phones and digital interactive TV (DTV) capable of connecting to the Internet

have focused policy makers' minds on how governments should respond to the increasingly pervasive presence of these technologies among the citizens they serve. Just as business has become more interested in exploiting e-commerce, so governments, too, have become more interested in e-government.

One reason for the widespread interest in electronic service delivery (ESD) and online democracy is the hope that they will help to restore the legitimacy of political institutions, by increasing their accessibility, responsiveness and comprehensibility. This objective is, however, likely to be badly undermined if the shift to online governance reinforces a new 'digital divide' between those people who have access to technology and those who do not. It will also miss its mark if citizens do not trust ICTs or if they fear the abuse of their personal data. For all these reasons, the successful exploitation of ICTs requires the establishment of effective technology dissemination policies, information management policies and regulatory regimes, thus raising issues that go far wider than the simple management of technological change.

Governments have used computers on a significant scale since the early 1970s, but over the past three decades there has been a marked shift of emphasis from the use of stand-alone computers to joining up computers in electronic networks. This trend fits well with

113

the current emphasis on holistic government (Perris 6 *et al.*, 2002). Joined-up government needs joined-up services, joined-up data and networked citizens, and ICTs seem to offer the means of achieving all these things.

LEARNING OBJECTIVES

- To be aware of the changing understanding of the significance of ICTs
- To be aware of the implications of managerial and institutional change associated with ICTs
- To understand the need for active policies to minimize the 'digital divide'
- To understand the crucial importance of trustworthy processing of personal data

---

THE STRATEGIC SIGNIFICANCE OF ICTS: FROM A FOCUS ON TECHNOLOGY TO A FOCUS ON INFORMATION

The vision of information-age government described in this chapter has been developed over the past fifteen years or so, in three main sets of publications, all aimed primarily at management academics and practising managers. Their influence on e-government reflects a (largely) one-way transfer of ideas from private to public sector and shows a gradual shift of emphasis from a preoccupation with *technology* as a strategic resource, through a focus on reforming *organizational processes*, to a growing interest in *information* and its exploitation.

Understanding the strategic significance of technology

The first set of publications constitutes, perhaps, the seminal writing on the relationship between IT and strategic management (e.g. Scott Morton, 1991). Its main purpose was to persuade managers that technology should cease to be regarded simply as a tool for *implementing* business strategy. Rather, the new information and communications capabilities associated with ICTs should be allowed to *shape* strategy. New, more speedy and direct ways of communicating with customers and suppliers would allow new marketing data to be collected and exploited, new distribution techniques to be developed and new supply chains to be constructed. Managers should ask not '*How can IT help me do my business?*' but '*How can I best do business now that I have IT?*' Businesses that failed to recognize the strong 'economic imperative of IT' would fall behind in an increasingly competitive world.

Re-engineering processes – towards joined-up electronic services

This is the literature that has most directly influenced the discourse through which e-government is discussed (Davenport, 1993). It offers a critique of the highly fragmented departmental structures associated with traditional bureaucracies and asserts that new information systems often fail, because they reinforce this fragmentation. The upshot is that customer data remain imprisoned in 'information silos', preventing public services from responding flexibly and holistically to customers' needs. 'Business process re-engineering' (BPR) implies, instead, that business processes and bureaucratic structures should be *fundamentally* 're-engineered' and this has a number of important implications. First, it suggests that processes should be integrated *horizontally* across departmental boundaries, and second, it encourages *vertical* integration between supply, production, distribution and consumption. For example, processing a welfare claim depends, at bottom, on the quality and timeliness of data about a claimant lodged by that claimant. Data input controlled by the customer himself – perhaps over the Internet – will not only be cheaper and faster but more accurate. 'Direct' services, in the manner of 'direct' banking or insurance services, are likely, therefore, to be both cheaper *and* better. Costs and red tape could be reduced still further if basic personal data (e.g. name, address, gender, marital status) are *shared* between information systems across government rather than collected anew by each department. Indeed, many governments worldwide are therefore becoming interested in developing a central register of residents and citizens that would be updated as they navigate certain 'life events', such as being born, getting married, becoming employed, moving house or entering into residential care.

Knowledge management: information as a strategic resource

'Knowledge management' (KM) has, in the past few years, become recognized as an increasingly strategic function (Davenport and Prusak, 1998). Its perceived importance stems from the distinction between:

- facts and figures held in computer systems and manual files (data);
- ordering of data into resources imbued with meaning and relevance (information);
- constructing a shared understanding of how information can be applied to solving problems and getting things done (knowledge).

KM involves 'knowing what an organization knows'. It depends on the insight that bringing better knowledge to bear on social or organizational problems is less a matter of collecting yet more data, and more to do with exploiting the vast quantities of data already held on computer systems as a result of day-to-day transactions with customers and suppliers. KM therefore involves knowing how these data can be transformed into a resource that is fully valued and used. In the public sector, KM is encouraging managers to understand their customer base (for example, who actually claims welfare benefits?); the incidence of particular social problems (for example, in which neighbourhoods are most crimes actually committed and when?) and the quality, impact or take-up of public services.

RE-ENGINEERING GOVERNMENTS FOR THE INFORMATION AGE: FORGING ELECTRONIC SERVICE DELIVERY

Over the past few years, many governments have drawn up information-age strategies based on these kinds of ideas. The British government's 'e-government strategy' was published in April 2000 (Central IT Unit, 2000), following several years' work on a long series of consultation papers and pilot projects by the Cabinet Office's Central IT Unit, now part of the Office of the E-Envoy. The implementation of the strategy has been supported by an increasingly stringent set of targets, culminating in the promise that 100 per cent of public services would be available electronically by 2005. This target has reinforced the strong focus on electronic service delivery (ESD) at the expense of other applications of ICTs, but some experiments are also beginning to occur in democratic practice and knowledge management. These, then, are the three headings under which I propose to explore changing attitudes to exploiting ICTs.

Innovations in ESD

The National Audit Office's study of *Government on the Web 2* (Dunleavy and Margetts, 2002) (available at www.nao.gov.uk) shows how the World Wide Web is being used for ESD. As this study points out, the relatively simple dissemination of information is much easier to deliver on the Web than interactive transactions (such as paying bills or lodging forms). The reasons for this will become clear below in our discussion of the *Government Gateway* and online voting. It is important to recognize, too, that some information-age services are better delivered through other electronic channels, especially the phone. Services for older and poorer people – such as social security claims, advice services or the NHS helpline, *NHS Direct* – will probably continue to be offered from call centres or in real-world offices, as well as on the Web.

One of the most pervasive themes in ESD is the aim of providing clusters of services through one-stop outlets. One-stop shops promise governments economies of scale and scope, while offering their customers more convenient access and more holistic responses to their needs and problems. One-stop shops therefore figure prominently in many countries' e-government plans. For example, the flagship of the British e-government strategy is the *UK Online Portal* at www.ukonline.gov.uk. This portal went live in 2000 and aims to offer a high-profile, convenient route into a wide range of public service information and trans-actions, regardless of which part of government provides them. By organizing services around common 'life events', the portal is intended to make them more comprehensible and easy to use. A particularly important innovation is the *Government Gateway*, a facility that enables companies or individuals to conduct transactions involving sensitive personal or commercial data, such as lodging tax forms or claiming government grants. Access to these transactions is secured either by the use of a PIN number and password or via a 'digital certificate', a device that, rather in the manner of a bank guarantee for a credit card, guarantees the iden-tity of the sender and makes the transaction legally 'non-repudiable'. Digital certificates are regarded as strategically important tools for the growth of e-government and e-commerce.

Nevertheless, as the British *Government Gateway* illustrates well, the development of portals has often been difficult and slow, because there are many critical success factors that are difficult to achieve. The issues relate to:

■ *Technical problems* – especially those involved in linking portals with the vast number of government computer systems pre-dating the World Wide Web.

- *Brand image* – for example, the British government has failed so far to establish a strong public profile for *UK Online*.
- *Portal design* – including the problems of covering an enormous range of government services, while also making it easy to find the combination of services a particular user needs.
- *Security and authentication* – including the problems of satisfying public service managers as to the integrity of personal data and the identity of their owners.
- *Low popular demand* – as illustrated by the low usage of the *Gateway*. Only about a thousand digital certificates were issued by 2002, and the E-Envoy's Office was also finding it difficult to persuade potential suppliers of digital certificates (e.g. banks) to enter this market.

In the UK, many of these problems are magnified by the complexity of the machinery of government. There is a vast range of departments and quangos and several tiers of government, including the new devolved administrations. In contrast, the online portal of the Australian state of Victoria – one of the acknowledged world leaders in e-government (see Case Example 9.1) – shows what can be done by forceful leadership operating on a simpler administrative system, serving a much smaller population. Readers may also be interested to compare the *UK Online Portal* with the *Service Canada Portal*, which offers a similar range of services at www.servicecanada.gc.ca.

Other governments, still, prefer to use ICTs to support the restructuring of 'real-world' public service outlets. One of the most prominent examples of this approach is the Australian Federal Government's Centrelink, the subject of Case Example 9.2.

FORGING ONLINE DEMOCRACY

If information is power, then ICTs offer huge opportunities for removing many of the barriers to accessing information and to participating actively in public life. The democratic applications of ICTs seem therefore to be immense, but writers on e-democracy have disagreed strongly about their likely impact. There are three main scenarios. ICTs could:

1   help reinvigorate representative democracy;
2   help establish more direct forms of democracy, by obviating the need for elected representatives to mediate between citizens and government;
3   reinforce the power of existing political elites, by giving them more powerful tools for political marketing and spin.

There is growing interest in democratic experimentation, but, thus far at least, little evidence that alternative models of democracy are being institutionalized into the fabric of Western states. On the contrary, research suggests that Internet technologies are being tamed by existing political elites (Margolis and Resnick, 2000), while, as we have seen, governments' own attention has been focused on ESD rather than on the health of the wider political system. Nevertheless, there are encouraging signs that e-democracy is beginning to claim a higher place on formal policy agendas than hitherto. In Britain, for example,

CASE EXAMPLE 9.1 **WWW.VIC.GOV.AU: A MINI CASE STUDY OF ESD**

In the mid-1990s, the Australian State of Victoria decided to invest heavily in the development of e-government as a way of providing cost-efficient, modern public services for a small population spread over a large geographical territory. Since then, Victoria has become one of the acknowledged leaders in ESD. The development of ESD was helped by a number of factors, including:

■ Strong political leadership in the form of a new Premier strongly committed to e-government.

■ Effective project management in the form of an energetic project manager operating with clear lines of accountability.

■ A population that was willing to engage with new technology.

A key feature is the extensive and well-designed website. This site clusters services by topic (e.g. arts, business, consumers, health) and by life event (e.g. getting married, going to school, having a baby, turning 18). It also allows citizens to carry out a wide range of functions involving both public and associated private services, including:

■ paying for services and licences

■ booking appointments or visits from tradesmen

■ registering a change of address with several organizations through a single transaction

■ ordering duplicate certificates

■ lodging completed forms

■ registering for a vote.

There is also a facility for providing feedback on services to the Premier of Victoria.

---

factors as diverse as the establishment of the new assemblies in Scotland and Wales and low election turn-outs, especially among the young, have stimulated growing interest in the democratic application of ICTs to strengthen representative democracy. Case Example 9.3 lists some recent innovations in the UK.

British government policy favours a twin-track approach to e-democracy (OGC/Office of the E-Envoy, 2002). One track is designed to lead to remote voting by electronic means (RVEM) in local and general elections, with electors casting their votes over the Internet or by texting on mobile phones. The government believes that RVEM will remove practical barriers preventing people from voting and help to modernize the image of democracy, particularly among the young. There are, however, a number of problems that need to be solved, including:

■ *supervision* – ensuring that voting in places other than polling stations is secret, private and free;

CASE EXAMPLE 9.2 **THE AUSTRALIAN CENTRELINK:
A MINI CASE STUDY OF E-ENABLED
ONE-STOP SERVICES
WWW.CENTRELINK.GOV.AU**

Centrelink was created in 1997, when the Australian DSS was split into two parts: a small policy department and a large service delivery organization, Centrelink. As well as delivering social security benefits, Centrelink also delivers services to its main client groups on behalf of ten other government departments, including the Commonwealth Employment Service.

This arrangement has a number of benefits, including:

- Services can be organized according to life events, rather than by the departments that own the programmes.
- Services are simpler and more comprehensible for clients to use.
- Delivery is more rational and cost-effective – Centrelink has delivered big efficiency savings.
- It makes possible the innovative use of ICTs.

Like the British DSS, Centrelink has relied mainly on a network of branch offices and call centres. However, it has also planned to invest heavily in ICTs, using both the Internet and advanced call centre technology. Among other innovations, its Online Action Plan calls for:

- Automated interactive voice response (IVR), to provide clients with details of their payments on demand.
- Decision support systems to help frontline staff deal with complex claims more easily.
- Telephone lodgement of claim forms.
- Multimedia payphones provided in rural areas to help clients access services more easily.
- A Web post office for communicating with Centrelink.
- Facilities for making integrated claims for a number of benefits when clients experience particular life events.

- *secure and robust* – protecting systems from hacking, viruses, technical failure and commercial failure of IT suppliers;
- *privacy* – protecting the secrecy of votes once cast and counted;
- *public confidence* – persuading voters to trust e-voting, and reassuring them that these problems have been addressed satisfactorily.

RVEM is therefore unlikely to be implemented nationally before 2008, though a number of pilots are planned (Pratchett, 2002).

The second track aims to exploit ICTs to increase public participation in politics and policy making (see Chapter 15). Since 1997, the British government has introduced systematic arrangements for public consultations, including the use of the Internet. It aims to extend

---

CASE EXAMPLE 9.3 E-DEMOCRACY IN BRITISH GOVERNMENT

This box gives examples of some recent experiments with using the Internet for e-democracy in different tiers of British government. Many of them are taken from the government's consultation document on e-democracy, *In the Service of Democracy*, first issued in July 2002.

■ *Citizen Space* (www.ukonline.gov.uk) – readers should particularly note the online discussions moderated by the Hansard Society. These have provided a forum for victims of domestic violence organized in association with a Parliamentary Select Committee investigation in 1999, and a discussion of the e-democracy paper in summer 2002. The site also provides a full list of current consultations by British central government. Facilities for discussion and feedback should develop rapidly over the next few years.

■ *Young Camden* (www.camden.gov.uk) – a website hosted by the London Borough of Camden specifically for young people to participate in surveys, discussions and online votes on issues that particularly concern them. The Council is committed to following up issues and providing feedback.

■ *The Welsh Assembly* (www.wales.gov.uk) – this site provides formal minutes of all the Assembly's committees, along with current policy papers out for consultation. Facilities for online feedback are also provided. Readers may be particularly interested in the consultation and feedback for the Welsh national ICT strategy at www.cymruarlein.wales.gov.uk/.

■ *The Scottish Assembly* (www.scottish.parliament.uk) – the Scottish Parliament offers relatively advanced facilities for online petitions. Citizens can create a petition, publicize it, invite signatures, submit it to the Parliament and join in online discussion.

■ *Number 10* (www.number-10.gov.uk) – the Prime Minister's Office also receives online petitions, but does not provide facilities for publicizing or signing them. The site lists petitions received, and the government's response. This site also provides briefings, press releases and links to discussion forums concerned with topical events.

these arrangements by requiring all departments to comply with an e-consultation toolkit. In particular, extensive use will be made of *CitizenSpace*, the public discussion forum hosted by the *UK Online Portal*. MPs are also being encouraged to develop e-mail links and online forums.

MANAGING KNOWLEDGE IN THE INFORMATION AGE

Public service computers hold data that could form a rich resource for policy makers and managers. Medical records could throw much light, for example, on the epidemiology of disease and social services; school, medical and police records could all help us understand why some neighbourhoods or people become socially excluded or become involved in crime. For this reason, there is growing interest in public sector applications of such data management techniques as:

- *Data matching* – comparing datasets to identify cases with particular parameters (e.g. matching social security and tax records to identify people who might be claiming benefits while undertaking paid employment).
- *Data mining* – analysing data already held on operational systems to yield new management or policy information (e.g. analysing records of educational institutions to uncover access trends).

In particular, the British government has taken an increasing range of data-matching powers to help fight such ills as social security fraud, crime (especially crimes involving violence or sex abuse) and illegal immigration. In some cases, these powers now include rights of access to the files of private organizations such as banks and building societies. Case Example 9.4 gives examples of proposals put forward in a recent government report. If enacted, they would significantly extend powers to share data.

The events in New York on 11 September 2001 have also stimulated interest in harnessing electronic data in the war against international terrorism. For example, in 2002 the European Parliament passed legislation allowing member states to require commercial companies such as Internet service providers to retain customer data (such as billing and service usage data) for up to seven years, despite data protection principles which dictate that personal data should be disposed of as soon as practicable. However, an attempt by the British Home Secretary to extend his powers to intercept Internet traffic was withdrawn pending public debate, a decision reflecting the strength of worries aroused by the spectre of electronic surveillance.

SOME KEY ISSUES

The assumption behind all these plans is that new technical infrastructures can be made to work as planned. This cannot be taken for granted as experience in the UK and elsewhere has painfully shown. Stronger project management is therefore recognized to be a crucial issue in delivering e-government, and governments worldwide have been forced to develop better arrangements to ensure that this is achieved (Cabinet Office, 2000; PUMA, 2001). Another crucial assumption is that citizens will be willing and able to use electronic channels for communicating with governments. A key issue here is whether citizens will have, and should have, confidence in electronic networks. For this reason, data privacy and security are now regarded as key objectives of, not as obstacles to, the development of e-government (Raab, 2001). There are several good reasons, however, why these objectives may be difficult to achieve.

Authenticating identity and protecting privacy

Network security arrangements and privacy enhancing technologies have improved immensely in recent years, although they need to be constantly updated to keep ahead of

121

CASE EXAMPLE 9.4 **PROPOSALS FOR EXTENDED DATA SHARING IN BRITISH GOVERNMENT**

These proposals are taken from a Report of the Performance and Innovation Unit on Data Sharing and Privacy, April 2002 (PIU, 2002). This report made nineteen specific proposals for new legal powers to share data between government agencies and beyond. They include proposals to share personal data between:

- the Children's Fund, local education authorities, social services and the police to ensure early identification of children and young people at risk of social exclusion;
- healthcare professionals in hospitals, GP practices and social care services, to enable them to have access to more complete medical histories of patients;
- DVLA and the insurance industry, to reduce the paperwork involved in taxing motor vehicles;
- GPs, social services, housing authorities, voluntary organizations and others, to deal with children who miss large periods of schooling and to ensure that they receive other public services they need;
- drug action teams and the Department of Health, to help the latter monitor the effectiveness of the fight against illicit drugs.

the game. An issue that is proving more difficult to resolve is the authentication of identity online – credit card companies, e-commerce businesses and public services all suffer increasingly from identity fraud. The British government has therefore toyed for years with proposals for identity cards (Home Office, 2002). It is particularly interested in 'smart cards' imprinted with a digital representation of a personal physical feature, such as the holder's fingerprint or iris. The card would record the holder's service entitlements (e.g. their season ticket to the local swimming bath or their electoral roll number or their entitlement to welfare benefits). The basic personal details of authorized card holders would be registered on a central database, as discussed above – a proposal that is bound to reinforce concerns about privacy.

Data quality

Another problem is that much of the data in government computers is inevitably inaccurate, out of date or incomplete, and could potentially cause huge damage if used for data-matching exercises such as those mentioned above. For example, sentencing an offender on the basis of an inaccurate criminal record, fingering the wrong man for paedophilia or accusing an upright citizen of social security fraud may cause the individuals involved untold anguish, and, if publicized, would also bring the service concerned into considerable disrepute. It is widely acknowledged, therefore, that a significant improvement in data quality is an essential condition for safe and effective data sharing.

PROTECTING DATA PRIVACY

All these issues serve to highlight the crucial importance of safeguarding the privacy of personal data. In Britain, data privacy is protected by the Data Protection Act 1998 and the Human Rights Act 1998, and is monitored by the Office of the Information Commissioner. Most public services also publish codes of practice on data privacy and data sharing. These policies are based on internationally accepted principles of data protection which may be consulted on the Information Commissioner's website at www.dataprotection.gov.uk/principl.htm.

There is, however, an uncomfortable fact: we simply do not know how far all these principles, codes and protocols are actually observed in day-to-day routines and how much uncontrolled, ad hoc data sharing takes place, especially between street-level bureaucrats. A second problem is that, as the references to social security fraud, crime and terrorism above illustrate, accepted principles of data protection can be overridden by 'public interest' considerations and some of the data sharing undertaken by public services cannot be subject to data subjects' consent or knowledge, both key principles of data protection. The question therefore arises: When are data protection principles *properly* overridden by the public interest, on what grounds and with what safeguards?

ACCESS AND EQUALITY – CLOSING THE DIGITAL DIVIDE

E-government strategies also assume that the public will have the means, the understanding and skill to access electronic networks. The success of e-government depends, therefore, on the effectiveness of strategies to address the 'digital divide'. In Britain, this issue is being addressed in two main ways (Office of the E-Envoy, 2000). First, the government is committed to near universal access to the Internet by 2005 and hopes that this will be achieved as much by the rapid dissemination of 3G phones and DTV as by the spread of personal computers. To stimulate the market, the UK was an early mover in liberalizing the telecommunications industry and issuing franchises for 3G phones. The result is that Britain is among leading nations for access to the Internet and to DTV (Dunleavy and Margetts, 2002). Nevertheless, the dissemination of broadband telecommunications capable of supporting high-speed Internet links has been slow and patchy, and the digital TV companies have suffered well-publicized commercial problems, casting doubts on the feasibility of market making for DTV.

Second, significant effort is being devoted to extending opportunities and support for people to go online. The government has financed projects for households in socially deprived areas to try out DTV, and is setting up some 1200 UK online centres throughout the country, offering Internet access, IT training and advice about education and job search facilities. Most of these centres are being located in FE colleges and community centres, and all 4300 public libraries will also be linked to a people's network offering similar facilities. UK Online is also being supported by a series of initiatives to place networked computers in all schools and to train children in e-citizenship.

SUMMARY

All this points to a rapidly changing agenda, one that raises serious issues for citizens and their political representatives as well as for public service managers. The focus is no longer on managing technological innovation to cope with well-defined tasks. Rather, the emphasis is shifting to the wider political significance of technologically enhanced methods of communicating, processing information and exploiting knowledge. This chapter has also raised important issues of principle, including ones that go to the heart of the meaning of such concepts as privacy, surveillance and citizenship. The exercises that follow are therefore designed to stimulate thinking and debate about these crucial issues.

QUESTIONS FOR REVIEW AND DISCUSSION

1   Assuming that facilities become available, what would be the main benefits and barriers for individual citizens in (a) voting in local elections over the Internet or (b) taxing a car online? What steps could public services take to maximize uptake of such facilities among a wide cross-section of the population?
2   Why have governments become more interested in e-democracy in recent years, and by what criteria would you judge its success?
3   Why have governments become more interested in data sharing (including data matching) in recent years? What benefits and dangers are there *for citizens and for governments* if this practice is extended in the ways suggested in Case Example 9.4?

READER EXERCISES

1   Visit the UK Online Portal, at least some of the websites cited in the section on ESD and the website of your own local council. Make a note of the main features offered by these sites. In the light of your notes, what would you consider to be the best site, and why?
2   Visit the websites listed in Case Example 9.3. How would you rate their contribution to the enrichment of democracy in the UK? Give reasons for your ratings.
3   Make a list of the government services that hold files containing your personal data. Make another list showing which files you would, and which you would not, consent to be shared between agencies, and why. In the light of these lists, consider whether there are sufficient safeguards in place to protect your privacy.

CLASS EXERCISES

1   Organize a formal debate on the proposition that 'this House supports the government's proposals for introducing identity cards'.
2   Organize a class discussion to explore the circumstances in which it is right for governments to cross-match sensitive personal data (such as social security records,

bank accounts, criminal records held on the Police National Computer, or medical records) without the consent of the data subject. Get a rapporteur to make a note of your main conclusions.

FURTHER READING

Christine Bellamy and John A. Taylor (1998), *Governing in the information age.* Milton Keynes: Open University Press, especially Chapters 1, 3 and 4.

Barry N. Hague and Brian Loader (1999), *Digital democracy.* London: Routledge.

David Lyon (1994), *The electronic eye: the rise of the surveillance society.* Cambridge: Polity Press.

Perris 6, Diana Leet, Kimberley Seltzer and Gerry Stoker (2002), *Towards holistic governance: the new reform agenda.* Basingstoke: Palgrave, especially chapters 2 and 7.

Chapter 10

Performance measurement and management in public sector organizations

Geert Bouckaert and Wouter van Dooren, Catholic University of
Leuven, Belgium

INTRODUCTION

> *Sir Humphrey*: Minister, you said you wanted the administration figures reduced,
> didn't you? *Jim Hacker*: Yes. *Sir Humphrey*: So we reduced the figures. *Jim Hacker*:
> But only the figures, not the number of administrators. *Sir Humphrey*: Well of
> course not. *Jim Hacker*: Well that is not what I meant. *Sir Humphrey*: Well really
> Minister, one is not a mind-reader, is one? You said reduce the figures, so we
> reduced the figures.
>
> (Yes Minister 2.1: 'The Compassionate Society')

Performance management is about both measurement and management, about information
and action (Hatry, 1999; Morley *et al.* 2001). The aim of this chapter is to explore the
concept, the potential and the practice of performance measurement and management in
public sector organizations.

LEARNING OBJECTIVES

- To be aware of the evolution of performance measurement and management in the
  public sector
- To understand the key concepts in performance measurement
- To understand the key concepts in performance management
- To understand the main lessons learned in performance management
- To be able to identify the main traps in performance management

THE EVOLUTION OF PERFORMANCE MANAGEMENT

The new public management (NPM) actively emphasizes the significance of performance
measurement as a management tool in government (OECD, 1997). Indeed, accurate performance information is needed for the implementation of management instruments such as

performance pay, performance contracts or performance budgets (Hatry, 1999). However, NPM did not originate the idea of measuring government performance. In both Europe and the United States, there had already been long-standing performance measurement initiatives (Bouckaert, 1995a). As early as 1949, the first Hoover Commission in the United States aimed at shifting the attention of the budget from inputs towards functions, activity cost and accomplishments.

> More important than efficiency in carrying out given tasks were initiatives, imagination and energy in the pursuit of public purposes. Those purposes were political and the administrators charged with responsibility for them, as well as many of their subordinates, had to be politically sensitive and knowledgeable.
>
> (Mosher, 1968, pp. 79–80)

This increased influence of civil servants cumulated in the development of planning and management techniques and systems such as the planning programming budgeting system (PPBS), and afterwards, management by objectives (MBO) and zero-based budgeting (ZBB) (see Chapter 8).

In the late 1980s and 1990s, there was a new emphasis on performance management, mainly because of rising fiscal deficits but often also inspired by ideologies of keeping the state as small as possible (see Chapter 3). In this phase, the main objective of performance measurement was to identify how to increase efficiency and/or to cut spending. By the mid- and late 1990s, government performance was increasingly seen as a key component of the competitive advantage of national economies and a contributory factor in overall societal performance. Minimizing the public sector was no longer the dominant public management reform strategy (Pollitt and Bouckaert, 2000). Effectiveness and quality concerns gained importance in many countries (see Chapter 11). For example, in 2000 the UK central government removed the compulsory competitive tendering regime in local government and replaced it with a Best Value approach, in which the quality of services has to be assessed (see Case Example 10.1).

Thus, the focus of performance measurement and management has changed over time in accordance with the dominant understanding of what constitutes 'government performance'. In times of shrinking public budgets and a discourse of the need for less government, as in the 1980s, performance measurement and management tends to focus on inputs and efficiency. At present, the decline in trust of public institutions is pushing performance measurement systems towards measurement of quality of life indicators and the quality of governance (see Chapter 13). In this respect, performance measurement and management are children of their time, with a new generation emerging about every decade.

KEY CONCEPTS IN PERFORMANCE MEASUREMENT

The input–output model of performance measurement

This section will look at how different types of performance may be measured. There are a number of levels at which performance measurement can operate – it may refer to the measurement of inputs, outputs or outcomes, and it may focus on economy, efficiency or

CASE EXAMPLE 10.1 **THE MOVE TO BEST VALUE IN THE UK**

The new direction of performance management in the United Kingdom is well illustrated by the current local government modernization programme, many elements of which have acted as pilots for the modernization programme in the health services and other parts of government. The first part of this programme, the 'Best Value' initiative, was introduced in local government in 1997 to replace the much-hated CCT legislation, first as a pilot initiative, then as a statutory duty, from 1 April 2000.

In practice, Best Value means (DETR, 1999a):

- Every part of the council's budget must be reviewed at least once every five years.
- Every review must apply the '4Cs' methodology to the service or the cross-cutting issue, which consists of the following steps:
  - **C**hallenge the need for the service and the way it is carried out
  - **C**onsult with all relevant stakeholders
  - **C**ompare the performance of the service with other providers
  - **C**ompete – test the competitiveness of the service.
- As a minimum level of comparison, each authority has to compare its performance with other comparable authorities against each of the 'Best Value performance indicators' (of which there are around one hundred in the case of the largest local authorities). These indicators include some which measure inputs, volume of activity, volume of output, productivity levels, unit costs, number of users, percentage of schoolchildren passing exams at 16 and 18, user satisfaction levels, reliability levels, numbers of complaints and so on – in other words, the whole spectrum from inputs to outcomes and from efficiency to quality.
- Each local authority must publish a plan to improve its performance significantly. Initially, these plans had to ensure that, within five years, each service would reach the performance level which the upper quartile of authorities achieved in 2000. (In 2002 this was amended to give more emphasis to 'stretch targets' agreed by each local authority with government departments across a range of priority issues.)

effectiveness. We can integrate these concepts in an input–output model of the policy and management cycle – see Figure 10.1 (Bouckaert *et al.*, 1997).

The input–output model gives a systemic view of the functioning of an organization. It starts with the strategic objectives (*field 1*). These are general 'end purposes' that are usually derived from the organization's mission statement or general policy documents. The next step in the policy cycle is to infer more specific and measurable targets from these general strategic guidelines (*field 2*). These are the operational objectives. Next we enter the management cycle, i.e. the daily operations of the organization. The management cycle consists of the inputs that go into the organization, the activities for which the inputs are used and the output that is realized by the activity (*fields 3, 4 and 5*). Personnel, infrastructure, finance and premises are some typical inputs. With these inputs, activities are undertaken.

129

For example, a school will organize lessons and a library will shelve books that may be lent out. The activities result in outputs (e.g. number of students passing exams or number of books on loan). Management should be concerned that the inputs yield the right amount and quality of outputs by organizing the activities in the best possible way. Therefore, the manager's feedback loop focuses primarily on inputs and outputs (*from field 5 to field 3*).

> The number of patients treated and discharged from a mental hospital (output indicator) is not the same as the percentage of discharged patients who are capable of living independently (outcome indicator).
>
> *Source*: Cited in Hatry (1999, p. 15)

When the outputs (i.e. the policy and management products) leave the internal organization, they enter society. The crucial question is whether and what outcomes result from the outputs. A sharp distinction must be made between outputs and outcomes. Outcomes are events, occurrences, or changes in conditions, behaviour or attitudes. Outcomes are not what the programme or organization itself did, but the consequences of what the programme or organization did.

A distinction is made between intermediate outcomes and end outcomes (*fields 6 and 7*). This is a pragmatic but important division between the ends ultimately desired and the interim accomplishments which are expected to lead to those end results (although, of course, they may not) (Hatry, 1999, p.15). Since a long time may elapse between the delivery of outputs and the occurrence of the end outcomes, the causality between the output and end outcome may be difficult to establish. The impact of the external environment (*field 8*) should also be assessed. Finally, the policy maker's feedback loop is the confrontation of the outcomes with the objectives (*fields 1 and 2*) which closes the circle. Finally it should be noticed that the clear-cut distinction between the policy and management cycle is valuable for analytical purposes but will not exist in reality. Managers need policy guidelines and the allocation of resources while policy makers need information on the feasibility of outputs and thus, expected outcomes.

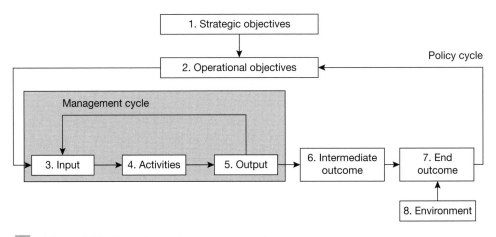

Figure 10.1 *The policy and management cycle*
Source Bouckaert et al. *(1997)*

130

Performance indicators

Different kinds of indicators can be derived from the input–output model – see Box 10.1.

The combination of the boxes in the input–output model allows us to formulate ratio-indicators.

- *Economy* is the cost divided by the input (e.g. the cost per employee, the costs per office).
- *Productivity* is the output divided by one specific input (e.g. bus hours on the road per employee (for public transport), closures per inspection (for food inspection), crimes cleared per police officer day).
- *Efficiency* is the ratio of output to input (or an index of inputs), e.g. crimes solved per police officer. Usually the only index of all inputs which is available is cost, which leads to the specific efficiency indicator of *unit cost* (e.g. cost per discharged patient, cost per crime cleared). Since *all* the costs of all the inputs used to obtain an output need to be calculated in financial terms, this can be properly calculated only if the organization has a high-quality analytical financial system.
- *Effectiveness* is outcome divided by output (e.g. number of complaints received about dirty streets per km of streets which receive regular cleaning).
- *Cost-effectiveness* is the ratio of cost to outcome (e.g. cost per successful college graduate).

Performance standards

A performance measurement system which focuses on the different steps in the input–output model should provide an organization with sufficient information to plan, monitor and evaluate both policy and management. The next step is to lay down standards that establish how well (or how badly) the organization is performing. Standards may be set in different ways:

- Politicians, for example, are sometimes tempted to set a popular standard as a symbol of how good their policies are, rather than as a yardstick for performance. The Kyoto standard for CO_2 emissions may be one high-profile example.

BOX 10.1 A TYPOLOGY OF PERFORMANCE INDICATORS

- *Input indicators*: e.g. number of employees, money spent, number of hospital beds, number of public buses.
- *Output indicators*: e.g. number of pupils taught, number of discharged patients, vehicle miles.
- *Intermediate outcome indicators*: e.g. new knowledge, increased skills, number of recovered patients.
- *End outcome indicators*: e.g. increased grades achieved in schools, reductions in unemployment, increased health and well-being.
- *Environmental indicators*: e.g. age structure, economic indicators such as growth of GDP.

- Another standard setting method is to use a scientific norm. For example, there is a scientific standard for the maximum quantities of dioxin allowed in the food chain.
- Mostly, however, the standards are set by comparison, usually either between time periods or across organizations. Time series analysis compares past performance with current performance. Cross-section analysis compares the organization with other organizations. Naturally, a comparison which combines both time series and different organizations will yield the most information.

The process of comparing performance across organizations is known as *benchmarking*. Where benchmarking is used to derive 'league tables', it requires a high degree of comparability between the organizations to be compared – otherwise the comparisons are likely to be regarded as unfair (especially by those shown up in a bad light). This is all the more serious if these league tables trigger government action (e.g. intervention by a higher level of government or loss of budgets). However, such comparisons do not tell us why the differences occur and, moreover, they may often leave out the most interesting comparisons (e.g. with high-performing organizations which are not 'comparable', but whose high performance is potentially transferable).

Statistical techniques for performance measurement

Several techniques might enhance the processing capacity of the organization. *Stochastic Frontier Analysis* is an example of a statistical technique in which the production function is based on the estimation of a priori specified parameters while allowing for some variation by the inclusion of random variables. Techniques such as *Data Envelopment Analysis* and *Free Disposal Hull* are also useful tools for comparing organizational performance both in time and place, while controlling for external variables. These are non-parametric methods in which the optimal production function is determined by the data. These techniques have been applied to compare public sector services such as fire services, local civil registry offices, hospitals, schools, prisons and courts, police forces and so on (e.g. Bouckaert, 1992; HM Treasury, 2000b).

KEY CONCEPTS IN PERFORMANCE MANAGEMENT

Performance measurement becomes valuable only when it is followed by management action – it is justified only if it is used. Performance management can be broadly defined as 'acting upon performance information'. In this section we will examine some of the most important functions of performance information in public sector management. Performance information may be used for different purposes – in the policy cycle, for accountability purposes or in financial management.

The policy cycle consists of four steps, i.e. policy preparation, decision, implementation and evaluation. Performance information may be used in all the different steps of the policy cycle. Analysis of predicted performance (against the background of past performance) can help in the development of better thought-out policies. Objectives are formulated, performance indicators are deduced from the objectives and targets are set. Next, performance information may be used by the management to monitor whether the policy is on track. The value of the monitoring will be highly dependent on the timeliness and frequency of the measurement effort. Finally, performance information may be used in policy evaluation.

Performance measurement provides a bird's-eye view, upon which action might be taken. However, it should be noticed that performance information often cannot provide all the information one needs for an evidence-based policy cycle (see Chapter 18). It may simply trigger in-depth examination of why performance problems (or successes) exist (Hatry, 1999, p.160). Generally, causal models and more qualitative research are needed to provide this in-depth information. This implies that performance management sometimes needs more information than routine performance measurement can supply. Effective performance measurement is a necessary but sometimes insufficient condition for performance management.

Performance management can also be used for accountability purposes. Different accountability relationships exist between stakeholders (see Box 10.2). Performance information can be used so that stakeholders can hold each other to account for how well they have each performed their assigned responsibilities.

SOME TRAPS AND LESSONS IN PERFORMANCE MANAGEMENT

Performance measurement opens up interesting possibilities for enhancing public sector management and policy making. However, it also contains some traps.

■ *Lack of interest of politicians and/or citizens.* The ownership of performance management initiatives usually lies within the administration. Politicians and the public often appear uninterested in the performance information which is provided – until things go wrong. One response to this frustrating situation is to tailor performance measurement to the demand, implying that citizens and politicians should become involved in defining performance indicators which interest them.

■ *Vagueness and ambiguity of goals.* This is often inherent in politics, and indeed may well be politically rational: clarifying and making objectives and indicators more concrete might lead to political conflict, in those situations where different stakeholders have different values and expectations. However, managers usually desire clarity of goals in order to maintain strategic direction. The tension between these political and managerial requirements may often be irresolvable.

■ *Games playing.* Sometimes organizations have an interest in portraying a flattering image of themselves. Of course, performance information can be functional or dysfunctional for an organization in this respect – some performance information may be very discomforting. Consequently, where some performance targets are especially important in public relations terms, organizations may be tempted to cheat in their performance reporting.

It appears likely that the risk of data corruption is higher when organizations see performance measurement as imposed externally. Local government, for example, tends to see, and resist, central government attempts at control through performance measurement and reporting exercises. Schools confronted with league tables may 'teach for the test' rather than to impart knowledge. Reported crime detection rates may be increased by spending more time getting

BOX 10.2 A TYPOLOGY OF ACCOUNTABILITY RELATIONS

Accountability of government to citizens and society: Government is responsible for a range of public services and other activities within society. Performance information may be a useful tool to enhance its responsiveness towards society and its citizens/clients. Until now this process of interaction has usually been unilateral (e.g. performance indicators have been published in the annual reports of governments and their agencies). However, this accountability may be more effective if citizens are involved in the performance measurement process in general and particularly in the definition of the indicators.

Accountability of the administration to politicians: The administration oversees the implementation of policies decided upon by politicians – it can therefore be required to demonstrate its performance level to politicians. Indeed, administrators themselves often demand the chance to provide performance information to politicians – often because it may offer an organizational defence against the irrationality (as they see it) of political decisions. However, if performance information is to influence politicians, it must be tailored to their interests and needs. Canadian civil servants, for example, recently took an initiative to make performance information more useful for parliamentarians by focusing on societal and quality of life indicators (Bennett *et al.*, 2001).

Accountability of decentralized agencies to central departments: A third accountability relationship exists between central government departments (e.g. ministries, regional or local offices of national government) and decentralized or devolved bodies (e.g. executive agencies of central government). Government, even when it operates more at 'arm's length', remains responsible for the outputs that are produced by its agencies, although how the agencies produce these outputs is no longer its concern. Consequently, performance information becomes crucial in the steering of these decentralized or devolved bodies. Indeed, in the case of a genuine devolution of responsibilities to an agency, the performance information captured in the management contract becomes the single most important tool for steering and direction. The *Next Steps* agencies in the United Kingdom, for instance, were set up under the terms of a framework agreement with their 'home' government department. Each year a Public Service Agreement, with performance targets, and a Service Delivery Agreement are negotiated between each government department and the Treasury, and one element of this relates to the performance of the executive agencies sponsored by that department. The achievement of these targets is taken very seriously by all the parties concerned, not least because failure could influence the Treasury's attitude to future budget changes. Similarly, performance indicators may be used in intergovernmental relations, for example, where central government exercises control on local authorities through the Audit Commission's Best Value indicators in the UK (Audit Commission, 2000). (This approach is not relevant, of course, in the many countries where local self-government is protected from central intervention by its constitutional position.)

Accountability of individual employees and teams to the top management: Performance information finally may be used to hold internal organizational units or individuals to account for how they discharge their responsibilities. Performance management in this case can help to motivate personnel to search for improvements (Hatry, 1999). Of course, this assumes that many employees are motivated by the desire to produce good results – in which case the mere provision of performance information combined with more freedom to organize their activities should provide them with sufficient scope to improve. However, on occasion, additional incentives are often used. Monetary incentives ('performance pay') are probably the most notorious example. Although performance pay exists in many public sectors (OECD, 1997), it remains controversial – it is said to be disruptive of team-working, insulting to professionals who believe themselves to be in 'public service' and difficult to calculate because so many external factors impact on the performance of any individual or team.

convicted criminals to confess to their past crimes rather than trying to solve current crimes. The performance figures of a drug offenders' rehabilitation agency may be raised by directing activity towards the easy cases and refusing to accept the more difficult cases. All of these abuses can be tackled partly by effective data auditing, which is a common tool to safeguard the accuracy, reliability and comparability of performance information. However, when incentives are high, abuse may become more ingenious to escape detection.

SUMMARY

This chapter suggests that performance management is possible, but not easy. Performance measurement and management in the public sector have evolved over time, with many ups and downs – they now attempt to cover a much wider range of concepts than forty years ago, from inputs through outputs to outcomes and addressing issues of economy, efficiency, effectiveness and quality. There remain significant difficulties but important lessons have been learned.

Performance measurement is useful only if it improves policy or management. Clearly, performance data must be reliable and should cover the dimensions of performance which really matter. Performance management has often been considered to be about the 'hard' data whereas quality management is often considered as a 'soft' management issue (see Chapter 11). Yet the focus on costs and efficiency at the expense of service quality can be dangerous, as the CCT regime in the UK showed. Indeed, the Citizen's Charter in 1991 may be seen as an implicit admission by the UK government that the emphasis on the 'three Es' – economy, efficiency, effectiveness – had been overdone. There is now an understanding in the UK, and in many other OECD countries, that performance management has to go hand in hand with quality management.

Finally, performance management is probably especially necessary in a turbulent organizational environment. Let us suggest a proof *ex absurdum:* if an organization does not measure its performance, it will understand only tentatively what its impact in society is and consequently its ability to respond appropriately will erode. Therefore, it is important to develop performance measurement systems in order to know at least a little more and to develop performance management systems in order to have a little more control over performance.

QUESTIONS FOR REVIEW AND DISCUSSION

1   What are the main types of performance which need to be measured and reported in the public sector? Who cares about these performance measures – and why do they care?
2   How can an organization decide whether its performance management system produces benefits at least as great as the costs it imposes?

READER EXERCISES

1   Take an annual report from a public agency with which you are familiar. Identify the performance indicators reported in it. Classify them according to the categories in Figure 10.1. Do you think that the balance between these types of performance indicator is appropriate for this agency?
2   Take one of the performance indicators identified in the above exercise. Consider how an individual, a unit or a whole organization might find ways of influencing the reported level of that indicator in order to make their work look more successful. For each of these possible abuses, suggest ways in which that kind of behaviour could be made less easy or less likely to succeed.

CLASS EXERCISES

1   Identify a case currently in the media where a public agency appears to have been changing its practices or its reporting approach in order to improve its 'league table' position, without necessarily improving its actual level of performance. Discuss how the performance measurement and reporting system might be changed in order to make such behaviour less likely in the future, while still producing useful information for the stakeholders who wish to hold this agency to account.
2   Discuss how your class, your tutor and your college assesses performance – of students, of staff and of the organization as a whole. What are the major limitations in this performance assessment? How could they be tackled?

FURTHER READING

Geert Bouckaert (1995b), 'Improving performance measurement', in Arie Halachmi and Geert Bouckaert (eds), *The enduring challenges of public administration*. San Francisco, CA: Jossey-Bass, pp. 379–412.

Harry P. Hatry (1999), *Performance measurement: getting results*. Washington, DC: Urban Institute Press.

Chapter 11

Quality management in public sector organizations

Tony Bovaird, Bristol Business School, UK and *Elke Löffler*,
Governance International, UK

INTRODUCTION

What is the likelihood that two or more strangers would have the same views when it comes to deciding what is a high-quality public service and what is not? In deciding on what is quality, we might assume that people consider various attributes of a given service or product and assign different weights to each attribute before reaching a decision (Bovaird and Halachmi, 1999, p. 145).

One person might look primarily to the fitness for use of the service, while another might look at whether the service was provided in timely fashion. Realistically, most individuals might be assumed to use some combinations of several factors to assess quality.

Clearly, quality is a complex concept. While it is already a difficult task to assess the quality of products and services, the assessment of organizational quality or of the quality of public policy making is even more difficult. The assessment of governance quality is likely to be most demanding and this area of analysis is really only in its initial phase.

LEARNING OBJECTIVES

- To be aware of the differences of quality management in the public and private sectors
- To understand the key issues associated with quality measurement in the public sector
- To be aware of the major quality assessment instruments used in the public sector
- To understand the key obstacles to and success factors in quality improvement in the public sector
- To understand how the quality of public governance might be assessed

DIFFERENCES IN QUALITY MANAGEMENT BETWEEN THE PUBLIC AND PRIVATE SECTORS

Quality management, as with many government reforms, has its roots in the private sector. There has been considerable debate as to whether private sector management principles can be transferred to the public sector. In the case of quality management, two issues have to be considered in this context.

First, most quality management approaches, including total quality management (TQM), have originally been developed for the manufacturing industry. Yet, goods and services have very different characteristics. For example, in the case of mass production, standardization is a key element of quality whereas, in the case of personal services, service quality often means variability in order to meet different customer needs (Gaster, 1995, pp. 36–44).

Second, given the private sector origins of most quality management approaches, there is an absence from the TQM vocabulary of many of the key concerns which have characterized debates about the provision of public services. For example, it is rare for the TQM literature to refer to 'citizens'. Its vocabulary is one of clients, customers, consumers and users (Pollitt and Bouckaert, 1995, pp. 6ff.). But unlike companies, public agencies cannot choose their customers – they often have to serve a rather large set of stakeholders with diverging interests. Moreover, even though many politicians like to pay lip-service to the ideas of the 'quality gurus', other loyalties and standards of excellence are also important to them. Service quality is unlikely to become the sole parameter for judging excellence in a public organization.

This does not mean that (private sector) quality management concepts do not work in a public sector setting. However, they have to be adapted to the context of public sector organizations.

WHAT WE MEAN BY 'QUALITY' AND HOW WE CAN MEASURE IT

As the context and drivers of public policy have changed over time (see Chapter 2), the meaning of quality has also changed. Bovaird (1996) has distinguished four key concepts of quality during its evolution as a concept:

1 quality as 'conformance to specification' (a meaning deriving from an engineering perspective and from the 'contract culture');
2 quality as 'fitness for purpose' (or 'meeting organizational objectives', essentially deriving from a systems perspective);
3 quality as 'meeting customer expectations' (or 'exceeding customer expectations', deriving from consumer psychology);
4 quality as 'passionate emotional involvement' – quality as that 'which lies beyond language and number' (the social psychology approach).

We can therefore say with confidence that there is no agreed definition of quality. Indeed, the 'gurus' tend not to define quality at all, except in very broad terms such as 'conformance to specification' or 'fitness for purpose'. It seems likely that organizations will find it difficult to bring about substantial quality improvement until they have fastened upon one definition of quality – whichever of the above four options they choose. Trying to run with two or more of these definitions in a single organization is likely to make the quality management process confusing and unconvincing – not only for frontline staff and service users but also for top and middle managers and for politicians.

However, it is certainly possible to analyse certain aspects of quality, even using quantitative methods in some cases. Scholars as well as practitioners have made various attempts to find a quality measure which can capture several dimensions of quality, incorporating the views of different stakeholders (employees, customers and so on). Yet relying on a single quality index is always risky for management (Bouckaert, 1995c, p. 26). First, it creates a 'quality score' which is not at all transparent as the different dimensions of quality are hidden. Second, it also allows for deficient dimensions to be compensated – for example, customer service may be traded off against additional features of a product. Such compensation is inappropriate if some stakeholders require minimum achievements of specific quality dimensions.

Given that quality is a multidimensional concept it is more meaningful to define a whole set of measures instead of relying on a sole index (see Box 11.1).

For example, the quality of a public swimming pool may be assessed on the basis of water cleanliness and temperature, equipment, reliability, conformance to professionally determined norms, friendliness of service, design and perception of the product.

The definition of a set of quality measures is only a first step in the process of quality measurement. Quality measures have to be made operational by means of quality indicators. Typically, quality indicators are categorized as quantitative versus qualitative and subjective versus objective:

- *Subjective quality indicators* can always be quantified. They are usually based on some type of survey which measures the reactions or expectations of a group of respondents.
- *Objective quality indicators*, however, cannot always be convincingly quantified.

BOX 11.1 CHARACTERISTICS OF SERVICE QUALITY

For services, the following quality dimensions influence a customer's view of quality:
- Tangibles
- Reliability
- Responsiveness
- Competence
- Courtesy
- Credibility
- Security
- Access
- Communication
- Understanding the customer

Source: Zeithaml *et al.* (1990, p. 23)

Let us look at an example. It is likely to be hard to construct an objective quantitative indicator measuring the comfort of waiting rooms in public agencies. Even though quantitative indicators such as the room temperature, the number of seats and the size of the waiting area may give some hints about the basic conditions of the waiting room, more qualitative information on its cleanliness, level of noise, decorative state, availability of private areas for confidential discussion and 'atmosphere' would be much more useful in allowing service providers to decide whether it embodied the appropriate quality level. Moreover, we would normally like to ask users of the service about their perceptions of these characteristics – a waiting room may look good to designers but be hated by the local mothers with young children who use it.

Once we start to explore subjective indicators such as user attitudes and satisfaction levels, we find, rather ironically, that significant quantification is usually possible – we can summarize the proportion of users who are highly satisfied (and dissatisfied), the proportion of users who think that the décor is attractive and so on. Ideally, a sound set of quality indicators should include both quantitative and qualitative indicators, and both objective and subjective factors. Moreover, we would suggest that no approach to assessing quality should contain *only* quantified or only objective factors – such assessments seem likely to miss some essential aspects of what me mean by 'quality'.

For measurement to be meaningful, it is often suggested that performance indicators have to be 'smart', i.e. they should fulfil certain criteria (see box). However, in quality assessment, we may wish to amend this list of criteria – 'measurable' may better be expressed as 'assessable', where the assessment is not necessarily quantitative.

'Smart' indicators should be:

- **S**pecific
- **M**easurable
- **A**chievable
- **R**elevant
- **T**ime-related

WHO KNOWS ABOUT QUALITY?

This discussion leads to an important admission – different stakeholders 'know' different things about quality, and this has to be built into any quality management system. In Table 11.1, we look at whether quality is privately experienced, or socially experienced, and whether what we mean by 'quality' in a particular context is simple or complex to specify. As may be seen, these dimensions lead to very different conclusions – sometimes users are likely to be the best arbiters of quality (where the service experience is essentially private, with few social knock-on effects, and where it is relatively simple to gauge its quality dimension). In other situations, however, we may well come to the conclusion that professionals or politicians might be the best arbiters. Finally, in very complex services, where there are also important knock-on effects of a service, we may well conclude that no one stakeholder group is likely to be a sound arbiter of quality – here it is likely that all stakeholders will need to be involved in the quality assessment process.

We may furthermore conclude that it is unwise to exclude any stakeholders from the quality assessment process, since they are all likely to believe that they understand aspects of quality which the other stakeholders neglect – and they will be reluctant to acquiesce to any quality assessment in which their voice was not heard. This is especially likely to be true of service users, since they often have an intense experience of what the service means to them and they will be reluctant to believe that their views should be entirely ignored, whatever other considerations are relevant to the quality assessment process.

MAJOR QUALITY ASSESSMENT INSTRUMENTS USED IN THE PUBLIC SECTOR

Since the search for the most appropriate quality indicators is time-consuming and requires long experience and detailed knowledge about the expectations of stakeholders and the purpose of the organization, 'ready-off-the peg' quality assessment systems have become popular in recent years in the private and (with some time lag) in the public sector.

In the following, the basic objectives and structure of several of these quality assessment systems will be described briefly – the ISO 9000 Series, citizen charters and quality excellence models. All of these instruments have become widespread, although sometimes used for rather dubious purposes.

1 The ISO 9000 Series and third party certification

ISO is the International Organization for Standardization, which is a federation of national standards bodies, and which is responsible for preparing international standards.

For details, see www.iso.org

The ISO 9000 Series is an internationally recognized standard for quality assurance. The international standard outlines how quality systems should be set up in organizations where a contract between seller and buyer requires the demonstration of a supplier's ability to supply to mutually agreed requirements.

Not surprisingly, the standardization approach has its roots in manufacturing and in the military sector. In the 1960s, the techniques of quality management practised in the USA were beginning to attract attention in Western Europe, and so the British Ministry of Defence introduced standards as a means of codifying the quality management systems of suppliers.

Table 11.1 *Who knows about quality?*

	Quality is privately experienced	Quality is socially experienced
Quality is simple to specify	Users know about quality	Politicians know about quality
Quality is complex to specify	Professionals know about quality (together with users)	No single group knows about quality – politicians must act as referee between different views

Source: Adapted from Kieron Walsh (1991b)

141

It is apparent that the main focus of the ISO system is on contracting situations. The recommended quality assurance system consists of compliance with twenty-three elements of 'good' quality management, which will allow an organization to formulate and deliver contracts at an appropriated and agreed standard. However, more recently ISO 9004 has been developed to adapt this approach to situations in which contracts are not put in place, which is often the case where TQM is being implemented.

The establishment of a quality assurance and management system along ISO 9000 guidelines involves considerable costs, particularly in setting up paperwork systems which clearly document all procedures in the organization. In view of this investment, organizations typically want to have their compliance to ISO 9000 standards to be verified. Independent, so-called 'third party' (i.e. external) certification offers the possibility of using quality as a marketing tool and avoids the disadvantages of second party (i.e. internal) subjective judgement. The desire to implement and achieve certification of ISO 9000 standards often derives from suppliers' needs to extend their markets into areas where their reputation is unknown or needs to be enhanced. Consequently, this approach has been common where the contract culture has taken root – private firms want to display their 'quality badge' in the public sector procurement process, while 'in-house' public sector providers want to demonstrate to the client department (and politicians) making procurement decisions that they are 'competitive' in quality terms with potential private sector rivals.

In December 2000 a revised version of the ISO 9000 Series was published by ISO (see http://www.iso.ch/). The new ISO 9001:2000 Series basically consists of the three former standards ISO 9001, ISO 9002 and ISO 9003. The ISO Technical Committee recommends that organizations should adopt ISO 9001:2000, which specifies requirements for a basic quality management system for any organization. The practices described in ISO 9004:2000 may then be implemented to reach higher levels of quality. Essentially, the revised 2000 version locates ISO closer to quality excellence models.

2 Citizen charters

The essential idea behind citizen charters, as introduced in the UK in 1991, was to introduce standards in the public sector. As the government put it, 'the citizen must be told what service standards are and be able to act where service is unacceptable' (HMSO, 1991, p. 4). The other basic principles of the UK citizen charter were: openness, information, transparency, non-discrimination, accessibility and redress.

The UK government's concept of citizen charters considered the market as the point of departure, with the general purpose being to increase competition and choice. The basic mechanism for quality improvement was meant to be pressure from service recipients on service producers to provide a satisfactory service experience. As Gaster (1995, p. 98) points out, this is a very different philosophy from the original citizen charters in the UK, which originated in local government in the late 1980s and were directed at meeting people's needs as willing or sometimes unwilling recipients of services, and at recognizing their rights as citizens. Interestingly, this latter concern was also very much the intention of the French and Belgian charters of the early and mid-1990s, which stressed the need to maintain an equilibrium of rights and duties between the various stakeholders.

This raises the question: Who defines the standards? It is striking that the first citizen charters were devised without much involvement of the public. Now there is much more awareness that the users have to be involved in the standard setting process (see Chapter 15).

It is evident that falling levels of public service quality in the UK have in many cases led to a lack of confidence in the realities of charters. Nevertheless, charters have prompted some service providers to think about what the public really wants in service quality. Moreover, they have stimulated debate about the rights of redress of consumers and citizens in relation to public (and privatized) services.

3 Quality excellence models: EFQM and the CAF

Quality excellence models may be used for self-assessment or as the basis of external assessment (often in the form of a quality award). Most quality excellence models have been developed first for the private sector and have been transferred to the public sector. In Europe, they clearly cluster around two core models – the 1999 version of the European Foundation for Quality Management (EFQM) Excellence Model (previously known as the Business Excellence Model, which in turn was partially adapted from the Malcolm Baldrige Award in the USA) and the Common Assessment Framework (CAF) of the European Member States and the EU Commission.

The EFQM Excellence Model (see http://www.efqm.org), on which a number of Western European national quality award schemes have been based (see Löffler, 2001), has become a widely used self-assessment instrument but an organization can also call in external assessors to judge their 'level of excellence' against the model. It includes the following elements:

- leadership
- policy and strategy making
- people management
- partnerships and resources
- processes
- people results
- customer results
- 'impact on society' results
- key organizational results

The first five of these factors are labelled 'enablers' (essentially critical success factors) and the last four are performance results. Naturally, the weightings given to these different components and the sub-criteria used within them vary between the EFQM Excellence Model and the different national variants (quality schemes or awards).

The Common Assessment Framework (CAF), which was designed specifically for public administration, is starting to become a common self-assessment instrument for public agencies (see http://www.eipa.nl/CAF/CAFmenu.htm). In contrast to the EFQM Excellence Model it is less demanding and therefore suitable for organizations starting with the implementation of TQM – but it is also rather less systematic.

QUALITY MANAGEMENT INITIATIVES

Many managers take the view that quality needs to be measured and controlled (sometimes even going so far as to use the old maxim 'If you can't measure it, you can't manage it'). We believe this is going much too far. Even though measurement and quality control is an important tool for improving quality in public administration, it is only a part of the process. As we can see from experience in the UK – where there are more inspectors, auditors and regulators than taxi drivers (Hood *et al.*, 1998) – a strong focus on measurement and monitoring can easily create a new bureaucracy in the public sector without much improvement in public services. We have to acknowledge that ultimately not all aspects of quality can be measured.

But how can quality be put into practice? Does it really need high commitment from the top, as many quality gurus believe, or can quality management be implemented as a bottom-up approach? Case Example 11.1 suggests that implementation depends strongly on the existence of 'champions' at all levels of the organization.

It will be interesting to see how the quality management initiative of the Courts Service evolves, as experience tells us that quality initiatives are difficult to sustain. Often they are simply imposed from above or by an external consultant as an 'add-on' process' and irrelevant to the individuals activities. As Lucy Gaster (1995, p. 9) stresses, quality management always has to do with values. If it is not embedded within an organization's values it is bound to fail. Getting the systems right – developing measurement systems and providing staff training – is only one precondition for implementation. In particular, when moving from public service quality to governance quality, the negotiation of values with different stakeholders becomes a crucial issue for quality management.

FROM HIGH-QUALITY PUBLIC SERVICES TOWARDS HIGH-QUALITY PUBLIC GOVERNANCE

There is empirical evidence that citizens who are reasonably satisfied with the quality of the public services which they receive are, at the same time, cynical about and mistrustful of government, Parliament and the civil service (see CCMD, 1998). This indicates that there is no linear relationship between service quality and trust.

From this wider perspective, an excellent public agency is not simply one which has the characteristics of an excellent service provider. It must also be excellent in the way in which it discharges its political and social responsibilities to its constituency (see Chapter 13).

As a consequence, quality indicators should not only focus on measuring service quality as provided by an individual organization but also on the quality of services provided by the overall service system, and the overall quality of life in a specific jurisdiction. Quality of life indicators will therefore be needed for a wide range of dimensions of the quality of life – for example, those measured by the Audit Commission (Box 11.2) and others such as the quality of life at work, the quality of culture, arts, entertainment, sports and other aspects of leisure, the quality of lifelong learning and so on.

Moreover, a high-quality public administration must not only be able to increase customer satisfaction with public services but also build trust in public administration through transparent processes and accountability and through democratic dialogue. In order

CASE EXAMPLE 11.1 **COURT SERVICE, UK**

A new Chief Executive took over in the Courts Service in 1998, with a mandate to produce major improvement in the Service. He appointed an experienced change consultant, who had worked with him in his previous organization, to carry out a benchmarking exercise, which took place in September 1998. It was seen as important that this process should have credibility, independence and should be 'owned' as far as possible by staff, many of whom (including all the directors) were interviewed during the exercise. The EFQM Excellence Model was used as a framework for the analysis. Strengths and weaknesses ('areas for improvement') were highlighted.

The two main strengths identified were the 'can do' culture, meaning that staff were willing to work long hours to solve delivery problems; and staff commitment, which meant that they cared about quality, results and a customer service. The 'areas for improvement' which emerged gave rise to a comprehensive action plan, to be carried out in nine 'strands' including strategic planning, leadership, putting people first, focusing on customers and the needs of the business, developing internal and external partnerships, centre/field relationships, resourcing and targeting for success, IT to support the business and communications. 'Strand leaders' were appointed to lead developments in each of the nine strands, generally comprising one senior member of HQ and one senior member of field staff. They were supported by cross-cutting steering groups composed of people from HQ and the field and were empowered to take the issue forward in whatever way seemed best, as long as it helped develop the new organizational culture and included consultation with people from different locations and levels within the organization.

At the same time, an internal appointment of Change Manager was made, supported by the continuing involvement of the external change consultant. The programme was publicly launched in early 1999, with a series of events involving about 1000 staff. The Chief Executive also visited about eighty locations in his first year, which made him and the programme very visible.

A second benchmarking exercise (again based on the EFQM Excellence Model) was carried out by the same consultant in late 2000. It found that many improvements had already occurred, particularly in strategic planning, leadership development (a top priority in the first phase, internal communication, and the achievement of Chartermarks). Local improvements had often been driven by local staff who had taken on the role of 'change champions'.

The exercise highlighted that more still needed to be done in the areas of customer service, project and programme management, implementing the IT strategy, managing external relationships, and involving more staff at every level.

Source: Adapted from Bovaird and Gaster (2002)

to do so, conventional business concepts of quality, which regard public agencies as service providers and citizens as customers, must be enriched by a political concept of quality which perceives public agencies as catalysts of a responsible and active civic society, through activation of citizens and other stakeholders.

BOX 11.2 KEY QUALITY OF LIFE INDICATORS IN UK LOCAL GOVERNMENT

The indicators used in a pilot by the Audit Commission included the following thirteen themes:

1 Combating unemployment
2 Encouraging economic regeneration
3 Tackling poverty and social exclusion
4 Developing people's skills
5 Improving people's health
6 Improving housing opportunities
7 Tackling community safety
8 Strengthening community involvement
9 Reducing pollution
10 Improving management of the environment
11 Improving the local environment
12 Improving transport
13 Protecting the diversity of nature.

Source: Audit Commission (2002a, p. 7)

BOX 11.3 A HEALTH CHECK ON LOCAL GOVERNANCE PROCESSES

- Strength of political institutions – voting, party membership, activism
- Strength of civic institutions – membership, volunteering, officeholding, fund-raising, donations
- Strength of sharing and collective behaviour – environmental protection, social care, crime prevention, sharing of household work
- Achievement of equity and equality – of opportunity, income, outcome
- Respect for diversity, tolerance of difference
- Level of openness and transparency in organizations – in public, voluntary, private sectors
- Levels of honesty and integrity in public domain
- Ability of the community to manage itself and meet needs not met by the state.

Source: Bovaird *et al.* (2003)

This is likely to be the focus of the development of quality management in the new era of public governance. In Box 11.3 we suggest some of the areas in which future quality indicators will need to be developed in order to assess the quality of local governance processes – and many of these will also be relevant at national level to assess the quality of public governance in a country as a whole.

SUMMARY

Not so long ago, quality was regarded as a topic which was essentially subjective and therefore not amenable to rational analysis – it was assumed that it was essentially 'a matter of opinion'. In recent years, many different ways have been found to bring the discussion of quality management into the centre of managerial decision making.

However, although there are now many useful tools and techniques available to examine quality in the public sector, it is essential that we remember that the essence of quality lies beyond that which can be described or measured. Consequently, we need to leave a space, in all our quality management systems, for the appropriate use of judgement and subjective assessment. The study of management is now much richer because this is better understood and accepted than it used to be.

In the future, we are likely to see discussions of 'organizational excellence' being extended beyond assessment of the quality of services towards assessment of the quality of life outcomes to which public organizations contribute and assessment of the quality of public governance processes.

QUESTIONS FOR REVIEW AND DISCUSSION

1   Consider the approach to quality which suggests that its appreciation lies beyond language and quantification (the approach which believes that quality involves 'passionate emotional involvement'). Are there any public services where this might be the most appropriate approach, in your view? If this approach were taken to quality management in one of these services, how do you think the achievement of better quality could be ascertained?

2   What are the arguments for using more than one approach to defining quality in an organization? How do you think the organization could avoid confusion in its subsequent quality management initiatives?

READER EXERCISES

1   Consider the different approaches to quality accreditation. Find a public agency in your area which has won accreditation under one of these schemes. Do you think that this has made any obvious difference to the quality of the service which it provides? If yes, think about how you have assessed the quality of service in your own mind – what definition of quality have you used? If no, think through the possible reasons why the accreditation process has not made a difference.

2   Take the example of a public organization with which you are familiar. Consider how the elements of the EFQM Excellence Model might be applied to this organization. Are there any other dimension of 'excellence' in the organization which you think are not captured in this model?

CLASS EXERCISES

1   How do you think quality should be defined in a university or college? Given this definition, how do you think it ought to be measured? What dangers do you think might emerge from such a measurement process? How would you suggest that they be minimized?

2   Divide into groups. Each group should look at one or two of the dimensions of local governance in Box 11.3 and suggest ways in which their achievement could be assessed – either quantitatively or qualitatively or both. Groups should then critique each other's suggestions in a plenary session.

FURTHER READING

Lucy Gaster (1995), *Quality in public services: manager's choices.* Buckingham: Open University Press.

Lucy Gaster and Amanda Squires (2003), *Providing quality in the public sector: a practical approach to improving public services.* Buckingham: Open University Press.

Christopher Pollitt and Geert Bouckaert (eds) (1995), *Quality improvement in European public services: concepts, cases and commentary.* London: Sage.

Chapter 12

Scrutiny through inspection and audit

Policies, structures and processes

John Clarke, Open University, Milton Keynes, UK

INTRODUCTION

Although publicly provided services have always been subject to forms of scrutiny, the emergence of new organizational forms and structures of service provision in recent years has made scrutiny an increasingly significant feature of their governance and management. In particular, the move towards more fragmented, dispersed and 'arm's-length' structures of provision has led governments to enlarge and enhance their repertoire of forms and practices of scrutiny.

Since the 1980s, we have experienced a period of innovation and reform in the organizational systems of providing public services (see chapters 2 and 4). Such changes have been uneven internationally, and have been most heavily concentrated in Anglophone countries (Australia, Canada, New Zealand, UK and the USA) where neo-liberal politics have had most impact to date. Nevertheless, the model of reform (towards the de-monopolization of public sector organizations; the move towards marketization and privatization of service provision and an enthusiasm for the model of new public management) has attained international currency (Flynn, 2000).

In this chapter, I explore the view that the reform of public services has driven an expansion of forms of scrutiny (particularly those of inspection and audit) and has simultaneously led to a blurring of boundaries between audit, inspection, organizational design and consultancy. The purposes and processes of scrutiny have become complicated in the effort to govern a dispersed system of public provision

THE 'POLITICS OF ORGANIZATIONAL DESIGN'

Associated with the rise of neo-liberalism as a dominant political force there has been a 'politics of organizational design'. This politics – or perhaps political ideology – has systematically challenged notions of the public (public interest, public services, public spending and public sectors) in order to 'liberate' private interests and markets from the growth of the state in the second half of the twentieth century. Although states have not been swept away, the programmes of reform in many countries have marketized, privatized and broken up public services in pursuit of the innovation, efficiency and choice promised by neo-liberal advocates.

149

at a distance. Expanded scrutiny – what Power has called the 'audit explosion' (1993, 1997) – emerges in this process of reform, and its continued spread has been driven by the problems of managing the organizational forms and relationships created by the reform process.

This chapter will explore the development of scrutiny, the changing forms and meanings of scrutiny, and the arguments about the necessity, desirability and effectiveness of such processes.

LEARNING OBJECTIVES

- To be aware of the conditions leading to the recent 'audit explosion' in the public sector
- To understand the new practices of audit
- To understand the changing roles of scrutiny agencies
- To understand the problems with and challenges to scrutiny of public sector organizations

LEVELS AND NEW FORMS OF SCRUTINY

Until the 1980s, the archetypal organizational form of public service provision was that of professional bureaucracy, in which hierarchical administration of policies and resources left spaces for professional autonomy, judgement and practice (Clarke and Newman, 1997). Combined with the governmental processes of representative democracy, such systems contained particular models of accountability and scrutiny.

These centred on vertical chains of accountability through the levels of bureaucracy to senior officials and upward to elected politicians (at local, regional or national level). They were supplemented by norms of administration and professional practice, often embodied within ethical codes of conduct which were supervised by professional disciplinary bodies such as the medical model of professional self-regulation (see Chapter 17). In some cases they were also subject to professional inspection to evaluate and advise upon standards of practice (e.g. in teaching, social work and policing; see Hughes *et al.*, 1996). Finally, the professional bureaucracies were typically subject to the practice of audit (in its traditional accounting meaning) to ensure that financial probity and good practice were being pursued in the handling of public funds.

The late twentieth-century reforms of public service organization disrupted these systems of accountability and scrutiny in two main ways. First, they fragmented and dispersed the organizations of service provision through the multiple strategies of decentralization, marketization and privatization, thus dislocating the possibilities of internal, vertical and hierarchical systems of control and scrutiny. The resulting complexity of organizational forms of public service provision – decentralized, semi-autonomous organizations linked in shifting webs of competitive and collaborative relationships, and subject to mixes of vertical and horizontal pressures for responsiveness and accountability – posed new problems of how to scrutinize service providers.

Second, however, neo-liberal advocates wove a compelling story out of the inadequacies, problems and frustrations of professional bureaucracies around the issue of trust. The combination of representative democracy and professional bureaucracy rested on assumptions about the effective articulation of the public interest through political representation, administrative neutrality and professional disinterest (Dunleavy, 1991; Clarke and Newman, 1997). Neo-liberal critics (especially public choice theorists) argued that none of these assumptions held – and that politicians, bureaucrats and professionals were better viewed as fundamentally venal, self-interested and seeking to maximize their own power, resources and status. Although neo-liberals certainly did not invent mistrust of, and challenge to, the practices of public service organizations, they did organize them into a coherent case for the dismantling of such institutions. In particular, this story of mistrust demanded new forms of discipline and scrutiny to supplement the introduction of market forces.

NEW PRACTICES OF AUDIT

Audit historically has meant the practice of scrutinizing financial control processes and financial decision making, as in the work of the National Audit Office in the UK (see Pollitt *et al.*, 1999) and national and regional audit courts in other OECD countries. The practice of fiscal scrutiny – the role of audit in its accountancy meaning – is concerned to verify the accuracy of financial statements and to check whether money has been spent for the purposes declared. In this narrow sense, audit is an effort to ensure sound financial management (see Chapter 8), and to stop fraud and corruption (see Chapter 17). The need for such financial scrutiny was reinforced in the 1980s by rising anxiety about public spending and, from a different perspective, by a drive towards 'businesslike' methods in public agencies, with the attendant dangers of financial malpractice. The establishment of organizations and procedures of financial scrutiny is still high on the agenda in other European countries such as Spain, and is currently regarded as a crucial issue in Central and Eastern European countries.

However, in more recent years the practice of audit in relation to public services has come to include a much wider range of evaluative and normative functions, most evidently in the work of the Audit Commission in the UK (see Case Example 12.1).

Cutler and Waine (1997, pp. 30–31) have argued that the Commission has developed

> a major extension of the role of audit, which traditionally has been mainly concerned with the accuracy of accounts and ensuring that public bodies were acting within their legal remit. Value for money (VFM) audit, however, involves an assessment of service performance, an area which, of course, intersects with professional judgements that were of limited or no relevance to the narrower financial and legal concerns of traditional audit practice.

The expansion of the meanings and practices of audit is a significant process in the context of UK governance and is echoed in some other national settings (see Pollitt *et al.*, 1999). In the UK, the Audit Commission's VFM studies have linked questions of accounting,

151

CASE EXAMPLE 12.1 **THE CREATION OF THE AUDIT COMMISSION IN 1983**

The Audit Commission was established in 1983 to appoint and regulate the external auditors of local authorities in England and Wales, paralleled by the Audit Commission for
Scotland. Some of these auditors are part of the district audit service, while others are
private firms which win the tender to do the external audit for the relevant public agencies. In 1990, its role was extended to include the National Health Service (NHS). The
Audit Commission's functions in local government have grown to include carrying out value-
for-money studies and the collection and audit of national statutory performance indicators
for councils, police and fire authorities. In 2000, the government placed a duty on all local
authorities to achieve Best Value in their activities and the Audit Commission was charged
with scrutinizing local councils' Best Value performance plans and carrying out inspections of their Best Value reviews.

More information about the Audit Commission is available at: www.audit-commission.
gov.uk.

---

evaluation, the identification of 'best practice', issues of organizational design, and management consultancy (Clarke *et al.*, 2000). That is, the Commission became an agency of policy
and organizational innovation, prescribing best practice, identifying dangerous deviations
and divergences, advising on the most effective organizational systems, structures and
cultures, and propounding the need for better management of public services. In many other
countries, the audit function of government has also expanded its role. One of the most
active (and widely published) Audit Courts is the Canadian Office of the Auditor General
(see Case Example 12.2).

Although not the focus of this chapter, a parallel blurring of boundaries may be observed
in the large private sector accounting firms which developed policy and management
consultancy practices alongside (and sometimes interleaved with) their audit work.

NEW ROLES OF SCRUTINY AGENCIES

This development of audit means displacing or coopting professional knowledge bases.
Displacement implies that they are subordinated to the specification of 'quality' by politicians
or managers. *Cooption* implies that the professional knowledge base is integrated into the
VFM audit or policy evaluation model (e.g. through processes of peer review).

The achievement of improved organizational performance has been increasingly viewed
as the province of 'good management' rather than professional standards. The pursuit of
'quality', 'excellence' or 'standards' means that evaluative agencies have come to colonize
organizational terrain that was previously the province of professional expertise (see also
Kirkpatrick and Martinez-Lucio, 1995). Different public services have seen different accom-
modations between professional expertise and evaluative agencies. Hughes and his colleagues

CASE EXAMPLE 12.2 **THE NEW ROLES OF THE AUDITOR GENERAL OF CANADA**

The Auditor General's responsibilities were clarified and expanded in the 1977 Auditor General Act. The Auditor General was given a broader mandate to examine how well the government managed its affairs, in addition to its continuing role of scrutinizing the accuracy of financial statements. However, the important principle was maintained that the Auditor General does not comment on policy choices, examining only how those policies are implemented.

The Act directs the Auditor General to address three main questions:

1   Is the government keeping proper accounts and records and presenting its financial information accurately? This is called 'attest' auditing. The auditor attests to, or verifies, the accuracy of financial statements.

2   Did the government collect or spend the authorized amount of money and for the purposes intended by Parliament? This is called 'compliance' auditing. The auditor asks if the government has complied with Parliament's wishes.

3   Were programmes run economically and efficiently? And does the government have the means to measure their effectiveness? This is called 'value-for-money' or performance auditing. The auditor asks whether or not taxpayers got value for their tax dollars.

In December 1995 the position of Commissioner of the Environment and Sustainable Development was established within the Office of the Auditor General and an obligation was placed on government departments to publish annual sustainable development strategies.

Source: Office of the Auditor General of Canada (2002. *What we do,* http://www.oag-bvg. gc.ca/domino/other.nsf/html/bodye.html). Reproduced with the permission of the Minister of Public Works and Government Services, 2003.

(1996) have suggested that the emergent audit-and-inspection regimes that operate in different welfare fields vary partly as a result of the relative power of the different professional groups. Box 12.1 illustrates three different types of UK inspection agencies.

The development of evaluation has been marked partly by a *shift from compliance to competition*. The evaluation of performance has centred on producing comparative information ('league tables' and the like) through which organizations are judged in terms of their relative success in achieving desired results. Hood *et al.* (1998, pp. 14–17) talk about these processes as involving a 'hybrid of oversight' and 'competition'.

The proliferation of types and agencies of scrutiny suggests that governments continue to have problems coordinating public provision. In particular, the fragmented and dispersed organizational systems developed during the past twenty years pose distinctive problems of control. There are also continuing arguments about whether scrutiny agencies are the most effective or appropriate method of coordination. The 'high cost/low trust' mix of external scrutiny poses questions about value and efficacy; while the competitive, intrusive and

153

BOX 12.1 THREE TYPES OF UK INSPECTION AGENCY

1 *HEFCE* (Higher Education Funding Council for England, with parallel agencies in Scotland, Wales and Northern Ireland) is a body that regulates higher education provision, combining funding, target setting and evaluation (such as the five-yearly Research Assessment Exercise that evaluates and grades research quality of all subjects in all UK universities). The Funding Councils were originally responsible for Teaching Quality Assessment, but controversies over method and process led to the establishment of a further body – the Quality Assurance Agency – to evaluate teaching standards.

2 *OFSTED* (Office for Standards in Education) was established in 1988 to set and to assess standards in schools. The agency inspects schools (and local education authorities that are responsible for some schools), provides evaluations of performance, produces 'league tables' of comparison between schools, and forms judgements on the 'best' approaches to teaching and school management.

2 *SSI* (Social Service Inspectorate) is a long-established 'professional' inspectorate. It was staffed originally by experienced social workers and social work managers who carried out inspections of local authority personal social services provision and engaged in professional support and development. The Inspectorate's function has become increasingly 'at arm's length' and more formally evaluative, culminating in the conduct of 'Joint Reviews' of social services provision with the Audit Commission (from 2000).

interventionist mode of scrutiny creates potentially antagonistic relationships (between provider organizations; between providers and scrutiny agencies, and between provider organizations and government). 'Audit', in its most general sense, has become the focus of controversy about whether it promotes better public services, and whether it is the best way to promote better public services. Some of these issues are discussed further in the following section.

CHALLENGES TO SCRUTINY

In this section, I explore three areas of challenge to the regime of expanded scrutiny of public service provision. The first deals with problems about the methods of scrutiny and evaluation; the second with problems of representing the 'public interest' in scrutiny processes; and the third examines challenges about the necessity and desirability of scrutiny as a means of controlling public services.

1 Methodological problems of evaluation

There is a growing literature that explores the political, organizational and methodological problems associated with evaluation (e.g. Boyne, 1997; Cutler and Waine, 1997; Newman,

2001b; Pollitt, 1995). The methodological problems concern the reliability and replicability of the knowledge that 'audit' produces. The technical notion of audit (in its accounting sense) aimed to produce reliable knowledge of organizations' financial performance and financial systems. Other forms of evaluative scrutiny have been criticized for using less robust methodologies. Such controversies came to a head over OFSTED school inspections in the late 1990s in the UK. Scrutiny organizations have tended to accept that there have been methodological problems, but that they will be overcome in the next, methodologically improved, round of evaluation. Other methodological problems concern the difficulty of identifying the causal variables associated with performance change (Pollitt, 1995).

The organizational consequences of the 'audit explosion' form a second focus of concern. Systems of evaluation, it is suggested, distort organizational performance, making it focus on what is being measured: 'what is counted is what gets done'. It is argued that public service organizations are typically multiple stakeholder and multi-objective organizations, but audit processes tend to focus on a limited number of objectives, usually those currently highly valued by central government (Newman, 2001b). In a different way, audit and inspection have had consequences for audited organizations in that they require them to divert scarce resources into the process of being evaluated (Power, 1993). Data have to be collected (often in new formats for different scrutiny agencies). Documentation and systems have to be made to conform to auditing requirements. On-site 'visits' have to be prepared for, stage-managed and performed. The outcomes of inspections, audits and evaluations have to be managed (particularly in relation to valued stakeholders). The 'audit explosion' has multiple costs – both in the creation and maintenance of the audit agencies, and in the organizations being audited.

Third, it has been a consistent point of criticism that public services were poorly documented, producing little reliable information about their performance other than accounting for 'inputs'. As a result, organizations have been required to produce auditable information about their activities, with a steadily increasing emphasis on outputs and outcomes (the effects produced by the organization's activities). Such information would allow the organization to be evaluated both intrinsically and comparatively (i.e. is it efficient, and is it more or less efficient than similar organizations?). These demands for auditable organizations have been framed by discourses of accountability and transparency – against the suspicion of 'producer domination' of organizational choices.

This concern with producing evaluative information creates a number of subsidiary dilemmas (at the intersection of the organization and the auditing agency):

- To what extent can the objectives of the organization be clearly and simply specified? (e.g. What is a school for?)
- To what extent is the performance of the organization measurable? (e.g. Do exam results measure school success?)
- To what extent is organizational performance a closed system in which outcomes reflect the effect of organizational activity? (e.g. Who or what else contributes to 'results'?)
- To what extent can comparability be guaranteed between organizations? (e.g. What unmeasured or unmeasurable factors within or outside organizations may differentiate organizational performance?)

155

Each stage of evaluation involves potentially contested processes of social construction. There are potential conflicts over the definition of objectives; over the choice of indicators; over the attribution of causal effects; and over how comparison is effected. More substantively, however, the construction of these evaluative processes requires an organization that produces auditable information.

2 The representation of public interest in scrutiny agencies and practices

There have been many political controversies surrounding the rise of scrutiny, which involve questions of social and political 'independence'. A different way of putting this is to ask what biases may enter into the systems of 'independent' evaluation. There are at least three possibilities that have been raised by critics. The first concerns social biases about the public interest: whom do 'auditors' have in mind when they see themselves as *representing the public*? Given the arguments over 'representation' in political life and public services (about the composition of organizational bodies in relation to the social composition of the nation), this is likely to become an increasingly significant question. Like the judiciary and magistracy, scrutineers may be scrutinized in terms of their ability to represent the diversity of the public's social composition and interests.

There are other controversies about the social biases of scrutiny that centre on the 'enthusiasms' of auditors within the sphere of organizational and occupational controversies. Can auditors or inspectors lay claim to know the 'one best way' in the face of contested choices that may be rooted in organizational, occupational or local-political knowledges and imperatives? Much of the controversy that surrounded OFSTED's role in schooling in the UK centred on its dogmatic insistence on one approach to teaching. Such partisan enthusiasms call the supposed independence of evaluation into question.

Finally, there are questions about the 'political' independence of scrutiny agencies. They typically occupy an ambiguous constitutional space, created by government but 'at arm's length' from it. The precise arrangements vary between countries and between different sorts of agency (see Hood *et al.*, 1998; Pollitt *et al.*, 1999). However, the increasing involvement in performance (rather than merely financial) evaluation aligns the agencies more directly with assessing organizations against current government policies and targets. Similarly, the blurring of boundaries between evaluation, consultancy and prescription narrows the distance between evaluation and government, creating possibilities for critics to challenge the claimed independence of scrutiny agencies. The shift away from the traditional audit function to being one of the key elements of the new governance implicates scrutiny agencies more directly in the business of government politics, policy and control.

None of these challenges has halted the rise of scrutiny processes. Indeed, they are typically dismissed as the defensive complaints of 'producer interests' unwilling to make themselves 'transparent' and 'accountable'. Nevertheless, they represent important political issues for the future development of governance relationships.

3 The necessity, desirability and effectiveness of scrutiny processes

Scrutiny processes are inherently 'low-trust/high-cost' models for controlling public services and they tend to be shaped by centralist assumptions and orientations. As a result, they accentuate some tendencies in the new governance, but restrict or even repress others. They fit less readily with diversification, innovation and participatory models of local governing of services. They are also more difficult to adapt to forms of network and partnership working: producing problems of overlap, integration and multiple 'ownership' (Newman, 2001a).

However, they seem likely to remain a favoured tool of central governments in the context of fragmented and dispersed systems of service provision. It may be that the most severe challenge to them emerges not from the public service sector, but from the misfortunes of audit in the private/corporate sector. The recent (2002) spectacular failures of audit to uncover or report fraud and malpractice in major corporate enterprises, and the blurring of lines between audit, consultancy and management in the activities of large accounting firms, have called 'audit' into question as an effective governance mechanism. Arguments have raged about the causes of such failures (weaknesses of the US model; bad management; overly 'cosy' relationships between auditors and auditees and so on). Similarly, arguments about how audit might be put right proliferate – including the inevitable suggestion that 'auditors need to be audited' (*Financial Times*, 3 July 2002). Whether such problems will have implications for the organization of scrutiny in its various forms in the public sector remains to be seen.

SUMMARY

In this chapter I have tried to outline the development of scrutiny systems as part of the new governance of public services. I have emphasized the appeal of processes of audit, inspection and evaluation as a means of government's exercising 'control at a distance' in dispersed and fragmented systems of service provision. I have suggested some of the instabilities and sites of potential challenge associated with the 'audit explosion', particularly those associated with the expansive blurring of roles towards organizational or management consultancy on the one hand and towards prescriptions of organizational practice on the other. As such, scrutiny processes are likely to remain a site of potential tension in the relationships between governments, public service organizations and the public. Much of this is likely to be concentrated in increasingly fractious relationships between central governments (committed to the reform of public services) and service providers (trying to lessen the 'burden' of scrutiny and concentrate limited resources on service provision). The balance of scrutiny – whether it intensifies or moves to what is sometimes called 'light touch' – is likely to depend on whether relationships of trust can be reconstructed around the triangle of public, government and public services. In the absence of such trust relationships, the 'audit explosion' is likely to continue.

QUESTIONS FOR REVIEW AND DISCUSSION

1   What conditions drove the 'audit explosion' in relation to public services?
2   What role do 'scrutiny' agencies play in the new governance?
3   To what extent does the practice of 'audit' distort organizational performance?
4   What challenges does the expansion of scrutiny face?
5   Is there a 'crisis of audit'? What are the implications for the scrutiny of public services?

READER EXERCISES

1   Obtain a report from a scrutiny agency. To what extent is it shaped by any of the issues discussed above?
2   How many forms of scrutiny has the organization in which you work (or in which someone you can ask works) experienced in the last two years? What are the different forms of scrutiny?
3   Talk to someone who has recently experienced audit, inspection or evaluative scrutiny in their work. What are the key features of their experience? Do they connect to any of the issues discussed above?

CLASS EXERCISES

In small groups, consider the questions about audit and control below.

1 Auditing public services

■   To what extent can the objectives of the organization be clearly and simply specified? (e.g. What is a school for?)
■   To what extent is the performance of the organization measurable? (e.g. Do exam results measure school success?)
■   To what extent is organizational performance a closed system in which outcomes reflect the effect of organizational activity? (e.g. Who or what else contributes to 'results'?)
■   To what extent can comparability be guaranteed between organizations? (e.g. What unmeasured or unmeasurable factors within or outside organizations may influence organizational performance?)

2 Controlling public services

■   How might governments evaluate the provision of public services if they did not use audit, inspection and other scrutiny agencies?
■   How might relations of trust be constructed between publics, governments and public services?

158

FURTHER READING

John Clarke, Sharon Gewirtz, Gordon Hughes and Jill Humphrey (2000), 'Guarding the public interest: auditing public services', in John Clarke, Sharon Gewirtz and Eugene McLaughlin (eds), *New managerialism, new welfare?* London: Sage/Open University.

Christopher Hood, Colin Scott, Oliver James, George Jones and Tony Travers (1998), *Regulation inside government: waste-watchers, quality police and sleaze busters*. Oxford: Oxford University Press.

Janet Newman (2001a), *Modernising governance: new Labour, policy and society*. London: Sage.

Michael Power (1997), *The audit society*. Oxford: Oxford University Press.

Part III

Governance as an emerging trend in the public sector

The third part of this book focuses explicitly on governance as an emerging trend in the public domain. It examines a number of themes central to public governance, and suggests how they are interlinked with public management and how these themes may evolve in the future, if public governance continues to acquire increasing importance.

Chapter 13 examines the relationship between governance and government. It suggests that the growing interest in public governance has arisen at least partly because of the modern necessity for governments to work in partnership with and to co-manage networks of external stakeholders.

The subsequent chapters explore how public leadership has developed from a concern largely with the management of public organizations to an interest in leadership within partnerships and networks (Chapter 14), how public agencies are finding new ways to engage with citizens and other stakeholders (Chapter 15), the changing agenda for management of equalities (Chapter 16), new concerns with and approaches to ethics and standards of conduct in public sector organizations (Chapter 17), and evidence-based approaches to developing and refining policy and practice in the public domain (Chapter 18).

Governance and government

Networking with external stakeholders

Elke Löffler, Governance International, UK

INTRODUCTION

There is a fast-increasing academic literature on public governance, public policy networks and network management in the public sector. Yet, at the same time, there is great confusion about these concepts. While social scientists find new ways to define and differentiate these concepts, for most practitioners many of these terms mean rather little. Does this mean that governance networks at different levels of government are simply the invention of political scientists and complexity scientists, and are of little importance in practice?

I want to argue that the reality is quite the opposite. As this chapter will show, public decision making and the production of public services have undergone fundamental changes in the past ten years or so. This is partly because we now have a more fragmented state, with far more public agencies (see chapters 2, 4 and 12). It is also partly because citizens now expect different types of information (see Chapter 10), better communication (see Chapter 6) and, in some limited (but very vocal) cases, are keener to engage in public decision making (see Chapter 15). Perhaps most important of all, it has come about because of 'wicked' policy problems, which make coordination and joint working a key for all agencies and managers working in the public domain.

As a result, public agencies no longer only have to be good at getting their internal management systems right – financial management, human resource management, ICT and performance management – but they also have to manage their most important external stakeholders well in order to achieve the desired policy outcomes and a high quality of public services. In other words, network management has become a key governance competence of public agencies.

SORTING IT ALL OUT: KEY GOVERNANCE CONCEPTS

Like most concepts in social sciences, governance is not a new term. Indeed, the term *governance* was first used in France in the fourteenth century where it meant 'seat of government' (Pierre and Peters, 2000, p. 1). The term became much more popular when the World Bank 're-invented' governance in a World Bank Report of 1989 (see Box 13.1). The use of the term *governance* by the World Bank signalled a new approach to development which

LEARNING OBJECTIVES

- To understand the key concepts of public governance
- To be aware of how the role of governments is changing from policy-making towards policy-moderating
- To be able to identify important stakeholders in public governance
- To understand networks as a specific mode of public governance

was based on the belief that economic prosperity is not possible without a minimum level of rule of law and democracy. At the same time, use of the seemingly apolitical term *governance* was valuable in preventing criticism that the World Bank was trying to interfere in the political decisions made by debtor countries.

Today, governance has become a highly topical issue for all international organizations – thus, for example, the United Nations, OECD and the EU produce policy-relevant advice and research related to various governance issues. The EU not only recommends 'good governance' to others but identified the reform of European governance as one of its four strategic goals in early 2000. For that purpose, the European Commission has produced a White Paper on governance (Commission of the European Communities, 2001) which specifies principles of good governance and makes proposals for changes in EU institutions, and their relationship to EU member states and to the world community.

At the same time, many governments have put governance – either explicitly or implicitly – on their public sector reform agenda (John, 2001). For example, the UK government has given a high profile to its 'public standards' committee to deal with issues of 'sleaze' in public life (see Chapter 17) and, on a different tack, set up a Social Exclusion Unit as a cross-departmental team based in the Cabinet Office 'to tackle in a joined up way the wide range of issues which arise from the inequalities in society today' (Prime Minister and the Minister for the Cabinet Office, 1999, p. 18). We can also observe the emergence of a wide range of new think-tanks and consultancy organizations aimed at fostering governance in the public domain.

Many governmental and non-governmental organizations have also focused on the attributes which they believe constitute 'good governance' (see Box 13.2).

It might be thought that the multiplicity of views on what constitutes governance in a positive and normative sense make it a less than useful concept. However, almost all definitions contain some common elements which show that governance (Bovaird and Löffler, 2002):

- assumes a multiple stakeholder scenario where collective problems can no longer be solved only by public authorities but require the cooperation of other players (e.g. citizens, business, voluntary sector, media) – and in which it will sometimes be the case that practices such as mediation, arbitration and self-regulation may be even more effective than public action;

BOX 13.1 DEFINITIONS OF GOVERNANCE

The exercise of political power to manage a nation's affairs.

(World Bank, 1989, p. 60)

Governance comprises the traditions, institutions and processes that determine how power is exercised, how citizens are given a voice, and how decisions are made on issues of public concern.

(Canadian Institute on Governance (www.iog.ca))

Governance is the way in which stakeholders interact with each other in order to influence the outcomes of policies.

(Governance International, UK (www.govint.org))

The pattern or structure that emerges in a socio-political system as a 'common' result or outcome of the interacting intervention efforts of all involved actors. This pattern cannot be reduced to [the outcome produced by] one actor or groups of actors in particular.

(Kooiman, 1993, p. 258)

BOX 13.2 DEFINITIONS OF 'GOOD GOVERNANCE'

We, the participants of the First World Conference on Governance, define good governance 'as a system that is transparent, accountable, just, fair, democratic, participatory and responsive to people's needs'.

(1999 Manila Declaration on Governance
(http://unpan1.un.org/intradoc/groups/public/documents/un/unpan000209.pdf))

Five principles underpin good governance and the changes proposed in the EU White Paper: 'openness, participation, accountability, effectiveness and coherence'.

(White Paper on European Governance
(http://europa.eu.int/comm/governance/index_en.htm))

The negotiation by multiple stakeholders of improved policy outcomes and agreed governance principles. To be sustainable, these have to be made operational and evaluated by multiple stakeholders on a regular basis.

(Governance International, UK (www.govint.org))

- ■ deals with formal rules (constitutions, laws, regulations) and informal rules (codes of ethics, customs, traditions) but assumes that negotiation between stakeholders seeking to use their power can alter the importance of these rules;
- ■ no longer focuses only on market structures as steering mechanisms, as in conventional 'new public management' approaches, but also considers hierarchies (such as bureaucracies) and cooperative networks as potential facilitating structures in appropriate circumstances;

165

- does not reason only in terms of the logic of ends and means, inputs and outputs, but recognizes that the characteristics of the key processes in social interaction (e.g. transparency, integrity, honesty) are likely to be valuable in themselves;
- is inherently political, concerned as it is with the interplay of stakeholders seeking to exercise power over each other in order to further their own interests – and therefore cannot be left to managerialist or professional decision-making elites.

The big challenge in practice is how to bring about 'good governance'. It follows from the above analysis that this cannot be achieved by good government alone. For example, in order to reduce crime it is important that the police service has sufficient resources, that it is managed efficiently and that it behaves in a fair and honest way and avoids racial and gender discrimination. If these prerequisites are not in place, crime levels can get out of hand in particular areas and inappropriate police responses may easily result in riots and an increase in lawlessness. However, the long-term solution to the problem of crime may not be within the power of the police (i.e. by means of better interventions designed by govern-ment and public sector organizations). At the root of the problem may be insufficient integration of immigrants, insufficient work and stimulating leisure opportunities for young people or simply a high rate of unemployment in a particular area. In this case, good gover-nance requires the cooperation of all relevant stakeholders in tackling the underlying problem. This certainly includes actions by various public agencies such as the police, schools, NHS and local authorities. However, it is also likely to require that people in local communities are prepared to be active in 'neighbourhood watch' activities, that commu-nity groups are prepared to launch initiatives to 'keep kids off the streets' and that local businesses are prepared to offer work opportunities to local people from disadvantaged and vulnerable groups, to avoid them becoming disillusioned with the economic and social institutions which shape their lives.

THE CHANGING ROLE OF GOVERNMENTS FROM POLICY MAKING TOWARDS POLICY MODERATING

If governance is much more than government, does this mean that governments no longer have an important role to play in local politics and service delivery? Or as the public gover-nance experts Jon Pierre and Guy Peters (2000) ask provocatively: 'Does government still matter?'

Such questions are misguided, since they consider governance issues out of context. More meaningful governance questions would rather be: When does government still matter? What functions could public agencies share with other stakeholders? What are the roles of different stakeholders, including the public sector, in solving different problems in society? There is a lot of empirical evidence that the public sector still has a very powerful problem-solving capacity with regard to some issues in some contexts (see Case Example 13.1).

Yet, even though governments still matter they are no longer necessarily the central actor but only one actor in the policy process (Scharpf, 1978). As Rod Rhodes (1997, p. 57) puts it, 'the state becomes a collection of inter-organizational networks made up of governmental and societal actors with no sovereign actor able to steer or regulate. A key

---

CASE EXAMPLE 13.1 THE BLARNEY STRATEGIC PLAN FOR SUSTAINABLE DEVELOPMENT

The Irish village of Blarney in the south of County Cork initiated a strategic planning process in 1994 in order to foster its economic success and to deal with a number of structural economic problems. In particular, the village had been split into a residential nucleus with few leisure facilities and a tourist area with congestion problems. Previous plans to deal with these problems had foundered due to objections raised by traders and local disagreements about the future of the village green.

The strategic plan had three objectives:

1   to ensure the village's progress into the future;
2   to address and solve the village's operational difficulties so that tourism did not strangle the village;
3   to sustain the environmental and social qualities of the village in the future.

Three separate village committees were set up to oversee progress against these objectives: the tripartite relationship between the council, the village steering group (comprising all local community groups and interests) and the planning consultants. A review of progress suggested that 75 per cent of stage 1 proposals have already been implemented. The strategic planning initiative of Blarney shows that even little villages have to deal with economic challenges in a cooperative and proactive way if they want to sustain economic success in the future.

Source: Adapted from Aodh Quinlivan (2002)

---

challenge for government is to enable these networks and seek out new forms of co-operation.' In other words, the importance of public governance does not so much pose the question of 'how much state?' but rather 'which state?' – where we have to deal with the state as the interaction of multiple stakeholders, each of whom has some public responsibility to influence and shape decisions in the public sphere.

Moreover, the move from government to governance requires all stakeholders to play a much more imaginative role in shaping the decisions in their communities or policy networks. This is exemplified in relation to local governance in Table 13.1.

IMPORTANT STAKEHOLDERS IN PUBLIC GOVERNANCE

Even though government remains an important player in most contexts, it is only one player in a multi-stakeholder context. Not only public agencies but also non-governmental stakeholders such as business and the media exercise an influence upon the way the rules of the game are formulated and how it is played out in the public domain. They also contribute to the outcomes of public policies, through their interactions with other stakeholders. So, for example, the press can change the view of a large part of the population on how important is the issue of asylum seekers (even in a country such as the UK where there are far fewer asylum seekers than in many other parts of the EU).

167

Table 13.1 *The move from local government to local governance*

Local government needs to consider	
not only . . .	*. . . but increasingly*
Organizational leadership	Leadership of networks
Developing organizations	Developing communities
Ensuring policy coherence across organizational departments and services	Ensuring policy coherence across organizational and sectoral borders and levels of government as well as over time (sustainable development)
Creating a set of values and a sense of direction, which leaves room for individual autonomy and creativity for mid-level managers and employees	Managing expectations of citizens, companies and other stakeholders
Policy and strategy	'Politicking': balancing strategic interests
Focus on the needs of customers	Activating civil society (through information, consultation and participation) in local policies and management
Separation of politics and administration	Public management as a process of interaction between elected officials, politically appointed officials, ad hoc advisers, career civil servants and external stakeholders
Annual plans, concentrating on current expenditure	Long-term plans, incorporating community plans, capital budget plans and asset management
People management	Management of the labour market
Increasing labour productivity through downsizing	Improving staff contribution to all the goals of the organization
Getting staff to focus on quality of service	Getting staff to focus on quality of life, in terms of quality of service outcomes for users and other stakeholders and also quality of working life for fellow staff
Motivation through more objective evaluation systems and more flexible pay systems	Motivation by allowing staff to contribute a wider range of their skills and aptitudes to the work of the organization
Recruiting and retaining qualified staff through transparent hiring processes	Recruiting, training and promoting staff in ways which increase the diversity of the public service in terms of gender, ethnicity, age and disabilities
Making better use of staff resources within the organization	Making better use of staff resources by increasing mobility within the public sector and also between other sectors and other areas
Resource management	Resource and knowledge management
Budget formulation as a top-down exercise (with fixed ceilings on total expenditures)	Preparation of local budgets with active participation of city councillors, including community representatives

Measurement of unit costs for performance improvement and performance monitoring	Measurement of money and time costs of the organization's activities, as experienced both by the organization and its stakeholders
Transparent financial reporting	'Fiscal transparency' to communicate with external stakeholders (business, citizens, media, etc.) on the value for money of activities
Improving technical efficiency	Improving social efficiency, including equitable distribution of budgets and services
Making ICT available to all staff for efficiency-enhancement purposes	Generating and sustaining new knowledge through knowledge management, both for staff and for other stakeholders interacting with the organization (including making ICT available to all stakeholders to improve effectiveness)
Processes	Internal and external relationships
Internal improvement processes (business process re-engineering)	Managing processes beyond organizational borders, including intergovernmental relations and constraints
Competing for tendered tasks	Managing multiple contracts and supplier relationships; building and maintaining accountable partnerships, with users, communities and other organizations where appropriate ('co-production of services with users, communities and other stakeholders')
Measurement of objective and subjective results	Measurement of multidimensional performance
Reporting systems based on needs of public managers and government oversight bodies	Publishing of performance information based on the needs of stakeholders in the community (social, ethical and environmental reporting)
Benchmarking results, internal processes or organizational performance against other local authorities	Involving stakeholder groups in the definition of performance standards and measurement of performance
Use of performance information for control purposes	Encouraging innovation and learning at multiple levels (individual, organizational, networks)
Functioning of the local authority	Developing good local governance
Serving the community by producing policies services and knowledge ('service provider')	Enabling the community to plan and manage its own affairs ('community developer')
Improving the internal efficiency of local authorities	Improving the external effectiveness of local authorities
Increasing user satisfaction of local services	Building public trust in local government through transparent processes and accountability and through democratic dialogue

Typically, public governance issues are likely to involve the following key stakeholders (among others):

- citizens (as individuals);
- community organizations, whether formally or loosely organized;
- nonprofit organizations (including charities and major non-governmental organizations);
- business;
- media;
- public agencies (e.g. different levels of government or elected bodies, including international levels);
- elected politicians.

It is obvious that the stakeholders who are most important in any public governance issue will vary, depending on the policy area, the geographic area or the community concerned. In order to solve 'wicked' policy problems successfully it is important to identify the most relevant stakeholders – and to decide how best to engage with them, to mobilize their efforts and to reconcile conflicts between them. This is the key role of public leadership (see Chapter 14).

NETWORKS AS A SPECIFIC MODE OF PUBLIC GOVERNANCE

For some academics, public governance refers to 'self-organizing, inter-organizational networks' (Rhodes, 1997, p. 53). Yet Pierre and Peters (2000, pp. 14–26) point out that, although networks have become an increasingly important aspect of public governance, they are only one specific mode of public governance. There are also other governance mechanisms which remain significant in the public, private and voluntary sectors. In particular, these include:

- hierarchies;
- markets;
- communities.

This means that public governance not only involves cooperation but also competition and conflict management. The key governance issues are not simply how to develop and maintain networks but which governance mechanisms are appropriate in which context.

But what do we mean by networks? In general, policy networks consist of a variety of actors who all have their own goals and strategies but who are also dependent on each other to achieve the desired public policy outcomes. There is no single actor who has enough power to ensure the achievement of the policy outcomes himself or herself. Obviously, the operation of networks will differ depending on the distribution of power and the institutional context which determines incentives or obstacles for cooperation (Kickert and Koppenjan, 1997, pp. 41f.). One famous typology of policy networks is the 'Rhodes typology' which focuses on welfare state services (see Table 13.2). Policy communities are at one end of the continuum and involve close relationships between a limited number of participants, while issue networks are at the other end and involve loose relationships between many participants with fluctuating interactions.

As the public sector has become more fragmented and the boundaries between public, private and nonprofit sectors have become more blurred, the nature of networks has changed. In the United Kingdom, functional policy networks based on central departments have expanded to include more actors, most notably from the private and voluntary sectors (Rhodes, 1997, p. 45). At the same time, the number of networks has increased significantly.

As a result, the implementation of public policies has had to adapt and the need for integration and coordination has increased. Hierarchical, top-down policy making typically does not work in networks, which have no obvious 'top'. In the academic literature, network management is seen as consisting of two major elements (Kickert and Koppenjan, 1997, p. 46):

1   direct management of interactions within networks (so-called *game management*);
2   influencing the institutional arrangements in order to improve conditions for cooperation indirectly (so-called *network constitution*).

If public policies are the results of the interactions ('games') between several actors with different goals and perceptions, improvements in public policies can be achieved through the effective management of these games. Klijn and Teisman (1997) identify three key network management strategies to improve the game management and the network structuring (see Table 13.3).

Given that the actors of a network have different goals and perceptions, there is a need to create some degree of alignment between the perceptions of different actors in relation to what needs to be done, which resources can be used, and the circumstances in which certain actions are acceptable (Goss, 2001). This process of identifying similarities and differences in actors' perceptions and the opportunities that exist for goal convergence is referred to as 'covenanting'. Whether or not a network achieves the jointly agreed outcomes depends on whether or not it includes all those actors who possess indispensable resources and also

Table 13.2 The 'Rhodes typology' of policy networks

Type of network	Characteristics of network
Policy community/ territorial community	Stability, highly restricted membership, vertical interdependence, limited horizontal articulation
Professional network	Stability, highly restricted membership, vertical interdependence, limited horizontal articulation, serves interest of profession
Intergovernmental network	Limited membership, limited vertical interdependence, extensive horizontal articulation
Producer network	Fluctuating membership, limited vertical interdependence, serves interest of producer
Issue network	Unstable, large number of members, limited vertical interdependence

Source: Rhodes (1997, p. 38)

Table 13.3 Key network management strategies

	Perceptions	Actors	Institutional arrangements
Game management	Covenanting	Selective (de)activation	Creating and implementing rules of the game
Network constitution	Reframing perceptions	Formation of new networks	Changing the rules of the game

Source: Klijn and Teisman (1997, p. 106) (modified by the author)

those actors who have the power to undermine achievement of the network's goals, if they have been left out (see Scharpf, 1978). Last but not least, the actors have to agree on institutional arrangements which facilitate the coordination of their activities. These arrangements may be highly formalized (e.g. covenants between different levels of government) or informal (e.g. agreements on working procedures within project teams).

In contrast to the game management strategies, changing the constitution of existing networks involves longer term strategies. Where different actors with indispensable resources are unwilling to cooperate, or even to communicate with each other (as happens sometimes, for example, in Belfast or in Jerusalem), it may be necessary to engage in activities to change the perceptions of these actors. In other cases, there may be a need to reconstitute a network and to bring in new actors. This is typically a problem of citizens' consultation processes, which often tend to be dominated by 'the usual suspects'. In many cases, minorities and 'inarticulate' groups find it hard to get a platform and to make known their perceptions (see chapters 15 and 16). Furthermore, existing institutional arrangements may prove to be weak in protecting the interests of the actors of a network. For instance, in e-government the major players may be 'techies', fascinated by the technology requirements to make e-government work, and 'marketeers', driven by the desire to promote government services online to their current users. In this case, a serious digital divide can open up, in which non-users of ICT services (often very vulnerable people who are actually high-priority clients of the services concerned) are seriously disadvantaged in the debate about service design and service delivery mechanisms (see Chapter 9).

Finally, there is still great uncertainty about the relative role of different stakeholders in improving quality of life, solving the 'wicked problems' in society and ensuring that public governance processes are improved. We cannot yet be clear about 'what works, where and when' in addressing these issues (Stoker, 1999). It is important, therefore, that we make appropriate use of that evidence, and take steps to improve the evidence available on public governance (see Chapter 18).

SUMMARY

This chapter has emphasized that the concepts of 'governance' and 'good governance' are contestable, but that they are central to the way in which government and the public sector relate to their society.

Government is not enough, since governance is enacted by many other stakeholders. However, good governance in society and in the polity will usually require good government.

The key question for governments is which role should it adopt in which context? Whereas in some situations it may be appropriate to take a leadership role, there may be other contexts in which stakeholders do not trust government sufficiently or when government does not have the necessary competence. In the latter case, it may be more effective for government to adopt the role of a moderator to help community leaders to deal with the problem or to take the role of a coordinator of a range of agencies.

The other question for government (and any other stakeholder) is to choose the right approach to deal with a problem. In some cases, the problem at stake can be solved through market mechanisms; in other cases, the problem should be delegated to the community. But there are still problems such as defence which are best dealt with by hierarchies.

QUESTIONS FOR REVIEW AND DISCUSSION

1   What does 'good governance' mean for you? Try to think of a number of attributes of good governance and how they could possibly be operationalized in order to assess the quality of public governance.
2   Describe how network management differs from the management of hierarchical organizations.

READER EXERCISES

1   Think of one key public policy area which concerns you. What are the main mechanisms by which non-governmental stakeholders can influence the outcomes. What are the main ways in which their influence could be strengthened?
2   Take a copy of a serious newspaper and identify the major public governance issues which surface in its stories (e.g. transparency, integrity or honesty of staff in public agencies; engagement of non-governmental stakeholders in policy decisions or management; ability to work in partnership with other agencies). Do the stories suggest any mechanisms by which these governance issues may better be tackled?

CLASS EXERCISES

1   Identify in class an important 'wicked' public policy problem which affects your quality of life (such as high pollution in your city, high levels of crime in your neighbourhood, discriminatory behaviour against the group to which you belong). In groups, discuss which stakeholders are likely to be most successful in solving this problem. Then discuss the obstacles which have to be overcome to give this stakeholder the ability to implement its solution. In the whole class, compare your analyses.
2   In groups, discuss which stakeholder(s) should take the lead in producing a healthier population in your city, and why. Compare your answers in a plenary session of the class.

FURTHER READING

Tony Bovaird and Elke Löffler (2002), 'Moving from excellence models of local service delivery to benchmarking of "good local governance"', *International Review of Administrative Sciences*, Vol. 67, No. 1, pp. 9–24.

Janet Newman (2001), *Modernising governance: New Labour, policy and society*. London: Sage.

Jon Pierre and B. Guy Peters (2000), *Governance, politics and the state*. New York: St Martin's Press.

Chapter 14

Public leadership

Mike Broussine, Bristol Business School, UK

INTRODUCTION

In today's interconnected and interdependent world, public leadership has to be more than just leading public sector organizations. Public organizations are often slow to address new problems, are hampered by all kinds of constraints, and have short time frames – usually election to election. 'Wicked' problems which cross organizational boundaries can be addressed successfully only by networks of public, private and non-profit organizations, community groups and citizens and other inter-organizational arrangements (see Chapter 13).

This means that the engagement of citizens in public issues (see Chapter 15) becomes a key attribute of public and community leadership. In order to solve complex problems, public leaders have to be able to initiate concerted action not only within their own organizations but among a set of stakeholders with different and competing interests. This means that traditional models of organizational leadership have their limitations, as they may help to make public organizations more performance- and customer-oriented but they are not adequate to address boundary-spanning public problems in a context of fragmented authority. Without doubt, the 'learning organization' requires a new concept of leadership (see Chapter 18).

The trouble is that there is no one view about what leadership is. There are several ways of looking at it. Those who have reviewed numerous studies (e.g. Horner, 1997; Yukl,

> ## LEADERSHIP IS . . .
>
> . . . about creating a sense of purpose and direction by gaining ownership for the right business vision and a powerful set of values; it's about communicating and legitimizing belief and passion, providing support, removing obstacles, and creating, not consuming, energy; it's about fostering creativity, focusing on results and building strong links between the organization, its clients, the community and front line staff; it's about developing people and teams, partnerships and coalitions; about being consistent but not inflexible, and most of all it's about building, winning and retaining trust.
>
> *Source*: Sir Michael Bichard, Rector of The London Institute (formerly Permanent Secretary at Department for Education and Employment)

2002), have concluded that, well . . . your view of leadership depends on where you are coming from and who you are. Yukl says, 'The definition of leadership is arbitrary . . . there is no single "correct" definition' (pp. 6–7). It is better to see leadership as a complex multifaceted phenomenon. The width of meanings about leadership is represented in this chapter by the boxed quotes from 'real' public service leaders. It may be difficult to define, but you recognize it when you see it, or are in it. Since most people agree that leadership is key to an organization's effectiveness, the lack of agreement about what it is should stimulate us to try to understand it more, especially, it ought to be said, in a public service context.

There are three further factors that complicate the study of leadership. The first is that leadership does not reside only with the women and men at the top of organizations, but is exercised throughout – by team leaders, senior practitioners, and by teams of managers and professionals. A second issue is that the language of organization is shifting away from management towards leadership: yet both of these functions are necessary for organizational functioning. Third, the omnipotence that we project on to our leaders has taken several knocks – our leaders are human, make mistakes, take risks, and do not know what is going on all the time. Many leaders of public organizations admit in their candid moments to feeling powerful and in control sometimes, but powerless and out of control at other times. These emotional boundaries – between omnipotence and impotence – are shared by leaders who are working under conditions of unpredictability and flux – a feature of today's public service organizations (see Chapter 4).

LEARNING OBJECTIVES

- To be aware of the current emphasis on leadership in public governance
- To be aware of the history of the study of leadership
- To understand the differences between leadership and management
- To understand the interrelationships between leadership, power and politics
- To be aware of the gender dimension in leadership
- To understand the key issues in community leadership
- To understand what leaders need to learn if they are to become effective

THE CURRENT EMPHASIS ON LEADERSHIP IN PUBLIC GOVERNANCE

The emphasis on leadership of today's public services is remarkable. A recent Audit Commission inspection report of a city council's corporate governance mentions leadership twenty-eight times in forty-eight pages. The Bristol Royal Infirmary Inquiry put the children's heart surgery scandal down in part to 'poor teamwork' and 'a clear lack of effective clinical leadership'.

The OECD (2001b, p. 13) suggests that a changing environment requires a new type of leadership because:

176

- the growing need to address interconnected problems in a public policy context of shared power demands leaders to pay more attention to policy coherence;
- leadership is a key component to make the public sector a competitive employer;
- a knowledge-intensive economy and public sector calls for a new type of leadership that inspires others to create and share knowledge;
- there is a continuing need for public sector organizations to adapt, which requires leadership not just among senior managers but amongst all public officials, elected and appointed.

LEADERSHIP IS . . .

. . . about challenging everyone in the organization to raise their game. It is about creating the energy and enthusiasm necessary to take the organization forward. The leader's role is to create, and then manage, the tensions between the short and the long term, current performance and future ambition, restructuring and revitalization. It is about injecting the necessary idealism and foresight to imagine possibilities of a better future for the organization combined with the pragmatism to recognize that while some people and systems may be outdated they still have a contribution that they can make.

Source: Hugh Burnard, Regional Head, Regional Business Service South, HM Customs and Excise

OECD concluded that the managerial skills which have been emphasized since the 1980s are not sufficient to cope with future challenges. In a similar vein, Hartley and Allison (2000) have looked at the role of leadership in the modernization of public services in the UK. They begin by outlining how important leadership seems to be in current thinking about the improvement of public services. Leadership has been included in the titles of influential government policy papers (e.g. DETR, 1998b, 1999b), and the government has promoted the setting up of new leadership academies – for school leadership, for the NHS and for local authority councillors. They ask, 'Why is leadership seen to be significant in the development of "modernized" governance and "improved" public services? Is it simply a mantra, or is there some logic to the promotion of leadership in public services?' (Hartley and Allison, 2000, p. 35). It is clear that leadership is seen as a significant underpinning of public service modernization.

Leadership is also seen as key to improving the outcomes of public policies. The recent White Paper on local government *Strong local leadership – quality public services* placed firm emphasis on leadership issues (DTLR, 2001b). DTLR suggests that strong and accountable political leadership is central to effective community leadership. Leadership is a central criterion for judging local authorities under the Corporate Performance Assessment scheme – 'a new type of assessment that seeks to assess the corporate capacity of the organization to provide the necessary leadership and direction to co-ordinate the provision of high quality services to local people' (Audit Commission, 2002b, p. 63).

In contrast to the government's concept of organizational leadership in central government, the local government White Paper emphasizes that leadership at local level should go beyond organizational borders of the local government sector. 'Such leadership helps to enhance the quality of life of individuals and communities, boost the local economy, improve the environment, and contribute to the achievement of wider regional and national policy goals' (DTLR, 2001b, p. 13).

The influential Performance Improvement Unit (PIU) report on leadership (Cabinet Office, 2001) started with the assumption that good leadership is too scarce in the public sector. While the PIU admits that there are many examples of good leadership, there is a scarcity of 'top-level' leaders, and the demands on leaders are growing (e.g. because of rapid technological change, greater organizational complexity, increased consumer expectations, and more demanding stakeholders).

The implicit meanings that are given to leadership in these developments differ significantly. To begin with, it is interesting to note how often 'strength' is associated with leadership in this discourse. It is mentioned in the titles of government papers on public services leadership (e.g. DTLR, 2001b). The PIU's study refers to 'strengthening' leadership; and 'stronger leadership with a clear sense of purpose' is cited as one of six key themes of the Civil Service Reform Programme.

It is also important to notice that many pronouncements on leadership are concerned with leaders at the top of their organizations. Leadership is conceived predominantly as, first, the attribute of an individual person or role; and second, as a top-down process. The White Paper on modernizing government (Cabinet Office, 1999) mentions 'the leadership needed to drive cultural change in the civil service' (p. 20). Such a view would suppose that leadership is not exercised anywhere else in the organization.

Critical analysis of the language used – an essential aspect of studying leadership – will reveal the 'theories-in-use' that policy makers adopt. Given the dominance of powerful voices which influence how public organizations are organized – with direct effects on the working lives of public service employees and users – it might be assumed that the idea of the strong top-level leader is the only legitimate view in town.

However, this suggests a simplified view of organizations that does not accord with reality. As Hartley and Allison (2000) point out, while the role of individual leaders in shaping events is clear, the 'lionization' of the individual leader assumes that she or he has pre-eminent capacity and power (p. 36). Vaill (1999) says: 'Leadership is not the behaviour of a person at all but rather a property of a social system' (p. 121). From a relational perspective leadership may be seen as arising from the support (or, at minimum, the acquiescence) of followers. That is why a definition of leadership which concentrates only on the qualities of individual leaders tells only half the story. A better definition of leadership is that *it mobilizes the capacities of others inside and outside the organization.*

LEADERSHIP IS . . .

. . . reminding people sometimes that if they think they are good, they may be comparing themselves to the wrong people

. . . encouraging your leaders to focus their enthusiasm on those that they lead and to share their problems with those that lead them.

. . . always treating people as you would wish to be treated yourself.

Source: Hugh Ross, Chief Executive, United Bristol Health Care Trust

A BRIEF HISTORY OF THE STUDY OF LEADERSHIP

A succinct and engaging summary of the various approaches to the study of leadership from the 1920s was given in a Royal Society of Arts lecture by Professor Gareth Jones of the Henley Management College in 1998:

> There have been three major schools of leadership study. The first is called *trait theory*, where behavioural scientists tried to identify effective leaders by looking at what they had in common. Trait theory broke down when an expensive American study stated, with a straight face, 'We have studied 400 effective leaders and we can conclude that they are either above average height or below'.
>
> By then the behavioural scientists had a new toy, the camera. They started to film people and said that effective leaders had a distinctive *style*. This approach was particularly associated with the human relations movement in the 1940s in America. The concept of leadership within this school was open, pseudo-democratic, personal, almost affectionate. Then the 1950s came along and with the world on the edge of thermonuclear destruction, a whole new leadership style seemed appropriate: the Cold War warrior. Managers were buying rimless glasses whether they needed them or not. That was the end of style theory.
>
> Then it was decided to study not leaders but leadership, i.e. the relationship between leaders and the led. It explains why you have different leaders in a ship-yard, a school, a hospital and an advertising agency. You first have to ask who you are trying to lead, then identify the critical parameters of the task. Finally you look for characteristics of the situation that can be turned to your advantage. These three issues form the basis of the latest and best theory, sometimes called *situation leadership theory*.
>
> (Jones, 1998, pp. 81–82)

Jones's brief tour gives a useful indication of the historical trends in the study of leadership. Horner (1997) and Yukl (2002) provide extensive and detailed reviews of these theories.

Situation leadership theory represents the most modern ideas about leadership. However, trait theory still has a major place in contemporary discourse about leadership, as does the notion of the *command-and-control* approach – born out of classical management principles in the early twentieth century. Whenever I ask a group of students or managers to give me their first thoughts about leadership, they invariably mention notable individuals from history such as Winston Churchill and Margaret Thatcher.

LEADERSHIP IS . . .

. . . willingness to

. . . keep on searching for excellence

. . . keep on believing that our students, our team, our staff group, our parents, our Board of Governors, this school, Cotham, are capable of achieving it.

Source: James Wetz, Principal, Cotham School, Bristol

179

The advantage of situational theory is that we can see how leadership depends on a relationship between the leader and the situation the leader is working in, including followers. Such theories are sometimes called contingency theories. This means that leadership can vary according to the situation – so that the British electorate rejected its wartime leader, Winston Churchill, in 1945, preferring new leaders in the immediate post-war era. This gives us a more realistic view of leadership (though admittedly a more complex one) because we now have to deal with several factors in addition to the charisma or strength of the individual leader. But, as we have seen, the notion of the 'strong' leader features to a considerable extent in the language of public service modernization.

THE DIFFERENCES BETWEEN LEADERSHIP AND MANAGEMENT

Any serious attempt to understand organizational leadership needs to deal with the difference between it and management. To put it succinctly: *Leadership shapes the future; management delivers it.*

There is now broad agreement that leadership and management are different. Of course managers lead, and leaders manage, so the distinction may be seen as just playing with words. However, to conflate the two processes would be wrong. Gabriel (1999, ch. 6) provides a useful analysis of the difference between leadership and management (Table 14.1). He adds, 'It is possible to manage inanimate objects – a diary, a farm, a stamp collection – but it is only possible to lead people' (p. 139).

LEADERSHIP IS . . .

. . . about having a clear vision based on core values and beliefs. Leaders must have conviction, drive, and commitment to empower others to work towards the achievement of the vision. Leaders must not falter in the face of difficulties. They must have self-reliance to persevere with resilience and tenacity to withstand setbacks, disappointments and failure and to lift and carry their people through disappointments to progress on towards success. These are the true strengths of leadership.

Source: Steve Pilkington, Chief Constable, Avon and Somerset Police

Table 14.1 *The difference between management and leadership*

What managers do	What leaders do
Focus on the present situation	Focus on the future
Organize our current resources so that we can use them effectively	Invent an image of the future that is so persuasive that we are willing to commit our efforts, time and resources to turn image into reality
Have a keen eye for detail	
Think of ways of stretching resources further	

Source: Based on Gabriel (1999, p. 139)

 180

The distinction between management and leadership frees us up to ask questions such as whether or not organizations are over-managed and under-led and whether or not the roles of leadership and management are invariably held by the same person.

The distinction between management and leadership represents an important boundary for the leader. How he or she sees the boundary is wrapped up in their self-identity and will affect the style with which the role is exercised. Will they see their role primarily as working with the new, the radical and risky, with uncertainty, encouraging creativity, and looking outside current parameters or constraints – in short, requiring leadership? Or, will they see their roles as mostly to do with acquiring resources, increasing efficiency, reducing costs, and solving today's rather than tomorrow's problems – requiring management? The answers to such questions have the potential to exert considerable influence on the culture and functioning of the organization.

LEADERSHIP, POWER AND POLITICS

I am obsessed with power! Let me rephrase that. We have to understand power and organizational politics if we are to approach an understanding about how leadership works, or does not. I am sure you have been asked to do something by your boss, and inwardly you think to yourself, 'What an idiot!' The authority, power and legitimacy of leaders are potentially contestable, and conflict suffuses organizational functioning. This is especially the case in public services where it is difficult to see the 'bottom line', and where there is much space for disagreement on aims and means. There is always a political (small 'p') dimension to leadership: organizational members will often seek 'to mobilize support for or against policies, rules, goals, or other decisions in which the outcome will have some effect on them. Politics, therefore, is essentially the exercise of power' (Robbins, 1987, p. 194).

The formal authority that goes with a leader's role is an important, usually hierarchically based, source of power (note that formal authority may be an attribute of a team, board or committee, not just a person). However, formal role authority is only one power base for organizational leadership. Burnes (2000, pp. 178–179) lists four other kinds:

1   Coercive power – the threat of negative consequences should compliance not be forthcoming.
2   Remunerative power – the promise of material rewards as inducements to cooperate.
3   Normative power – the allocation and manipulation of symbolic rewards such as status symbols, as inducements to obey.
4   Knowledge-based power – the control of unique information which is needed to make decisions.

You can understand an organization's politics and power structures by seeking to find out who is included, and who is excluded, from decision making. Except in the most authoritarian organizations, authority for decision making will be delegated throughout the organization. Similarly the four power bases, to greater or lesser extents, may be distributed through all levels of the hierarchy. Knowledge-based power, especially, goes with the professional expertise that is the basis of much of the front-line work of the public services.

181

Indeed, something will have gone wrong if the chief executive and his or her board try to deny the utility of front-line knowledge-based power. However, we may know of instances where 'constructive dissent' among workers was not listened to by formal leaders with the result that the solutions to organizational problems – already known to the workers – took a long time to implement: 'a solution to excessive waiting times and chronic staff shortages is to allow the "subordinate" nurses the freedom to solve the problems that they could have solved years ago – if only someone had thought to ask them and to implement their suggestions' (Cabinet Office, 2000, Annex D). Leadership occurs among groups of people as well as highly placed individuals. Power is more diffuse than we might at first imagine, and does not operate only through orthodox hierarchy. A corollary is that leadership is exercised in a political environment – a seen and unseen network of relations and tactics people employ to either commit to, or dissent from, decisions that affect them.

THE GENDER DIMENSION OF LEADERSHIP

It is important to study leadership from the gender point of view for several reasons. First, a large number of public service employees are women. Second, public service organizations purport to have advanced equal opportunities policies. Third, the main users of public services tend to be women: for example, women live longer than men on average, and therefore feature more than men among elderly healthcare patients and social care clients. For these reasons, you might expect that women are at least equally represented in the leadership of UK public services as men – if so, you would be wrong (see Reader exercise 3 at the end of this chapter).

The belief that there are distinguishable 'male' and 'female' styles of leadership is widespread. Many people feel, for example, that women especially hold 'people skills' and those associated with bringing about transformational change. Care is needed in jumping to such conclusions. Women in recent research (Broussine and Fox, 2002) emphasized that they did not have a monopoly of these skills and attributes. The idea of male and female approaches to leadership could itself be stereotypical, denying both men and women the opportunity to exercise different skills. Furthermore, appreciation of womanly qualities (usually described as caring and relational) could be another way of restricting women to certain kinds of roles, for example, careers in the personnel function. Nevertheless, despite such caution, it was clear that for many female senior managers, and their male colleagues, the gendered distinction in leadership styles was based in some kind of reality.

Our research in UK local government showed that the perpetuation of classical 'command-and-control' and 'macho' assumptions about leadership was strongly associated with stereotypical views among those responsible for appointing women chief executives. The range of blatant and subtle discriminatory behaviours that many women experienced had the effect of marginalizing or belittling their authority as leaders. Even in authorities with good equal opportunity initiatives the informal organization could continue to transmit cultural messages about the 'proper place' for women. Almost all women chief executives reported that even after they had been in a post for a while they often felt under scrutiny and judged in different ways to men.

A particular tension centred on the issue of change. Coffey *et al.* (1999) identified an 'organizational schizophrenia' by which an organization can promote a woman to senior management, 'and genuinely welcome that appointment, and can at the same time manifest . . . behaviours that make it very hard for her to succeed' (p. 73).

The growth in recent years of performance targets and other managerialist approaches may create more 'macho' – individualistic and competitive – organizational cultures. In addition, as argued above, it is likely that traditional so-called 'male' command-and-control assumptions about leadership are being perpetuated by the emphasis on 'strong' leadership in the 'modernizing government' agenda. It is not surprising that this kind of environment has led some female junior managers to question whether promotion is worth going for. Many in our study thought it was not.

COMMUNITY LEADERSHIP

Public leadership is as much about relationships with external stakeholders and communities as it is about mobilization of internal organizational capacities. Public leaders – at whatever level in the organization – need to be able to operate at the boundaries between the organization and its environment. In the public services this is not easy, because that environment is complex. For one thing it consists of a range of stakeholders (citizens, service users, customers, community groups, individuals) whose needs and wants cannot be presented in a uniform way. Second, in these days of 'partnership working' between public agencies and communities, the idea of a clear line of demarcation between an organization and its environment is unhelpful.

Case Example 14.1 demonstrates how community leadership may be seen as the mobilization of others' leadership capacities. It also shows that community leadership is about providing an environment that enables different professions, working with those most affected, to act together to resolve social problems. We may therefore see public leadership as *working at boundaries*, developing effective relationships between professions, between agencies and organizations, and between all these and the communities they serve. Thus, public leadership cannot only be seen as the relationship between leaders and followers (in the case study, just who are the leaders, and who are the followers?). It needs to be seen also as resulting from collaboration and cooperation resulting possibly in new and unexpected forms of leadership.

KEY LEARNING FOR PUBLIC LEADERS

We arrive finally at the question of what leaders need to learn if they are to be effective. Given the complexities of leadership

> ## LEADERSHIP IS . . .
>
> . . . sometimes about stepping out in front of the crowd offering a vision to follow. More often it's about carving out and holding open a space for the ideas and expertise of others to grow and take shape. This is the challenge – leadership is about making a space for the leadership of others to come through.
>
> *Source*: Liz Kidd, Planning and Development Manager, Children and Families Division, Wiltshire County Council

CASE EXAMPLE 14.1 SOLVING LOCAL PROBLEMS THROUGH COMMUNITY LEADERSHIP

In a major residential area of Falmouth in Cornwall, concerned professionals in the local authority, Carrick District Council, and the health authority, working together with a small number of activists in the community, helped to initiate major improvements to the condition of the housing, especially in respect of heating and insulation. As residents saw the improvements in quality of life which were brought about by this programme, they became more interested in working on a series of further initiatives on the estate, covering estate management, housing repairs, crime watch, youth training schemes, etc. These schemes were largely led and managed by the residents themselves. As the initiatives proved successful, the strength of resident involvement grew and some of the residents decided to become politically active on a formal basis, e.g. getting elected as councillors. One of the strengths of the approach was that residents always had a majority on the project management committee, which was an independent legal entity, but the committee also included all the main public sector organizations with responsibilities for services provided in the housing estate.

Source: Bovaird and Owen (2002, pp. 57–73)

in public organizations, our contention is that *leadership and learning go together*. This view suggests that leaders get their authority from their ability to learn and their ability to develop the organization's capacity to learn. Thus organizations with good leaders are more likely to respond effectively in providing appropriate services to the public and to work effectively with other stakeholders in the public policy arena.

This view is not often mirrored in practice. Leaders are often set up, or set themselves up, as people with all the answers. Their followers become highly dependent on their omniscience – they wish to hear the 'path to the future' articulated with confidence and eloquence. Such leaders present themselves as leaders who can 'take a grip' and, consequently, they mask all the uncertainty and fallibility inherent in the system.

In such situations leadership is the antithesis of learning. Leaders 'know', and therefore do not need to learn. Indeed admission of a need to learn will evidence vulnerability, and threaten the image of certainty and security offered by such leadership. However, such an illusion of infallibility is difficult to sustain. When reality is inescapable, some leaders fall.

An alternative view holds that uncertainty pervades any complex human

LEADERSHIP IS . . .

. . . to look far ahead without losing sight – not only hearing but listening, not only working but creating.

Source: Prof. Dr Marga Pröhl, Head of Department, Democracy and Civil Society, The Bertelsmann Foundation, Germany

system. Leadership needs to acknowledge this and to engage with uncertainty in a positive way. It needs people to build resilience to deal with the uncertainties. The ability to learn is a vital tool in the context of change and uncertainty (Vaill, 1999). Furthermore, 'It is not enough for one or two individuals to develop these [leadership] skills. They must be distributed widely throughout the organization' (Senge, 1998, p. 302). Of course, this view of leadership differs greatly from that of the charismatic decision maker, a view based in trait theory.

So what capacities do today's public service leaders need to learn in practice? I think they need the capacities to:

- tolerate ambiguity and uncertainty;
- recognize the impossibility of omniscience;
- maintain personal perspective and self-knowledge;
- critically reflect – to ask oneself continuously whether current ways of leading need changing according to changed circumstances;
- develop leaders and leadership throughout the organization, and in the community in which their organization is embedded;
- watch out for 'dependency cultures';
- recognize that leadership and learning go together.

Many public service leaders now recognize the value of finding the space to reflect critically on how they are doing. Action learning sets, personal role supervision and mentoring, each in their own way provides this space. As public services continue to change rapidly, organizational leaders need increasingly to see their roles as requiring self-knowledge, inner confidence and a 'good enough' sense of identity. They need to be able to think . . . but also to act.

SUMMARY

A strong political emphasis on good leadership lies at the heart of the governance agenda. However, we need to look critically at some of the assumptions and language about leadership. Leadership is not the property of only one person. Leadership may be found at all levels of the organization, as well as outside the organization in the community. It is often a function carried out by teams and committees. Another key to understanding leadership is to distinguish between management and leadership.

Leadership occurs in a complex political environment in which different bases of power are at play in visible and invisible ways at different levels of the hierarchy. To see leadership only in terms of formal authority and hierarchy leads to a limited view. However, classical, orthodox and 'male' views of leadership – especially 'command-and-control' – prevail in the public services.

More inclusive views of leadership need to be developed in the public services, and there is evidence that this is happening in practice. There is growing recognition that, in a complex and changing system, we need to see leadership and learning as simultaneous if not synonymous activities. Finally we need to see leadership as the mobilization of stakeholders – in terms of financial and staff resources, their expertise or 'everyday' knowledge and their willingness to cooperate to solve interconnected problems which impact upon their lives or organizations.

QUESTIONS FOR REVIEW AND DISCUSSION

1   Explain why the *command-and-control* notion of leadership remains influential in some public agencies at the beginning of the twenty-first century.
2   Do you see yourself as a *leader* or as a *manager*? Give reasons for your answer.
3   How can leaders lead when they don't know everything that's going to happen?
4   What might leaders do to address the 'dependency culture' in their organization and in its stakeholders?

READER EXERCISES

1   Interview two organizational leaders, one in the private, and one in the public sector. You might ask:
- Do you see yourself as a *leader* or as a *manager*?
- How would you describe the responsibility of being a leader?
- What do people expect of you as leader?

Can you deduce any differences between public and private sector leadership?
2   Pick out two of the boxed *Leadership is* . . . quotes that seem to contrast with each other in some way. Examine each quote carefully. What are the assumptions and values about leadership that attach to each quote? What are the differences in emphasis?
3   Explore the statistics on female representation in leadership of public sector organizations at www.eoc.org.uk. What are the statistics for your particular public service?

CLASS EXERCISE

Work as a team with three other students on this three-part task:

1   Research sources in the library, and find an article or paper which reports on some recent research into organizational leadership. Your chosen study should have been carried out no earlier than the year 2000.
2   Write a summary of this study.
3   Present your summary to your colleague students. Include in your presentation something about what you have learned about your own leadership approaches and styles as you carried out this exercise.

FURTHER READING

Cabinet Office (2001), *Strengthening leadership in the public sector: a research study by the Performance and Innovation Unit*. London: The Cabinet Office.

Melissa Horner (1997), 'Leadership theory: past, present and future', *Team Performance Management*, Vol. 3, Issue 4, pp. 270–287.

OECD (2001b), *Public sector leadership for the 21st century*. Paris: OECD.

Gary A. Yukl (2002), *Leadership in organizations*. Englewood Cliffs, NJ: Prentice-Hall.

Chapter 15

Engaging with citizens and other stakeholders

Steve Martin, Centre for Local and Regional Government Research, Cardiff University, UK

INTRODUCTION

Public participation is not new. There were attempts to promote local involvement in planning decisions in the UK as long ago as the 1960s. User involvement has long been a feature of some social services, and 'community involvement' is a pre-condition of funding from most UK and EU regeneration programmes. Until relatively recently, though, many mainstream services remained under the control of expert professionals who, it was assumed, acted in the best interests of service users and the public at large. Voters could remove unpopular politicians through the ballot-box, but they were not expected to take much of a direct interest in policy debates or the management of public services between elections.

Current attempts to improve services and modernize governance systems have, however, placed public engagement centre stage. Policy makers in Western democracies appear united in the belief that it offers an important means of rebuilding trust in government and ensuring that services are responsive to users' needs and aspirations. Local politicians have seen engagement with the public as a means of substantiating their claim to be 'close to the citizen'. Meanwhile, in the age of 'spin', ministers and their advisers have turned to assorted panels, opinion polls and focus groups to help inform political priorities, policy development and presentation.

LEARNING OBJECTIVES

- To be aware of the arguments in favour of engagement with service users and citizens
- To be aware of the main forms of public engagement
- To be aware of practical approaches to public engagement
- To understand the obstacles to effective engagement and ways of overcoming these

WHY ENGAGE WITH THE PUBLIC?

The OECD (2001a) argues that engaging with citizens is 'a core element of good governance'. It claims that the benefits include:

- improving the quality of policy-making by allowing government to tap wider sources of information, perspectives and potential solutions;
- facilitating greater and faster interaction between citizens and governments;
- increased accountability and transparency which increases representativeness and public confidence.

The current UK government also sees engagement with the public as vital. The assumption is that increased participation will act as a force for service improvement, bringing pressure to bear on otherwise unresponsive and inefficient public bureaucracies. It is believed that this will increase the perceived legitimacy of government by encouraging more effective 'community leadership' (see Chapter 14).

Pressure for increased engagement has been fuelled by low, and falling, levels of turn-out in local elections in the UK (see Table 15.1). In contrast, there has been a rapid growth in *direct* participation at local level (Lowdnes *et al.*, 1998). In particular, Agenda 21 has proved an important trigger, as have regeneration initiatives, such as the New Deal for Communities programme, which has spawned a plethora of local community-based partnerships (see Case Example 15.1).

There has also been a much greater emphasis in recent years on direct public involvement in planning and delivering services. Clause 3.1 of the 1999 Local Government Act requires local councils, police and fire authorities and a range of other statutory agencies to consult not only service users and taxpayers (both individuals and businesses) but also anyone else who they deem to have legitimate interest in the area (which might, for example, include commuters, tourists and representatives of voluntary

> At its heart *Best Value* seeks to reshape the relationship between government and the electorate.
>
> *Source*: Hilary Armstrong, former Minister for Local Government and the Regions

Table 15.1 *Turn-out in local elections (%)*

	Pre-1995	Post-1995	% change
Italy	85	80	−5
Sweden	85	79	−6
Germany	72	70	−2
France	68	72	+4
Netherlands	54	47	−7
UK	40	35	−5

and community organizations). In addition, councils must ensure that their 'staff are involved in any plans to change the way in which services are provided' (DETR, 1998c).

Councils must involve the public in reviewing current services and setting targets for future improvement. They must publish annual 'performance plans' giving details of current service standards, targets for year-on-year improvement and action plans to achieve them. They also have to gauge resident satisfaction using performance indicators imposed by central government. Failure to fulfil any of these requirements can lead to censure by auditors and inspectors, and direct intervention in the running of an authority's services by the Secretary of State.

The early signs are that these new requirements have increased both the scale and scope of engagement by local authorities with local people. Most councils have introduced consultation in services that previously have not had much direct contact with the public. Many have adopted new, more interactive approaches and sought to reach communities and groups with which they previously had only limited contact (Martin *et al.*, 2001).

At national level, there has been a strong emphasis on 'listening' to the public. The 'People's Panel', consisting of a representative sample of 5000 people, was used as an important 'sounding board', and ministers toured the country attending so-called 'listening events' at which 'ordinary people' could air their views (see Case Example 15.2).

FORMS OF PUBLIC ENGAGEMENT

The rhetoric of public service 'modernization' and public service improvement, including many of the initiatives outlined above, frequently conflates very different kinds of public participation. Recent government statements in the UK have, for example, referred to the importance of 'consultation', 'listening', 'being in touch with the people', 'involving users' and strengthening 'accountability to local people', almost as if these very different activities were synonymous or interchangeable. In fact, they represent a wide spectrum of different types of interaction.

One of the most widely quoted typologies of public participation is the hierarchy of approaches developed by Sherry Arnstein (1971). On the lower rungs of a 'ladder of participation' she placed manipulation of the public. What she saw as 'tokenistic' activities

191

CASE EXAMPLE 15.2 **THE PEOPLE'S PANEL**

The People's Panel was set up by the UK Cabinet Office in 1998 to provide feedback on levels of public satisfaction with public services. It was wound up in 2001 but ministers claim other departments have now developed their own mechanisms for public engagement.

An independent evaluation of the panel concluded that it had provided a useful 'high-level feel' for public opinion, stimulated new consumer research and demonstrated the government's intention to better engage citizens. However, it found weaknesses in the design of the panel and criticized the newsletter produced by the Cabinet Office for being unduly self-serving. For further details see www.cabinetoffice.gov.uk/servicefirst/1998/panel/ppsummary.htm

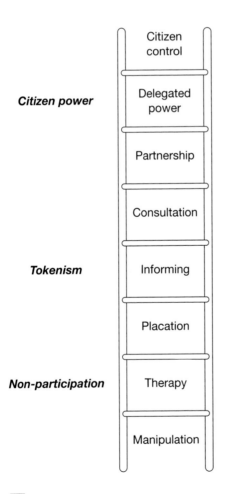

Figure 15.1 'Ladder of participation'
Source: Adapted from Arnstein (1971)

Citizen control

Delegated power

Citizen power

Partnership

Consultation

Informing

Tokenism

Placation

Therapy

Non-participation

Manipulation

– 'informing' and 'consultation' – came in the middle section. At the upper end were approaches that empower the public. This typology is misleading, however, in that it implies that some forms of engagement are inherently superior. In practice what matters most is that the form of participation used is fit for the purpose. A more useful typology is perhaps that shown in Figure 15.2.

All three of these activities are likely to be important components of an organization's strategy for engaging with its service users and other stakeholders.

Communication

Some commentators have echoed Arnstein's scepticism about insincerely motivated forms of participation. Pollitt (1988), for example, dismisses what he dubs the 'charm school and better wallpaper end of the spectrum'. However, honest and effective communication with the public is a legitimate and necessary function, providing people with the means to access services and engage in an informed dialogue. At the very least the public needs clear information about what services are on offer, when and where, in

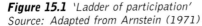

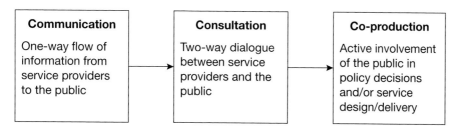

Figure 15.2 *Public participation spectrum*

order to be able to access them. Anyone who wants a greater level of involvement in policy decisions is likely to also need information about current service standards, standards achieved by other providers, the reasons for resource allocation decisions made by their provider, and any constraints operating on services in their area.

This is important in the UK where research has shown alarmingly low levels of awareness of which agencies are responsible for the delivery of local public services. One survey found that in some areas almost half the population believed that the local council managed hospitals (Bromley and Rao, 2000). Opinion polls have shown that young people in particular feel they lack information about their local authority, and there is evidence of a link between public satisfaction and the degree to which people feel that they are being kept informed by government (ODPM, 2002).

Consultation

Consultation differs from communication in that it involves a two-way flow of information and views between governments/service providers and the public. It covers a wide range of activities involving widely differing levels of engagement. In some cases, the public is presented with a narrow range of options and asked to decide which it prefers. In others, people are consulted at a very early stage and may be given the chance to shape and play a role in conducting the consultation exercise. Typically, though, service providers remain in control – initiating the consultation, setting the agenda, determining the consultation methods, selecting the consultees and deciding what, if anything, needs to be done in response to the views expressed by the public.

Co-production

The efficacy of many public services depends not only on the performance of the providers but also on the responses of users and the communities in which they live (Bovaird, 2002). Raising levels of educational attainment, for example, is not just a question of good classroom teaching. It also depends on the capacity and willingness of students to learn and levels of parental support. Similarly, mortality rates depend not only on the efficacy of medical treatments provided by health services but also on the lifestyle choices of the public (including diet, exercise, smoking and so forth). Many services therefore benefit from the active involvement of users in design and production. This can help to increase the chances that services meet users' needs. It can also play an important part in the 'social role valorization' of, for example, people with learning disabilities. Co-production therefore seeks to go beyond an attempt to attune public services to the wishes of passive recipients. Its aim is to empower users to take greater control over, and responsibility for, their lives.

PARTICIPATION BY WHOM?

Another important issue is with whom governments and service providers need to engage (see also chapters 6 and 11).

- *Customers* – In some cases the input of users/clients will be the most valuable form of engagement; for example, in informing detailed operational issues relating to the delivery of particular services.
- *Citizens* – In others, the citizenry as a whole has an important stake in the decision-making process. For example, taxpayers who do not use a service may have a legitimate interest in the relative costs of alternative approaches to service delivery (and their preferences may well be at odds with those of service users).
- *Communities* – In the case of initiatives designed to benefit particular neighbourhoods or sections of the population it may be important to engage with specific communities of place, identity or interest.

Combining the three levels of interaction identified in Figure 15.2 with this threefold categorization of the main stakeholder groups provides a useful typology of different modes of engagement (see Figure 15.3).

Experience suggests that it is important to be clear from the outset about what the objectives of each exercise in public participation are. This helps to ensure that the right tools and techniques are used. It can also help to clarify what level of influence is being offered to the public, thus reducing the risk of disillusionment among consultees who come to believe that engagement has delivered less than they expected.

PRACTICAL APPROACHES TO PUBLIC ENGAGEMENT

There is a plethora of good toolkits and consultation manuals for practitioners wishing to engage with the public. The aim of this section is not therefore to give a comprehensive guide but to provide a flavour of the range of techniques currently in use.

Communication tools

Governments at local and national levels use a wide variety of media to provide information to the public. Traditional approaches include noticeboards, council newspapers, service directories, videos, roadshows, exhibitions and public awareness campaigns. In recent years electronic information and communications technologies have provided new ways of disseminating information – including websites, community information points (e.g. in libraries) and

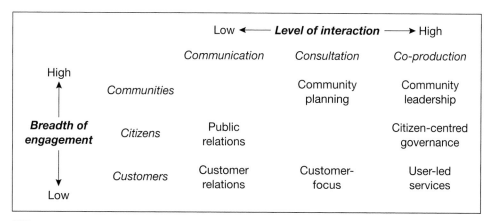

Figure 15.3 *Modes of public participation*
Source: Adapted from Martin and Boaz (2000)

CD-Roms. Some rural local authorities see the internet as an important new means of serving the needs of sparcely populated areas.

Increasing attention is being given to improving communications by local authorities in the UK. A report published by the Office of the Deputy Prime Minister in the UK in 2002 stated that this is central to the achievement of effective governance and service improvement (ODPM, 2002), and central government has worked with the Local Government Association and the Audit Commission to produce a 'Communications Toolkit' for use by all authorities (for details see www.idea.gov.uk/knowledge).

Bristol City Council is one of many local councils to have set up *multimedia kiosks* around the city which provide free access to its website and other sources of information.

'*Herefordshire in Touch*' aims to use government funded regeneration programmes to provide *broadband access to information about council services*. The county council is also developing a joint website with the police, health service, chamber of commerce and voluntary sector which will enable residents to access information about all services through a single address.

CONSULTATION METHODS

Lowndes *et al.* (1998) found that the vast majority of British local authorities used traditional consultative mechanisms. Nine out of ten held public meetings, ran complaints/suggestions schemes and undertook written consultations. Two-thirds organized service user forums, 62 per cent had area forums and half had forums focused on particular issues or services. Many were developing more 'deliberative methods'. Half reported using focus groups, a quarter had involved the public in 'visioning exercises' or community appraisals and 5 per cent had held citizens' juries.

Some councils have arranged 'listening days' during which senior managers and councillors have gone out into the streets to talk to shoppers and householders. Others have opened up council meetings to local people and scheduled regular public question times. Some have begun to broadcast committee meetings on the Web. Free phone lines to enable citizens to record comments and suggestions are now widespread, and at least one UK council has installed video booths in the town so that residents can record video messages.

Although they were relatively rare ten years ago, almost all local councils, and many other local service providers, now conduct residents' surveys regularly to gauge public satisfaction with existing services. Central government has also invested heavily in recent years in surveys of the general public (see Case Example 15.3).

CASE EXAMPLE 15.3 **MAJOR SURVEYS IN THE UK**

The *Home Office* commissions an annual 'British Crime Survey' of 40,000 people to assess attitudes to and experiences of crime, the police and the courts.

The *Department of Health's* 'Through the Patient's Eyes' survey assesses hospital in-patients' views on the way they were treated in hospital.

The *Strategic Rail Authority* runs a twice-yearly 'National Passenger Survey' which analyses the views of train passengers about the punctuality and frequency of trains and the level of ticket prices.

Many local councils, police forces and health authorities in the UK have used citizens' panels (representative samples, typically of 1000 to 2000 local people) as sounding boards whose views are sought regularly about key policy issues. Panels of service users and particular communities are also now commonplace.

Citizens' juries bring together a small group of laypeople (selected as a representative sample of the population as a whole) to consider evidence from experts on a specific policy or service issue and to produce recommendations. Juries have been used in the USA and Germany for some years (see Renn *et al.*, 1995) and have recently been used by health authorities and local authorities in the UK (see below).

Some agencies have also developed what are in effect larger citizens' juries, often called 'public scrutiny workshops' or 'consensus conferences', to explore key policy issues.

Interactive information and communications technologies are being used to consult individual local people; for example, through message boards and online discussions with policy makers, and an increasing number of local councils are consulting the public about budget decisions. Some have held referenda on the level of council tax. Others have sought the public's view about allocations between services.

Milton Keynes and Bristol City Councils have both held *referenda on the level of council tax* offering residents a range of options and spelling out the implications for service budgets.

Co-production

Co-production is less common than consultation but can take a number of different forms – including public involvement in formulating strategies (e.g. 'planning for real', 'visioning exercises' and community appraisals), designing services, co-managing them and monitoring performance. User groups can have roles in providing services, working in partnership in developing services and campaigning for more resources and policy change (Barnes *et al.*, 1999).

OBSTACLES TO EFFECTIVE ENGAGEMENT

Power to the people?

Increased public participation does not enjoy unqualified support among public officials and politicians. Not surprisingly, some see it as a threat to their professional judgement or democratic legitimacy, fearing 'governance by referendum' in which their role is reduced to that of 'rubber-stamping' decisions made by the public.

> Unravelling the interests of different groups in our services will be one of the key roles of councillors; their job will be to act as community leaders and to act as brokers, balancing the different interests of different groups and developing integrated policies which meet local needs best.
>
> *Source*: City of York Council

However, in practice, engagement with users and citizens does not obviate the need for service experts or for political judgement. In most cases, it simply provides more information about the range of, often conflicting, views among the public. Politicians and senior managers still need to decide how best to reconcile competing interests and to allocate resources accordingly.

Have we got the right approach?

Many public sector organizations focus a great deal of effort on choosing the 'right' approach to public participation. In practice, however, there is rarely one correct method. Some of the approaches described above, for example, public meetings, citizens' juries and focus groups, offer high levels of interaction but reach only a small proportion of the population. They are also relatively costly, time-consuming and require skilled facilitation. Other methods, such as citizens' and users' panels and resident's surveys, offer breadth of coverage and are relatively cheap, but they provide less in-depth interaction.

Most organizations therefore need to have a balanced portfolio of approaches that are tailored to the:

- objectives of engaging with users and citizens;
- resources available to those managing the process;
- timescale;
- capacity of respondents.

197

Let's work together

It is quite common for several local agencies, or even several service departments within the same agency, to pursue their own individual consultation exercises in isolation from each other and unaware that effort is being duplicated. This is problematic for two reasons. First, it is a waste of resources. Second, it increases the risk of 'consultation fatigue' among the public.

> We usually ask a question ten times and use the information once. We must learn to ask once and use the answer ten times in different settings.
>
> *Source*: Local authority chief executive

In order to avoid duplication and bring together disparate initiatives, some organizations have developed databases of previous consultations. In some areas joint consultation strategies are being developed by local councils, health authorities, the police and other agencies to ensure that they coordinate their initiatives.

Overcoming apathy

Another problem is that many members of the public are unwilling to engage in the ways and to the degree that governments wish. Research suggests, for example, that only one in five citizens in the UK wants to engage more closely with their local authority (Box 15.1).

By definition the minority who do get involved are therefore unlikely to be unrepresentative of the community as a whole, particularly because the most vulnerable groups, those on lower incomes, young people, older people, members of households with a disabled person and members of ethnic minority communities, are usually the least inclined to be involved. Moreover, most people express a strong preference for relatively passive forms of engagement. In a recent survey in the UK the public strongly favoured one-off consultations via postal surveys and face-to-face interviews. Very few were prepared to participate in in-depth consultations – only 13 per cent said they would be willing to go to public meetings, just 6 per cent said they would participate in a citizens' panel and only 3 per cent would take part in a citizens' jury (Martin *et al.*, 2001).

BOX 15.1 PUBLIC ATTITUDES TO PARTICIPATION

- ■ I'm not interested in what the Council does, or whether it does its job – 1 per cent
- ■ I'm not interested in what the Council does as long as it does its job – 16 per cent
- ■ I like to know what the Council is doing, but I'm happy to let it get on with its job – 57 per cent
- ■ I would like to have more of a say in what the Council does and the services it provides – 21 per cent
- ■ I already work for/am involved with the Council – 3 per cent
- ■ Don't know – 1 per cent

One way of alleviating this problem is to focus on those policies and issues which citizens say they care most about – typically services such as community safety, street cleaning, leisure facilities for young people. Another is to use the consultation methods that members of the public say they are most comfortable with. It is also vital to give feedback on how results were used, what decisions were taken and why, so that people can see that their views were taken seriously and made a real difference. Finally, some public service providers that have made important strides in engaging with the public have been less adept at consulting their own staff. This is a missed opportunity because many front-line staff live locally and use local services. They are therefore in a position to provide valuable feedback on their own and their families' experiences.

Ensuring it makes a difference

One of the major reasons for citizens' unwillingness to engage is widespread scepticism about whether governments and public service providers are willing to respond to public opinion. In many cases the scope for action will be constrained by the fact that an agency has only limited control over a policy area. Local authorities in the UK, for example, have little or no direct influence over many of the key issues about which local people feel most strongly including health, community safety and employment, and often have limited room for manoeuvre in terms of the services they do provide directly due to centrally determined performance targets and 'ring-fenced' budgets.

> If voting changed anything, they'd abolish it.
>
> *Source*: Ken Livingstone, Mayor of London

It is therefore important to make clear at the outset what the parameters of engagement are, what issues are up for negotiation, what changes are possible and what is 'off-limits'. It is also crucial that there is effective communication with users and citizens throughout the process and, where possible, that some early 'wins' are achieved and celebrated – communities often complain that decision-making processes are too slow, and lose interest if improvements do not materialize fairly rapidly.

Evaluating participation

There is now a strong body of knowledge about public participation, its potential and pitfalls – both in the UK and in many other Western countries. For example, Coote and Lenaghan (1997) and McIver (1997) evaluate the use of citizens' juries in the health service. Hall and Stewart (1997) provide a detailed account of early experiments with juries in six local authorities in England covering subjects as diverse as library services, waste management, drugs in the community, community facilities in rural areas and regeneration.

However, public service providers often fail to tap this reservoir of knowledge or to reflect on their own experiences of public participation. The result is that they risk 're-inventing the wheel' and repeating mistakes made elsewhere.

199

It is therefore important to take time to evaluate the results of previous attempts to engage with users and citizens, assessing what is already known about what the public wants, how people wish to be involved in decisions and which approaches work best. It is also important for policy makers and practitioners to consider carefully the scope for coordinating their actions with those of other local agencies and to look further afield to gain new ideas about engagement from other service settings and other countries.

SUMMARY

Engaging service users and citizens in policy making and the design and delivery of services is not new, but it is being seen increasingly as a key to good governance in most Western democracies. As a result there has been a plethora of new programmes and initiatives designed to ensure greater public participation.

Engagement can take many forms. Less interactive approaches involve communication – the one-way flow of information from policy makers and managers to the public. More interactive approaches include consultation – a two-way flow of information, views and perspectives between policy makers/managers and users/citizens, and co-production – involving active partnership between providers and the public to develop strategies, design and deliver services and monitor standards.

Participation may include a range of different stakeholder groups. In some circumstances it is appropriate to engage first and foremost with service users. In others it is necessary to involve the public as a whole. In some cases it is important to work with particular communities of place or specific groups.

There is a vast array of techniques for public engagement. What matters most is that the tools used by an organization are fit for the purpose and are appropriate to its own capacity and that of the groups with which it is seeking to engage.

Public participation offers a range of potential benefits but also entails formidable challenges. There is a lot of experience that can be tapped from across a range of services and different national settings. It is important that policy makers, politicians and public service managers draw upon this growing body of evidence in developing their own organizations' approaches to public engagement.

QUESTIONS FOR REVIEW AND DISCUSSION

1   In what ways can engagement with users and other stakeholders enhance public services?
2   Which methods are likely to be most useful in consulting:
    ■   service users;
    ■   citizens;
    ■   businesses.
    Explain your choice of approaches.

3 What are the benefits of representative democracy? How can these be reconciled with increasing direct public participation in policy decisions?

4 How might public engagement undertaken by public organizations need to differ from engagement with stakeholders by private sector organizations?

READER EXERCISES

1 Think of your own experience as a user of public services. What services or issues would you like to have more influence over? How might the organization(s) responsible for these services engage most effectively with you?

2 Interview a local councillor to get his or her views as to how his or her role has changed as a result of more public engagement.

CLASS EXERCISES

Work in groups on these exercises.

1 Access communications provided to its residents by a local authority (ideally the council that serves the area in which you study, work or live). You may want to look at:
- its website;
- the information it provides with council tax bills;
- the most recent summary Best Value performance plan;
- the council newspaper (if it has one);
- information about council services provided in local libraries or council offices.

2 Write a short report on the strengths and weaknesses of the council's communications – How easy was it to obtain information? How user-friendly is it? Is it sufficiently comprehensive? In your view is it likely to be useful to local people? Is there adequate provision for those with particular needs (e.g. are translations and large-print versions available)? Does it communicate a clear sense of the organization's values and mission? Does it make clear how local people can contact the council with queries and complaints? Is there provision for people to feed back their views to the council easily?

3 Imagine that you have been hired to prepare an action plan for addressing any weaknesses you observe in the council's communications. Present and explain your proposals to your colleague students.

FURTHER READING

Local Government Association (1998), *Democratic practice: a guide.* London: LGA.

Steve Martin and Annette Boaz (2000), 'Public participation and citizen-centred local government', *Public Money and Management*, Vol. 20, No. 2, pp. 47–54.

OECD (2001a), *Engaging citizens in policy-making: information, consultation and public participation*, PUMA Policy Briefing No. 10. Paris: OECD.

Chapter 16

Changing equalities
Politics, policies and practice

Janet Newman, Open University, Milton Keynes, UK

INTRODUCTION

Concepts of equality and inequality are fundamentally *political* concepts that have become institutionalized in the public sector in particular ways. Yet, along with concepts such as 'fairness', 'social justice' or, more recently, 'social exclusion', they are historically rooted and mutable. In recent years the meaning of such concepts has shifted, reflecting changing social, economic and political conditions. These include the demise of taken-for-granted assumptions about the welfare state as the guarantor of universal rights and benefits; the increasing importance of social movements around disability, age and sexuality; the changing role of women both in the labour market and public life; and, in the UK, the fundamental reassessment of institutional cultures and practices following the Macpherson Report of 1999. This reported on the failure of the police to deal effectively with the death of a young black teenager, Stephen Lawrence, in 1993. It introduced the concept of 'institutional racism' into the political lexicon and led to the amendment of UK legislation on race relations. Each of these movements and events is framed in broader patterns of political change, notably the shift in language away from redistributive meanings of equality and towards the more cultural interpretations implied in the idea of social exclusion; and from the formalized concept of equality to more fluid notions of social diversity.

These transformations have produced major challenges for the public sector. Its capacity to respond is influenced by a number of different issues, not least the ways in which new business and management practices have been adopted; the ways in which notions of consumerism have reshaped relationships between public services and the public; and the effects of the emerging patterns of governance described in chapters 2, 4 and 13. Where are we at the beginning of the twenty-first century? And what is the capacity of the public sector to deliver equality goals in the midst of these profound social and political transformations?

CHANGING POLITICS: ADMINISTRATIVE JUSTICE OR SOCIAL JUSTICE?

Equality is not an essential, unchanging and universal principle of public management. Equality legislation and equality policies are the product of struggles by particular groups to overcome patterns of structural inequality – around social divisions such as class, gender, race, disability and sexuality. Most of what we take for granted as citizens is the product of such struggles. The politics of equality is not settled, but is the continued focus of social action as groups face new forms of disadvantage or attempt to enlarge the opportunities open to them. It is also open to various forms of 'backlash' as those whose power bases are threatened mobilize their resources – ideological, legal and institutional – to resist change. Equality, diversity and social justice are, then, all *political* concepts that are the focus of different interpretations and give rise to different strategies of enactment and resistance.

The form of equality that became enshrined in the public sector was based on the concept of administrative justice – a concept that tended to strip it of these political inflections (see Box 16.1).

Administrative justice is, however, a poor means of redressing inequality. Subjecting everyone to the same rules is not enough to compensate for injustices inherited from the past. Providing opportunities for individuals to transcend the patterns of inequality formed around social divisions does little to address the divisions themselves. Administrative justice gives rise to an individualized and passive conception of equal opportunities that enables dominant cultures to reproduce themselves. That is, to succeed, individuals may take on the characteristics of the dominant groups in whose image organizational cultures have been moulded over successive generations. In this way, little structural change – the shifting of power relations – can take place, and the same groups of staff, users or citizens tend to remain excluded from the centres of power and decision making. Despite the rules of

BOX 16.1: THE TWO PRINCIPLES OF ADMINISTRATIVE JUSTICE

The first principle derives from the notion of citizenship in welfare democracies. All citizens are considered to have equal claims on welfare services, so that, given the same circumstances, they could expect to receive the same benefits, wherever – and to whomever – they made their claims.

The second principle is that of the impartiality of public service officers – an impartiality guaranteed by the bureaucratic rules and norms of the organizations in which they work.

impartiality and equality, some groups may perceive that their interests are marginalized, their voices unheard, or that they are treated unjustly.

The politics of equality has been through two key shifts in recent years. The first has been an increasing emphasis on diversity – that is, a recognition of the need to respond to difference rather than simply providing equality of opportunity. The second – less embedded – has been an attempt to transcend the passive and formalized notion of equality with a more active and dynamic concept of social justice (see Box 16.2). This shifts attention to the outcomes of policies and practices rather than to the processes through which they are delivered.

CHANGING POLICIES: DIVERSITY AS A BUSINESS ASSET?

The emergence of the diversity agenda

In the 1980s and 1990s, public services went through profound changes with the introduction of markets and extension of contracting out, a new emphasis on efficiency goals and 'value for money', increasing downward pressure on public sector pay and a series of attacks on trade unions' powers (see chapters 2, 4 and 7). Many organizations introduced flexibility strategies that adversely affected their lowest paid workers, among whom women and black and ethnic minorities were disproportionately represented. Despite some notable exceptions, equality goals became subordinated to business and efficiency goals. However, more recently there has been a resurgence of interest in the possible benefits of diversity strategies for organizations across the private and public sectors. Consider the three studies given in Box 16.3.

The rhetoric in these extracts is that equality can be aligned with efficiency in an unproblematic way – equality considerations are aligned with good business practice. However, alongside this sense of fit, the increase in competition in public services (for funding and legitimacy) may emphasize efficiency above equity considerations. This is not necessarily the case: equity and efficiency are not polar opposites but may be combined in different ways in service design, implementation and outcomes (Harrow, 2002). It has to be recognized, however, that these combinations are context specific and depend on the way in which organizations link equality goals to business goals at both strategic and operational levels.

In the public policy literature the ethos is that equality and diversity are simply a case of being 'responsive' to the different needs of diverse groups of users or citizens (Audit

---

BOX 16.2 THE DIFFERENCE BETWEEN ADMINISTRATIVE AND SOCIAL JUSTICE

Administrative justice is about processes and rules: for example, the process of staff selection; the rules by which resources are distributed.

Social justice is about the outcomes of policies and practices: for example, the overall profile of a labour force; the extent to which resources are redistributed.

BOX 16.3 EXAMPLES OF DIVERSITY STRATEGIES IN THE PRIVATE AND PUBLIC SECTORS

Extract 1 Diversity drive at BP targets gay staff

Britain's biggest company, BP, is targeting gays and lesbians for recruitment as part of a drive to ditch traditional business prejudices. It is also seeking women and foreign nationals in a determined bid to rid itself of the 'golf club culture' it believes encourages only Anglo-Saxon men. The company's chief executive, Lord Browne . . . said 'human capital [is] more important than all the plants and equipment needed for exploiting oil and gas reserves. . . . If we can get a disproportionate share of the most talented people in the world, we have a chance of holding a competitive edge.'

Furthermore, yesterday, Patricia Hewitt, the Trades and Industry Secretary, urged companies to review their employment policies to make sure that workers from ethnic communities were given a chance of jobs. 'It is clearly the right thing to do but also makes sound business sense to cast the net as wide as possible when fishing for new talent' she said. Her call came as a survey of ninety-nine leading British companies and public sector organizations identified only forty-four people from ethnic minorities in positions at Board level. . . . More than one-third of the organizations surveyed . . . said their race strategy 'made a measurable impact on their bottom line in terms of customers'.

Source: Adapted from the *Guardian* (20 June 2002, p. 2)

Extract 2 How diversity can improve your performance

A recent research report ('The Business of Diversity') has revealed more than a hundred of the UK's leading organizations now recognize the development of diversity as an important contributor to their overall business performance. Whether your business is commerce or the delivery of better public services, 80 per cent of the respondents saw a direct link between good diversity policies and improved performance.

In another research project, undertaken by the specialist consultancy Schneider-Ross, 140 leading organizations from both the private and public sectors were questioned about their equality and diversity business priorities and what links they saw between this and their overall business performance. The report found that successful equality and diversity policies deliver significant business results including: 'better recruitment, increased retention, improved understanding of markets and communities, an enhanced reputation and cost savings'.

Source: Adapted from Cabinet Office Diversity website (www.diversity-whatworks, gov.uk)

Extract 3 The vital connection

Equality and fair treatment are central to the UK government's goals to tackle inequalities and improve the health and well-being of the population. Its comprehensive programme to modernize health and social care is targeted on achieving high-quality, fair, accessible and responsive services. Furthermore, in modernizing services and employment, the government is committed to inclusiveness – ensuring that public services meet the needs of all citizens. However, these goals will be achieved only if the NHS builds a commitment to equality and inclusiveness into everything it does – not only in delivering services but also in employing the right people with the right skills and diversity, with the leadership to match.

Source: Adapted from *NHS Executive* (p. 2)

Commission, 2002c). However, the academic literature suggests that responsiveness may not always deliver equality considerations: the results of public consultation exercises may displace professional notions of equality, and consumer power tends to be weak as a driver of equality (Harrow, 2002). The solution to this dilemma is to develop strong, rather than weak, notions of diversity and forms of consultation, each linked to concepts of social, rather than administrative justice (Young, 1990). A positive notion of diversity acknowledges the wide plurality of interests and complexity of identifications among the public, rather than resting on crude conceptions of 'consulting the whole (i.e. undifferentiated) community' or dividing the public into distinct categories ('the black and ethnic minority community', 'women', 'the elderly' and so on). Rather than simply sampling pre-formed 'opinions' through survey techniques, consultation should enable different groups to be informed about the issues and to engage in dialogue – with each other and with public agencies.

Diversity policies have been criticized because of their focus on individuals, rather than groups; and because of their focus on assimilation. That is, diverse groups may be absorbed or incorporated into the mainstream and so lose their distinct forms of identity and patterns of allegiance (Prasad et al., 1997). The existence of a diverse workforce will not yield the benefits of enhanced innovation, responsiveness, market sensitivity and so on if the organization is modelled on an image of a holistic, consensual culture in which all sign up to the 'ownership' of the same goals and values and are expected to adopt the dominant ethos. A diverse organization is necessarily a dynamic organization: one in which there is likely to be conflict between different values and norms, in which minority voices are able to raise challenges to conventional practice, and in which power imbalances and discriminatory practices are recognized and discussed. That is, it is one which recognizes that change involves politics as well as management.

Despite these difficulties, the links being made between diversity and business effectiveness provide a springboard for securing a place for equality agendas at the core of organizational strategies, rather than their consignment to the backwaters of personnel management. However, politics and business make uneasy partners, and it is important to hold on to the idea that equality and diversity are contested ideas around which a number of conflicts are played out. Only then can we understand why, while equality and diversity are concepts to which everyone may ascribe in principle, few translate into practice in a way that makes a real and sustainable difference.

207

CHANGING PRACTICE: BARRIERS TO CHANGE

Why, given the centrality of equality in public services over many decades, has so little been achieved? The data here are compelling; see e.g. Audit Commission (2002c) and documents from the Commission for Racial Equality, the Equal Opportunities Commission and other official bodies. The barriers to change may be explored at three different levels of analysis: the institutional, the organizational and the personal.

Institutional explanations

Institutional explanations explore the ways in which organizations adopt norms and practices in order to enhance their legitimacy in the eyes of external stakeholders (Newman, 2002a). Equality policies are part of a dominant 'logic of appropriate action' within public services. These logics are based on norms and conventions developed through interaction with peers and within particular professional groups (personnel officers, equality officers, professional associations, trade unions and so on). These norms differ subtly between different services (with, for example, social service organizations talking about 'anti-oppressive practices' while police services may be oriented towards eradicating 'institutional racism'). They also vary geographically (with a higher legitimacy afforded to equality issues in, say, metropolitan rather than rural areas).

Equality policies and programmes may be partly ceremonial, their function being to secure organizational legitimacy in the institutional environment. There may be a host of signs and symbols (e.g. 'we are an equal opportunity employer' statements on job adverts, photos of black officers in publicity materials, or perhaps a lone woman promoted to an otherwise all-male senior management team). However, these signs and symbols may be 'loosely coupled' to the realities of everyday practice (Meyer and Rowan, 1991). Loose coupling allows multiple goals to be pursued in different parts of the system independently of each other. A delicate balance has to be struck between being seen to support equality goals while not allowing them to get in the way of operational efficiency. So, for example, there may be a formal jobshare policy, but an informal set of rules about where this policy can, and cannot, be applied. In order to secure efficiency goals new working practices may be introduced that adversely affect the pay and conditions of low-paid workers, so further disadvantaging women and ethnic minority staff. The corporate centre may adopt a policy on social exclusion that has little impact on service planning or operational management. Tighter coupling brings a closer alignment between policies and outcomes, with outputs monitored and outcomes evaluated.

Organizational explanations

Organizational explanations tend to focus on the intractibility of organizational cultures (Itzin and Newman, 1995). This focus stems from a recognition that individuals and groups may be disadvantaged not by overt discrimination (e.g. the old height rule in the police force, or the bar on married women in the civil service) but by norms and practices that influence their experience of the workplace. Expectations about working hours, access to flexible working and jobsharing opportunities, norms about an appropriate work/life balance, may all be applied 'fairly' (i.e. even-handedly) but may be profoundly discriminatory in their effects. Issues of language, humour, and normative assumptions about lifestyle and relationships can all contribute to the marginalization of particular groups and disable them from making an effective contribution. Assumptions about the characteristics of users and communities – about young black males, Asian women, young single mothers, travellers, the homeless – may be enshrined in the culture and passed on from one generation of practitioners to the next. Such assumptions may not be held consciously by any particular individual, but nevertheless may become institutionalized in the culture, influencing myriad informal practices that may be experienced as discriminatory by the groups concerned.

However, culture change strategies are rarely successful on their own – the hearts and minds of those whose power and status may be threatened by equality issues cannot necessarily be won by a succession of mission statements and corporate goals. People may learn a new language without changing their behaviour. There may be a backlash against those promoting equality values and actions, coupled with subtle strategies of resistance. Culture change programmes need to be supported by 'harder' organizational change strategies such as equality audits, targets linked to performance indicators, careful use of disciplinary procedures to signal behaviours that are unacceptable, resource allocation strategies that reward positive outcomes, and the monitoring and evaluation of outcomes.

Personal explanations

Personal explanations explore the ways in which individuals experience the implementation of equality policies. Change is threatening, not only to established power bases but also to workers' views of their competence and professional expertise (Lewis, 2000b). For example, a black hospital worker may experience racial abuse from a white patient, or a white worker may be asked to collude in racist comments about a black colleague, but neither may feel able to respond because of the patient's vulnerable or dependent status. A care worker's sense of competence may be challenged by the distressing behaviour of a client – or carer – from a different cultural background to her own. A white social work manager may feel that her authority is threatened by the claims of her 'multiracial' team and may feel tentative about exercising proper performance management in the case of black colleagues. A male police officer may marginalize a gay or lesbian member of the team from the informal bonds of collegiality on which the team's proficiency depends. Such personal fears, emotions and responses tend to be viewed as outside the domain of rational management practice. Yet they may lead to strategies of avoidance that further marginalize groups which are already disadvantaged. Only in organizational cultures that acknowledge the emotional, as well as the managerial, dynamics of change, and where there is a culture of learning rather than blame, can these fears be confronted and addressed.

CHANGING FORMS OF GOVERNANCE

In the new governance literature, notions of networks, partnerships, participation and involvement all tend to be conceptualized in terms of a predominantly optimistic reading of change in the public policy system, i.e. as a welcome release from the inflexibilities of hierarchy or the fragmenting consequences of markets (see Chapter 13). There is, however, a need for more careful attention to be paid to the patterns of inclusion and exclusion they may produce or reproduce.

One of the key characteristics of network forms of governance in the public sector is the dispersal of power among a plurality of interdependent actors. Public sector organizations are, then, not simply the recipients of *dictats* from above but are active agents in shaping the new agenda and influencing the experience of those drawn into new forms of network-based relationship. A host of actions, which appear to have little relationship to issues of difference, are likely to be highly significant in terms of their consequences for patterns of equality and inequality, both within the organization and in the wider 'community'. These include the way in which organizations set up consultation exercises; the way in which they are represented on partnership bodies; the strategy chosen to implement modernizing reforms such as Best Value or clinical governance; the means through which staff are selected to develop new projects or initiatives that require network-based working; the way in which community strategies are forged and local strategic partnerships established; the way in which contracts with voluntary or community sector organizations are written; and the conceptualizations of 'community', 'diversity' and 'difference' that inform each of these practices (Newman, 2001a, 2003).

Networks and partnerships are viewed as a response to the increasing complexity and ambiguity of the public realm. As the site of action shifts, so equality agendas must be renegotiated. In Newman (2002b, 2003) I suggest two alternative scenarios for what the outcomes of these negotiations might be. The first is a pessimistic reading in which the power dominance of statutory agencies means that radical perspectives from 'outside' are absorbed, deflected or neutralized. For example, organizations may engage in forms of consultation in which the rules of debate are firmly set by the statutory body, thus excluding or marginalizing alternative forms of dialogue. Dissenting or difficult voices may be dismissed as 'unrepresentative', and groups likely to challenge the mainstream consensus may be excluded through a range of informal strategies.

The second scenario is one in which the public sector becomes more open to challenges from groups historically marginalized from decision-making processes. This scenario also emphasizes the possibility of socially oriented action on the part of public service workers committed to equality goals. The opening up of organizations to greater influence by users, citizens and communities – including community activists and politicized user groups – can be a major impetus for innovation. It also potentially provides new forms of legitimacy for those public service professionals seeking to engage with social and political change.

SUMMARY

Concepts of equality and inequality are fundamentally *political* concepts. In recent years, the language has tended to shift away from redistributive meanings of equality and towards the more cultural interpretations implied in the idea of social exclusion; and from the formalized concept of equality to more fluid notions of social diversity.

Equality is not an unchanging and universal principle of public management. Equality legislation and equality policies are the product of struggles by particular groups to overcome patterns of structural inequality – around social divisions such as class, gender, race, disability and sexuality. In recent years there has been an increasing emphasis on diversity – that is, a recognition of the need to respond to difference and to pursue a more active and dynamic concept of social justice.

As diversity becomes seen as contributing to business effectiveness, equality agendas are to be found more frequently at the core of organizational strategies. However, it remains the case that equality and diversity are contested ideas. This may be part of the reason why rather less has been achieved than hoped for in recent years. Barriers to change may be identified at three different levels of analysis: the institutional, the organizational and the personal.

Finally, network forms of governance in the public sector mean that a host of actions, which appear to have little relationship to issues of difference, are likely to be highly significant in terms of their consequences for patterns of equality and inequality – including network approaches to consultation; representation on partnership bodies; the selection of staff to develop new projects or initiatives; methods of developing community strategies and local strategic partnerships; the type of contracts with voluntary or community sector organizations; and the ways in which 'community', 'diversity' and 'difference' are conceptualized.

QUESTIONS FOR REVIEW AND DISCUSSION

1   Why do policies or practices based on the concept of administrative justice fail to deliver change in historical patterns of discrimination or exclusion?
2   Reread the extracts in Box 16.3 and identify the main links and arguments that are being made. What are the strengths and weaknesses of these arguments?
3   How might 'equality' and 'efficiency' goals be in conflict, and how might organizations attempt to reconcile them?
4   Why do new forms of governance mean rethinking the traditional conception of equal opportunities in the public sector?

READER EXERCISES

1   'Bureaucracy' has become unfashionable as an organizational form. What are the implications for ensuring fair treatment for citizens – and staff – in more flexible, devolved organizational forms?
2   What strategies or practices might your organization or service adopt to enhance its legitimacy in the eyes of particular groups who may have been subject to institutionalized patterns of discrimination or exclusion in the past?
3   The 'welfare state' is undergoing important shifts as demand on some services exceeds the capacity – or willingness – of the state to supply them. Services are

increasingly being targeted to particular groups, rationed through various means, or subjected to the logic of the marketplace. It is also argued that the receipt of services should be conditional on service users being prepared to act responsibly or being clearly 'deserving' of the service – in the familiar phrase of new Labour, that 'rights' come with 'responsibilities'. What ideas of equality or justice do you think underpin such measures? And what might be the implications for our understanding of citizenship in the twenty-first century?

CLASS EXERCISES

1   Look up the definition of 'institutional racism' set out in the Macpherson Report (Macpherson, 1999). Consider how the concept of institutional bias might influence practice in relation to other forms of discrimination – for example, in terms of gender, disability, age, sexuality – in your own organization or service or a service you use.
2   Obtain a recent report from an organization such as the Commission for Racial Equality or the Equal Opportunities Commission on the distribution of top jobs in the public and/or private sector (or find press reports or websites summarizing such data). Explore how far each of the three levels of analysis (institutional, organizational, personal) might be used to explain these data, and identify strategies that might be used to bring about change at each level.
3   Research the way in which a sample of large public and private sector organizations develop and monitor their equality policies. Are there any differences between the public and private sectors? How might such differences be explained?

FURTHER READING

Janet Newman (2003), 'New Labour, governance and the politics of diversity', in J. Barry, M. Dent and M. O'Neill, eds, *Gender and the public sector: professionals and managerial change*. London: Routledge pp. 15–26.

Jenny Harrow (2002), 'The new public management and social justice: just efficiency or equity as well?', in Kate McLaughlin, Stephen P. Osborne and Ewan Ferlie (eds), *New public management*: current trends and future prospects. London: Routledge, pp. 141–159.

Chapter 17

Ethics and standards of conduct

Howard Davis, Warwick Business School, UK

INTRODUCTION

Concern to ensure high standards of behaviour is by no means a new phenomenon. Indeed, demands for ethical conduct on the part of politicians and public officials pre-date the modern concern for the rule of law (the *Rechtsstaat*) and can be traced back to at least Greek and Roman times. These concerns have risen to prominence again in recent years because of the changing context of public policies (see Chapter 2), and because of changes both in the management and governance arrangements in the public sector (see chapters 4 and 13).

In spite of some evidence of improved efficiency in public sector organizations as they implemented the first wave of public sector reforms (see Chapter 4), citizens' trust in government by and large has fallen in most industrialized countries in recent decades – for example, in the USA in the 1990s about three in four citizens did not trust the government to do the right thing, whereas it had been only one in four in the 1960s (Putnam, 2001, p. 47). One factor behind this – though by no means the only one – is the public perception of lower standards of conduct on the part of politicians and public officials.

The growth in recent years of 'sleaze', corruption scandals and allegations of dishonesty may not only have affected the confidence and trust which citizens have in public representatives and officials but also citizens' attitudes to democratic activity. In many OECD countries, there is low voter turn-out at elections (with less than 50 per cent turn-out of eligible voters in the US presidential elections of 2000 and often less than 25 per cent turn-out in local elections in the UK), sinking membership of political parties, general disinterest in politics and even open disrespect towards politicians.

There is concern, too, that a high level of corruption decreases economic performance, since it means that the costs of service production go up, less efficient providers are used, discriminatory behaviour favours certain groups and harms other groups, and there are significant losses of potential tax income (with the knock-on effect of lower public expenditure).

Consequently, many governments have taken action to increase levels of trust in the public sector. These initiatives have taken many forms: for example, some governments have stressed the value of increased engagement with citizens and other stakeholders (see Chapter 15), while others have focused on increasing transparency and ensuring fair and honest behaviour of individuals and organizations acting in the public domain.

LEARNING OBJECTIVES

- To understand the reasons for the current emphasis on ethics and standards of conduct in the public sector
- To understand the mechanisms by which corruption can operate in the public sector
- To be aware of the rationale behind the recent move to strengthened codes of conduct in the United Kingdom and elsewhere
- To understand the pros and cons of control-oriented and prevention-oriented mechanisms to ensure ethical behaviour
- To understand the role for transparency as a mechanism for fighting unethical behaviour

ETHICS AS A KEY GOVERNANCE ISSUE IN THE PUBLIC SECTOR

As the definitions of 'good governance' illustrate in Chapter 13, ethics is considered either explicitly or implicitly to be part of what makes 'good governance'. How does this renewed emphasis on fair, just and ethical behaviour come about?

There are no empirical grounds for claiming that managerialism, as an ideology or a codified set of practices, has given explicit incentives which would encourage unethical behaviour. Nevertheless, it seems fair to say that the switch to a focus on results (outputs and outcomes), and away from processes, may have some unfortunate side-effects. The simple truths that 'processes matter' and that 'the ends do not necessarily justify the means' seem to have been forgotten. If processes are not regulated, then some unfair and dishonest processes can occur.

Consequently, the stronger focus on economically driven values and business management methods in the public sector – which has been stronger in some countries such as the UK and much weaker in other countries such as France – has generated fresh discussion about the values and (written and unwritten) norms of the public service. Indeed, one of the immediate issues which have to be discussed in each country is whether a public service ethos still exists or whether the culture of the public service has become almost identical with business culture.

Furthermore, the introduction of contract management (see Chapter 7) and the increasing blurring of boundaries

STANDARDS IN PUBLIC LIFE

Decentralization and contracting out have varied the format for organizations giving public service. There is greater interchange between sectors. There are more short term contracts. There is scepticism about traditional institutions. Against that background it cannot be assumed that everyone in the public service will assimilate a public service culture unless they are told what is expected of them and the message is systematically reinforced. The principles inherent in the ethic of public service need to be set out afresh.

Source: Committee on Standards in Public Life (1995, p.17)

between various sectors (see Chapter 3) mean that decision makers in the public sector face new, unfamiliar situations and dilemmas, which require new guidelines to clarify how they should be tackled properly from an ethics perspective.

In particular, the following changes in public management have raised questions as to what are the 'new rules of the game':

- New levels and intensity of interactions between the public, private and nonprofit sectors have led to all kinds of partnerships. This brings the associated danger of a blurring of responsibilities. Therefore, there is a need for clarity of roles and transparency in decision making, not only inside the partnerships but also for external stakeholders.

- Increased managerial freedom for managers – and also to some extent for front-line staff – have arisen from increased flexibility in the use of financial and staffing resources. For example, in some continental European countries many public agencies such as utilities now operate within a private law framework which gives managers much more flexibility than did the previous public sector framework, with its rather rigid staff regulations and financial accounting systems. However, the extent to which these agencies must observe a 'public service obligation' is much less clear than in the past.

- With deregulation taking place in many OECD countries, including the UK, many new regulatory agencies have been created. In many cases it is not really clear to whom the regulators are accountable. Given the power of these bodies, and the individuals who serve in them, it is not surprising that some instances occur where they abuse their position. In the UK, this has been seen most frequently in the case of special drugs squads in the police forces and in some branches of Customs and Excise, both of which have access to high-value goods which are being traded illegally.

- Increased mobility of staff between different sectors introduces new values into the public sector. While this may have been useful in inculcating a more entrepreneurial spirit in the public sector, it has also meant the dilution of traditional understandings of 'public service'. It also raises the thorny issue of how to deal with the passing of confidential information on to the new workplace – a particular difficulty when public officials move on to jobs in the private sector.

The increasing involvement of the private sector in the provision of local services is useful in illustrating some of the ethical issues involved. For example, Seal and Vincent-Jones (1997, p. 7) summarized one set of concerns about the extension of trust-based, relational contracting to local government services, arguing that:

> [The] positive image of trust that emerges from the literature is based on an implicit assumption that trusting relationships are somehow welfare-enhancing. Less obvious are the negative aspects of trust – trust between members of self-serving elites which may flourish within bureaucracies whether they are located in town halls or Communist Parties.

215

Davis and Walker (1997, 1998) have argued that different parties in any contract inevitably have different primary objectives. The first objective for a contractor has to be to survive. A contractor's staff ultimately is not there to provide the best possible public service, but to provide the best possible public service *according to the contract* – however else this may be dressed up. Profitability and survival are the key contractor objectives, service being a means to achieving that 'greater' goal.

As a result of these changes to the basic value system operating in the public sector, public officials and political representatives often find themselves in hazy areas, where it is no longer clear what constitutes proper behaviour. Of course, there are also cases of deliberate wrongdoing in spite of clear guidance through legal regulations or standards of conduct. However, these are likely to be only the tip of the iceberg, with many other undesirable behaviours occurring more through ignorance or confusion.

CORRUPTION AND OTHER FORMS OF UNETHICAL BEHAVIOUR

As the examples below illustrate, media attention gleefully focuses on corruption scandals (see Case Example 17.1). But there are many other forms of unethical behaviour which are usually not reported by the media, such as disadvantaging citizens who do not have a strong voice or excluding certain user groups from access to public services. Therefore, the question arises as to what distinguishes corruption scandals from other forms of unethical behaviour?

Defining corruption is far from straightforward. Corruption cases, as with all problems in the arena of ethics, involve an actor who does not behave in conformance with legal norms or with what is expected of him or her by other stakeholders in a specific situation, who have a right to believe that this behaviour will not occur. It is evident that what is defined as corruption is also culture-bound. For example, while it is totally unacceptable for any public officials in the UK to accept gifts, this is a part of many Asian cultures.

Nevertheless, a key question must always be: In whose interests does a particular arrangement or relationship operate? In any relationship the full details of it, and what makes it work successfully, may well be opaque to outsiders. In public service there is a continuing difficulty ensuring that arrangements and relationships work in the public interest and are clearly seen to do so. The closer any relationship becomes, the greater the potential for corrupt practice and corruption of purpose. Cosy and exclusive relationships sit uneasily with public probity expectations. The move from cliques to cosiness to collusion to corruption is all too easy without adequate safeguards.

Transparency International measures corruption by carrying out large-scale surveys measuring the perception of corruption in different countries (see Box 17.1).

However, there is still room for argument about the underlying trends. There is little empirical evidence to suggest whether or not the level of corruption in most OECD countries has increased in the public sector in the past ten years. Indeed, one line of argument is that the public sector has become more transparent in recent years, so that more cases of corruption have been exposed, which does not mean that the underlying level of corruption has increased (Reichard, 1998, p. 129). The picture is complicated by the possibility that lower standards of conduct may themselves be the result of new public management

CASE EXAMPLE 17.1 RECENT CORRUPTION SCANDALS IN THE UK

The 'Donnygate' scandal is one of the highest profile local government corruption scandals of recent years. A four-year police investigation from 1997 concerning Labour-controlled Doncaster Council in South Yorkshire involved seventy-four arrests and 2000 interviews. The investigations led to twenty-one councillors, including two former mayors and two former council leaders, being convicted of expenses fraud. The sums involved were often small but there was said to be 'a wholesale culture of corruption' affecting the authority in the mid-1990s. In addition, a former chair of planning and a local property developer were sentenced to four- and five-year prison terms respectively in relation to bribes and planning permission. . . .

'Flagship' Conservative-controlled Westminster City Council in London has been the subject of a long-running alleged 'homes for votes' scandal. In May 1996 auditor John Magill accused former council leader Dame Shirley Porter and five others of 'wilful misconduct' and 'disgraceful and improper gerrymandering' between 1987 and 1989. He also made them jointly and severally liable to repay the £31.6 million that he estimated to have been wrongly spent as they allegedly tried to 'fix' election results in marginal wards by selling council homes cheaply under the right to buy scheme to people thought to be more likely to vote Conservative. The 'surcharge' was later reduced to £26.5 million. After appeal hearings going in different directions the House of Lords, in December 2001, reimposed the surcharge on Dame Shirley and her former deputy. In April 2002 Dame Shirley lodged a formal complaint against the ruling with the European Court of Human Rights. August 2002 saw Westminster City Council win a High Court summary judgment to help it recover the £26.5 million plus some interest. However, at the time of writing the affair had yet to be brought to a conclusion.

Source: Adapted from *Guardian* (various dates)

practices, particularly the growth of contracting to the private sector, which has always been one of the arenas in which the potential for corruption is particularly high.

THE ROLE OF CODES OF CONDUCT IN THE PUBLIC SECTOR

It is important to note that not only what is defined as unethical behaviour is strongly culture-bound but Western countries also have different traditions regarding the combat of corruption and other forms of unethical behaviour. In particular, two major traditions may be identified: 'Westminster-type' countries such as the UK, New Zealand and Australia (and also the USA) tend to take a 'direct line' to ethical issues, i.e. these countries have a long tradition of addressing questions of values and moral behaviour directly. In continental European countries such as Germany and France, ethical issues are normally addressed

BOX 17.1 PERCEPTION OF CORRUPTION WORLDWIDE

Transparency International is an international nonprofit organization which is dedicated to increasing the transparency of decisionmaking in the public and nonprofit sector around the world and to exposing and combating corruption. One of its activities is the compilation and publication of an international Corruption Perceptions Index (CPI).

The CPI is a poll of polls, reflecting the perceptions of business people and country analysts, both resident and non-resident. First launched in 1995, the CPI in 2002 drew upon fifteen surveys from nine independent institutions. In a rolling survey of polls taken between 2000 and 2002, the CPI included only those countries that featured in at least three surveys.

In 2002, this index ranked 102 countries: more than seventy countries scored less than 5 out of a clean score of 10. Corruption was perceived to be rampant in Indonesia, Kenya, Angola, Madagascar, Paraguay, Nigeria and Bangladesh, countries with a score of less than 2. While some countries in transition from communism – most notably Slovenia, which had a cleaner score than EU member countries Italy and Greece – were perceived to be increasingly less corrupt, many countries in the former Soviet Union remained 'ridden with corruption'.

Countries with a score of higher than 9, with very low levels of perceived corruption, were predominantly rich countries, namely Finland, Denmark, New Zealand, Iceland, Singapore and Sweden. The UK ranked 10th (with a score of 8.7) and the USA ranked 17th (with a score of 7.7).

Source: Transparency International – Corruption Perceptions Index, 2002 (www.transparency.org/pressreleases_archive/2002/2002.08.28.cpi.en.html)

indirectly through various sets of laws. For example, the *Public Administration Times* (the monthly magazine of the American Society for Public Administration) always includes a case study dealing with some ethical issue and some model solution from a managerial or political perspective. In the corresponding journal for German civil servants, there is always a case of disciplinary law with the respective model solution or the rulings of some court.

Because of the lack of a comprehensive legal framework for dealing with unethical behaviour, in recent years there has been an 'explosion' of codes of conduct and/or expectations in 'Westminster-type' countries. These have typically been drafted either for public organizations or for professional associations whose members work in public organizations. A well-known example of such a code is the 'seven principles of public life' set out by the Committee on Standards in Public Life (see Box 17.2). This UK Committee, chaired initially by Judge Lord Nolan, was established by John Major's government in 1994 following a series of allegations about parliamentarians (such as 'cash for questions', sexual liaisons and alleged dishonesty) and concerns at the cumulative effect of these events on public confidence in politicians and the system of government.

The Committee was established on a standing basis and was given a wide remit to examine

BOX 17.2 THE SEVEN PRINCIPLES OF PUBLIC LIFE

Selflessness	Holders of public office should take decisions solely in terms of the public interest. They should not do so in order to gain financial or other material benefits for themselves, their family, or their friends.
Integrity	Holders of public office should not place themselves under any financial or other obligation to outside individuals or organizations that might influence them in the performance of their official duties.
Objectivity	In carrying out public business, including making public appointments, awarding contracts, or recommending individuals for rewards and benefits, holders of public office should make choices on merit.
Accountability	Holders of public office are accountable for their decisions and actions to the public and must submit themselves to whatever scrutiny is appropriate to their office.
Openness	Holders of public office should be as open as possible about all the decisions and actions that they take. They should give reasons for their decisions and restrict information only when the wider public interest clearly demands it.
Honesty	Holders of public office have a duty to declare any private interests relating to their public duties and to take steps to resolve any conflicts arising in a way that protects the public interest.
Leadership	Holders of public office should promote and support these principles by leadership and example.

Source: Committee on Standards in Public Life (1995, p. 14)

current concerns about standards of conduct of all holders of public office, including arrangements relating to financial and commercial activities, and make recommendations as to any changes in present arrangements which might be required to ensure the highest standards of propriety in public life.

(*Hansard*, 25 October 1994, col. 758)

In assessing whether these principles are honoured, none of them can be assumed to be in place – all must be demonstrated to be honoured in practice. Furthermore, the assessment of whether these principles are in place will often throw up systemic issues which need to be considered across the sector, not just in one organization. For example, the first principle, 'selflessness', is undoubtedly threatened by some of the fragmented ways of working in the mixed economy of provision that characterizes modern local government, particularly where contracting is the norm (see Chapter 7).

It is also interesting to note some omissions from these principles. They do not, for example, include either *competence* or *representativeness*. *Competence* is arguably central to 'proper' public service activity and there must be grave doubts about the ethics of an organization providing a service where it no longer has the competence to deliver it to the desired standard. *Representativeness* is recurring and problematic. At the heart of the matter is the question of whether those in the public service (politicians and officials) should more accurately reflect (in terms of gender, age, ethnic origin and so on) the populations they are there to serve. On one side, there is the need for different groups in society to feel that their group is represented properly in the decision-making process, at both political and officer level. On the other side, there is the strong desire to pick the right person for the post, irrespective of their background.

Codes of conduct have also been exported from the UK to other countries, in particular to Central and Eastern Europe (even though most of these countries follow the German legalistic tradition). In many CEE countries, it is unclear what is the legal standing of such codes of conduct.

Some see the standards agenda as a new bureaucracy but behind the agenda are some important considerations. The regard with which politicians and public servants are held influences both the credibility of government bodies and their ability to act. Thus the desire to see probity and 'proper' behaviour is mirrored by a concern to prevent corruption and improper behaviour. Nevertheless, expectations as to appropriate standards of behaviour can vary, e.g. between the personal domain and the public domain, between the public sector and the private sector and between one country and another (a factor of some relevance to, for example, cross-national contracting).

Another problem is ownership of standards. In many cases, codes of conduct are drafted by a committee, the members of which may represent different backgrounds and values from those espoused by those who have to conform to the standards. Nor is this the only potential value clash. Eleanor Glor (2001) stresses the differences in values between different generations. To this we might add the different value systems which may be observed between people from different genders, races, religions, regions and so on. Clearly, getting ownership of a single set of standards is often going to be difficult. There is currently no argument against the view that expectations as to what constitutes ethical behaviour have to be made explicit. Nevertheless, there is a strong argument that these standards still need to be negotiated between the various stakeholder groups of each public sector organization, rather than being imposed by some external body.

CONTROL-ORIENTED AND PREVENTION-ORIENTED MECHANISMS

There is general agreement that ethics management should always involve both control-oriented and prevention-oriented mechanisms. A strategy against corruption should look for ways to ensure accountability, limit and clarify discretion, and increase transparency and awareness of unethical behaviour.

An OECD survey in 1999 showed that control-oriented mechanisms, such as independent financial and legal scrutiny, were considered to be the most important mechanisms for combating corruption (OECD, 1999, p. 22). Many OECD countries have also taken measures to protect whistle-blowers and to encourage staff to report wrongdoing. Much less common are participatory approaches to counter unethical behaviour by involving citizens in the policing of public activity (see Case Example 17.2).

CASE EXAMPLE 17.2 **THE INDEPENDENT COMMISSION AGAINST CORRUPTION (ICAC) IN HONG KONG**

In the 1970s, the newly elected Governor of Hong Kong set up an Independent Commission against Corruption (ICAC) which reported directly to him. The ICAC had powerful investigatory capabilities, but from the beginning it emphasized prevention and citizen participation. The ICAC had three sections: one in charge of investigations, one in charge of helping other administrations to take remedial measures and one which involved the people of Hong Kong in the fight against corruption. In order to mobilize citizen participation and support, citizens' advisory committees were set up as well as local offices to gather information about corruption from civil society and to engage in grass-roots educational activities about corruption's evils. It included school programmes, publicity campaigns, filmstrips, TV dramas, a radio call-in show, special pamphlets and exhibitions.

Source: Klitgaard *et al.* (2000)

It is clear that controls are always costly and can never be watertight. Consequently, most countries have focused their efforts on risk management. This implies that controls are particularly frequent and intensive in areas where the risk of corruption is high such as in public procurement and public finance. For example, most organizations place ceilings on the amount of expenditure that can be authorized by any individual manager and contract authorizations invariably have to be agreed by more than one person.

Besides more effective controls, many countries have also taken prevention measures. Meanwhile, there exists a comprehensive set of instruments which are used in order to prevent unethical behaviour such as:

- measures to avoid conflicts of interests (or at least to make them open) such as declarations of financial and business interests of public officials and politicians or regulations for staff moving between sectors;
- affirmative action by supporting disadvantaged groups (e.g. ethnic minorities, women) to gain access to managerial positions or to bridge the digital divide by making them fit for the information society;
- public education programmes which aim at raising awareness about desirable forms of behaviour and perceptions of unethical behaviour.

This latter group of prevention measures reminds us that ethics are always concerned with values. All control mechanisms will fail if actors do not try to live up to the values which are implicit or explicit in various standards of conduct. But can values be taught? Both in the US and in the UK, it appears that academics, at least, think so – ethics typically form an important part of public management education and training curricula.

221

TRANSPARENCY

There is common agreement that transparency is important in order to fight corruption and other forms of unethical behaviour. The assumption is that an increase of transparency brings about a decrease of corruption. Indeed, most OECD countries have recently passed freedom of information laws which give third parties access to government information. In many cases, freedom of information laws also provide remedies for citizens who believe that their right of access to information has not been respected – in some cases, citizens may complain to an information officer or an ombudsman or ask courts to enforce their access rights. Without any doubt, in each case a balance needs to be made between requirements to protect personal privacy and other reasons for confidentiality of information. For example, in Canada, most freedom of information legislation does not apply to public–private partnerships. It is argued that this could impinge on private interests and endanger the confidentiality of commercial information.

Again, the degree to which various stakeholders in different countries wish to be transparent is culture-bound. Scandinavian countries have a comparatively high degree of transparency in the public sector. For example, the Swedish Tax Agency is obliged to provide information about the income tax declaration of any citizen if requested to do so by any other citizen.

Without doubt, the media also play an important role in this context. In particular, in the information age, they are often considered to be the 'fourth power' in the political system. Of course, the media also come under attack when they abuse the freedom of the press to violate personal rights to privacy.

E-government may also be used to increase the degree of transparency as entire documents and accounts can easily be widely and instantly disseminated – at least to those who have electronic access. However, electronic security is a recurring concern and cross-border 'scams' can potentially take place with great ease and speed.

SUMMARY

The standards and conduct of public representatives and officials significantly affect the standing in which they are held. This in turn affects the confidence and respect in which governmental systems are held. High standards of conduct and public confidence go hand in hand. As the Standards Board for English local government says,

> At the heart of good . . . democracy is a bond of trust between the community and the people who represent them – a bond which depends greatly on the conduct of those people. The public have a right to expect the highest standards of behaviour from their representatives and those responsible for the delivery of . . . public services.
>
> (www.standardsboard.co.uk)

Many people maintain these standards most of the time. Nevertheless, the need to be vigilant and alert remains as important today as ever.

QUESTIONS FOR REVIEW AND DISCUSSION

1   Why are high standards of conduct thought to be important for those in public life?
2   What degree of disclosure of private interests is needed from those in public life? How far should such expectations extend to their friends and families?
3   Are ethics and standards of conduct matters for enforcement or education and guidance?

READER EXERCISES

1   Is it right to expect higher standards of conduct from those in public life than we would apply to ourselves?
2   Can you provide a 'watertight' definition of conflicts of interest? Are there any circumstances in which this definition might be relaxed?

CLASS EXERCISE

Consider 'The seven principles of public life' (see Box 17.2). Are there any principles which you consider inappropriate? Are there any additional principles that you would include? Can these principles be defined in a meaningful way?

FURTHER READING

Committee on Standards in Public Life (1995), *First report,* Vol. 1. Cm 2850–1. London: HMSO.

DETR (2001), *Allegations of misconduct in English local authorities.* London: DETR.

OECD (1999), *Public sector corruption: an international survey of prevention measures.* Paris: OECD.

Standards Board for England website (www.standardsboard.co.uk, as of 5 July 2003).

Chapter 18

Evidence-based policy and practice

Annette Boaz, Queen Mary, University of London, UK and *Sandra Nutley*, University of St Andrews, UK

INTRODUCTION

There is growing interest in the UK and elsewhere in the use of evidence to improve policy making and public service delivery. Of course, researchers and analysts have long worked with and in governments. However, in the UK the election of a Labour government in 1997 revitalized interest in the role of evidence in the policy process. In setting out his modernizing agenda, the Prime Minister has frequently asserted that '*what matters is what works*', a theme developed in subsequent government publications.

The 1990s also saw reduced public confidence in public service professionals, partly because service users are themselves increasingly educated, informed and questioning (see Chapter 17). Moreover, clients are demanding more information about their service choices. The development of evidence-based practice is one way of addressing these concerns.

This chapter seeks to demonstrate that it is both desirable and practical to ground policy and practice in more reliable knowledge about social problems and what works in tackling them. This does not mean that we have simple faith in the achievement of progress by reason. However, it does suggest that effective governance of complex social systems requires opportunities for social and organizational learning, which in turn rely on systems for gathering and using evidence (Sanderson, 2002).

LEARNING OBJECTIVES

- To understand what counts as evidence for what purposes
- To understand how evidence can be used to improve public services
- To be aware of the obstacles to improved use of evidence
- To understand how evidence-based learning can be encouraged

WHAT COUNTS AS EVIDENCE FOR WHAT PURPOSES?

There are two main forms of evidence required to improve governmental effectiveness (Sanderson, 2002): evidence to facilitate *accountability* (information about the performance of government) and evidence to promote *improvement* (knowledge that enables the design and delivery of more effective policies and programmes). Chapter 10 has discussed the issue of accountability and the role of performance information in facilitating this. Here we consider the use of evidence for improvement purposes – referred to frequently as 'evidence-based policy and practice' (EBPP).

Discussion of EBPP has been focused predominantly on the question of 'what works' – what interventions or strategies should be used to meet specified policy goals and identified client needs (Davies *et al.*, 2000). However, policy and practice improvement entails a broader range of knowledge than this, including knowledge about the nature of social problems, how potentially effective interventions can be implemented, and who needs to be involved in this process. Furthermore, evidence is also required about the costs of action and the balance between those costs and the likely benefits.

Knowledge about some of these issues is often based more on tacit understandings than on evidence derived from systematic investigations. So, it is no surprise that the UK Cabinet Office works with a broad and eclectic definition of evidence:

> Expert knowledge; published research; existing statistics; stakeholder consultations; previous policy evaluations; the Internet; outcomes from consultations; costings of policy options; output from economic and statistical modelling. . . . There is a great deal of critical evidence held in the minds of both front-line staff . . . and those to whom policy is directed.
>
> (SPMT, 1999)

HOW CAN EVIDENCE BE USED TO IMPROVE PUBLIC POLICY AND PRACTICE?

In this section we consider how research and evaluation evidence can be used. We focus on four main uses of research:

1   to design and develop public policy;
2   to assess the impact of policy interventions;
3   to improve policy implementation;
4   to identify tomorrow's issues.

Using evidence right from the start: to design and develop public policy

Research has an important role to play at the start of the policy process. It can help to identify the issues to be addressed and whether there are interventions that are likely to be effective in tackling recognized problems.

The choice of a particular policy direction should be informed by existing evidence on what has been tried elsewhere and whether it has been demonstrated to deliver the desired benefits. Typically, this involves commissioning literature reviews and in recent years the techniques for undertaking such reviews have come under increased scrutiny (see Case Example 18.1).

Consultation exercises and market research are often used, alongside more formal research, to explore the views and priorities of key stakeholders and the public (as discussed in Chapter 15).

Research may also be used to understand more fully the context and challenges facing a proposed policy. At this stage a range of techniques may be used. These may assess the likelihood of alternative future scenarios (e.g. the 'Scenarios for Scotland' project), or they may focus on forecasting more specific impacts of a proposed policy, such as health and environmental impact assessments.

In recent years pilots have been used increasingly in the design and development of public services. A policy can be trialled with a small group of organizations to identify potential problems and refine the policy before wider implementation – this is sometimes referred to as 'prototyping' (Sanderson, 2002). Pilots are usually subject to some form of evaluation, often with the aim of distilling the learning from pilot sites to feed into the subsequent roll-out of the policy. Recent UK examples of policy development through evaluated pilots include Best Value (see Chapter 10) and the New Deal for Communities programme (see Chapter 15).

Finally, the design of policy implementation strategies requires consideration of how to bring about practitioner change. Evidence may be used to develop detailed guidance for practitioners, with a view to modify current practice, particularly by promoting quality and

CASE EXAMPLE 18.1 SYSTEMATIC REVIEWS OF THE EXISTING KNOWLEDGE BASE

A distinct feature of systematic reviews is that they are carried out to a set of pre-agreed standards. The main standards are as follows:

- Focusing on answering a specific question(s)
- Using protocols to guide the review process
- Seeking to identify as much of the relevant research as possible
- Appraising the quality of the research included in the review
- Synthesizing the research findings in the studies included
- Updating in order to remain relevant

The international *Cochrane Collaboration* prepares, maintains and disseminates the results of systematic reviews of research on the effects of healthcare. Building on the experience of Cochrane, the *Campbell Collaboration* has been established to carry out reviews of interventions in the fields of education, criminal justice and social work.

For more information, visit http://www.cochrane.org and http://campbell.collaboration.org

consistency in service delivery. For example, in the UK the National Treatment Agency has been established to review the evidence base relating to the effective treatment of drug misuse and produce summaries of this evidence base which feed into guidelines both for those commissioning services and those providing them.

Using evidence right to the end: evidence of effectiveness/impact

Existing knowledge about the effectiveness of many policy and practice interventions is partial at best (see also Chapter 10). Hence, while systematic reviews of the knowledge base may suggest promising policy directions, there is still a need to evaluate their impact in specific contexts, which in turn adds to the evidence base.

Evaluating evidence of effectiveness often involves the use of experimental methods, such as randomized controlled trials (RCTs). Although RCTs have been used mainly to measure the effectiveness of clinical interventions, they have also been applied in other areas including continuing education, quality assurance, and organizational and regulatory interventions. Within healthcare an established 'hierarchy of evidence' for assessing what works has evolved. This places randomized experiments (or, even better, systematic reviews of these) at the apex; observational studies and professional consensus are accorded much lower cred-ibility. In contrast to the hierarchical approach in healthcare, in other sectors such as education, criminal justice and social care there are major disputes as to what constitutes appropriate evidence of effectiveness.

Furthermore, divisions between qualitative and quantitative research paradigms run deep (Davies *et al.*, 2000). This happens in part because of the more diverse and eclectic social science underpinnings in these sectors (in comparison to the natural sciences underpinnings in much of healthcare), and in part because of the multiple and contested nature of the outcomes sought. Thus knowledge of 'what works' tends to be influenced greatly by the kinds of questions asked, and is in any case largely provisional and highly context depen-dent. This has led to calls for a realist approach to social policy evaluations (Pawson and Tilley, 1997), which begins with a theory of causal explanation and gives research the task of testing theories of how programme outcomes are generated by specific mechanisms and contexts. This involves making inter- and intra-programme comparisons in order to see which configurations of context–mechanism–outcome are efficacious. It also attempts to embody knowledge, held by the different stakeholders in the policy process, which has iden-tified what works for whom in what circumstances.

Using evidence throughout: improving policy implementation

Impact studies need to be complemented by research to explore progress towards goals, to assess the costs involved in the intervention, to understand the processes involved and from this to learn the lessons that will improve policy implementation. This calls for rigorous, ongoing monitoring and evaluation throughout the life of a policy or programme.

There is a long tradition of evaluating process and implementation issues, using a wide variety of research methods and approaches. For example, action research models involve practitioners in designing and carrying out research. One of the strengths of this approach is that the practitioner does not have to wait for a final research report, but is in a position to integrate learning into his or her work as it emerges.

Using evidence to break the mould: identifying tomorrow's issues

Alongside the increased emphasis on building an evidence base for policy and practice, there has been a plea that researchers continue to explore a wider set of ideas than those defined by the current policy agenda – 'blue skies' thinking, keeping sight of the 'bigger picture', looking more widely for ideas and problems, and challenging current thinking. The way in which pure research can help reframe current thinking is illustrated by the design of the auction of third generation mobile phone licences in the UK. Pioneering research on game theory at the Centre for Economic Learning and Social Evolution, at University College London, was used in 2000 to design a new style of auction for mobile phone licences, which raised £22 billion for the UK Treasury, much more than had originally been expected.

Because of their distance from policy and practice, academic researchers are in a good position to challenge current thinking. Research councils and independent organizations such as the Joseph Rowntree Foundation in the UK and the Rockefeller Foundation in the USA currently take a lead role in supporting and nurturing curiosity-driven research.

Overall, we can see that research and evaluation may be used for many different purposes, each requiring somewhat different evidence-gathering techniques and methodologies (see Table 18.1).

Table 18.1 Evidence uses and methods

Purposes	Methods and approaches might include:
Identify key issues	Review existing literature, surveys, group discussions, interviews
Understand the views of stakeholders	Interviews, group discussions, surveys
Explore contextual factors (including opportunities and costs)	Impact assessment, cost benefit analysis, interviews and discussion groups
Prepare guidance for those implementing a policy	Synthesizing the best available evidence, consulting key stakeholders, cost benefit analysis
Evaluate the effectiveness of a policy intervention Understand what works with whom and in what circumstances	Experimental and quasi-experimental studies, economic evaluations, realist evaluations, evaluations of pilots
Evaluate the processes involved Explore the issues involved in implementing the policy	Case studies, observations, documentary analysis, interviews, group discussions and surveys
Monitor progress	Management data, surveys and interviews
Generate new ideas and alternatives, highlight issues for future consideration	'Blue skies' research, syntheses of existing research, interviews, group discussions

WHAT ARE THE OBSTACLES TO THE IMPROVED UTILIZATION OF EVIDENCE?

Many have argued that it is self-evident that policy and practice benefits from being more rather than less informed by evidence (Hammersley, 2001). However, studies of utilization have frequently expressed concern about the apparent underuse of research (Weiss, 1998). How should this problem of *underuse* be tackled, where findings about effectiveness are either not applied, or are not applied successfully? Conversely, should we also be concerned about *overuse* of research, for example, the rapid spread of tentative findings, and about *misuse*, especially where evidence of effectiveness is ambiguous?

Walter *et al.* (2002), in a review of ways of increasing the impact of research, found evidence of a number of generic barriers to increased research use (see Box 18.1). The problem of underuse is frequently considered to stem from the fact that researchers and research users (policy makers and practitioners) occupy different worlds: they operate on different time-scales, use different languages, have different needs and respond to different incentive systems. This leads to a call for better dissemination strategies to bridge the gap between the two communities and enable research to be communicated effectively to policy makers and practitioners.

BOX 18.1 BARRIERS TO THE USE OF EVIDENCE

Barriers to researchers engaging in research impact activities:

- lack of resources – money and time
- lack of skills
- lack of professional credit for disseminating research.

Barriers to users' engagement with research:

- lack of time – to read journals, attend presentations or conduct their own research
- low priority in relation to internal and external pressures
- poor communication of research within organizations
- perceptions of research – for example, internally conducted or commissioned research is more likely to be seen as relevant and hence considered
- research is not timely or relevant to users' needs
- research is less likely to be used where findings are controversial or upset the status quo
- other sources of information may be valued more highly, particularly by policy makers
- individual resistance to research, especially when viewed as a threat to 'craft' skills and experience – which can have a wider effect if it occurs at management levels
- failure to value research at an organizational level, or an actively hostile organizational culture.

Source: Walter *et al.* (2002)

However, this conceptualization of the problem is in danger of overplaying the potential role of research evidence and underplaying the role of other forms of knowledge and experience in the development of policy and practice. Delafons (1995) suggests that potential sources for new policy ideas include: political parties, Ministers, Parliament, pressure groups, lobbyists, international bodies, academics and the research community. Ideas from each group will have a relationship (whether formal or informal) to existing research evidence, knowledge and/or experience. For example, a minister is likely to be influenced not only by formal research, but also by the views of constituents, the results of opinion polls, the party manifesto on which he or she was elected, his or her formal learning, and knowledge gained through both work and personal experience. As a consequence, one of the problems facing decision makers is the sheer volume of evidence available to them. As John Maynard Keynes famously concluded, 'there is nothing a government hates more than to be well informed; for it makes the process of arriving at decisions much more complicated and difficult' (Skidelsky, 1992: 630).

In addition to information overload, decision makers have to wrestle with political and organizational factors. They have to 'conciliate between all the interests and institutions of the society, and between the institutions represented in the policy-making process' (Perri 6 et al., 2002: 2). All stakeholders are likely to use evidence both strategically and politically – we can view this as part of their 'game-playing' (Perri 6, 2002). It should be stressed that while it is tempting to think of evidence entering the policy process as part of a rational decision-making process, reality is often far more messy and overtly political than this.

There are at least four ways in which evidence might influence policy (see Box 18.2) and the instrumental use of research is in fact quite rare. It is most likely where the research findings are non-controversial, require only limited change and will be implemented within a supportive environment: in other words, when they do not upset the status quo (Weiss, 1998).

In general, there is more cause for optimism about the use of evidence if research use is defined more broadly than its direct translation into changes in practice.

HOW CAN EVIDENCE-BASED LEARNING BE ENCOURAGED?

In the UK, although there is a prominent debate about the use of evidence in many policy areas (e.g. criminal justice, education, healthcare and social care), there are important differences both within and between sectors in the concept of EBPP being promoted (Davies et al., 2000).

Here we limit discussion to two of the dimensions that characterize EBPP: the *type of evidence* being used (evidence from research versus evidence from routine data); and the *focus of attention* (the individual practitioner versus the broader organization/system for service delivery). Together, these give four ways of conceptualizing EBPP (see Table 18.2).

- *The evidence-based problem solver* – here the emphasis is on the ways in which individuals use research evidence to make decisions and solve problems on a day-to-day, case-by-case basis. This is evidence-based medicine's view of what EBPP should entail.
- *The reflective practitioner* is one who uses observational data (including that arising from routine monitoring systems) to inform the way he or she learns from the past and makes adjustments for the future.

BOX 18.2 FOUR MAIN TYPES OF RESEARCH UTILIZATION

1 Instrumental use

Research feeds directly into decision making for policy and practice.

2 Conceptual use

Even if it seems impossible to use findings directly, research can provide new ways of thinking about a situation and offer insights into the strengths and weaknesses of particular courses of action. New conceptual understandings may then sometimes be used in instrumental ways.

3 Mobilization of support

Here, research becomes an instrument of persuasion. Findings — or simply the act of research — may be used as a political tool, to legitimate particular courses of action or inaction.

4 Wider influence

Research can have an influence beyond the institutions and events being studied. Research adds to the accumulation of knowledge which ultimately contributes to large-scale shifts in thinking, and sometimes action.

Source: Adapted from Weiss (1998)

- *System redesign* emphasizes the importance of using evidence to reshape total systems. This tends to mean a top-down, centrally driven concept of evidence-based practice — for example, the *What Works* initiative in probation.
- *System adjustment* refers to organizational or system-level use of monitoring data in the cybernetics mould, sometimes referred to as single-loop learning.

These are pure types and practice is likely to spill across these boxes. However, many of the existing strategies for promoting EBPP (particularly those which centre on issuing practice guidelines, backed up by audit and inspection regimes) would seem to focus on system adjustment (and occasionally system redesign). There is a danger that such an approach will inhibit rather than promote individual and organizational learning. The generation of new knowledge often relies on local invention and experimentation, which may be stifled by centralized control both of what counts as evidence and what practices are condoned. The concept of organizational learning suggests that an approach to EBPP which casts the practitioner as a problem solver (as in evidence-based medicine) may be better

Table 18.2 *Types of evidence-based practice*

	Evidence	
Focus	Research	Monitoring data
Individual	Problem solver	Reflective practitioner
Organization/system	System redesign	System adjustment

Source: Nutley *et al.* (2003, Figure 2)

suited to the development of learning organizations than the top-down implementation of detailed guidelines and protocols.

Building upon this line of thinking, in the field of education there has been a call to rethink research utilization in terms of 'knowledge transformation', which is described as a 'knowledge-led, problem-constrained learning process' (DesForges, 2000). It is argued that four conditions are necessary for such learning to take place:

1   A knowledge base.
2   A problem definition related to that knowledge base.
3   Transformation/learning strategies involving various modes of representing 'old' knowledge as well as the acquisition of 'new' knowledge.
4   Appropriate motivation.

The promoters of EBPP have to learn how to balance the continuing need for individual innovation and experimentation with system-level concerns about compliance and consistency of service. There are no easy solutions to this conundrum. However, a better understanding of how public service organizations manage knowledge and how they encourage individual and organizational learning is likely to lead to better long-term service improvement strategies (see Box 18.3).

SUMMARY

We have argued in this chapter that evidence may be used both to facilitate *accountability* and to promote *improvement* in policy making, programme development and service delivery. We have focused on the latter and have considered four main uses of research for policy and practice:

1   To design and develop public policy.
2   To assess the impact of policy interventions.
3   To improve policy implementation.
4   To identify tomorrow's issues.

Research has important insights to offer in each of these areas. Each requires different forms of evidence, which in turn employ different methods for gathering evidence. Thus

233

BOX 18.3 SOURCES OF INSIGHT INTO HOW TO ENCOURAGE EVIDENCE-BASED LEARNING

Knowledge management

Knowledge management is concerned with developing robust systems for storing and communicating knowledge. There are two main approaches to the management of knowledge: a codification strategy and a personalization approach (Hansen *et al.*, 1999). Codification strategies tend to be computer-centred; knowledge is carefully codified and stored in databases. In a personalization approach it is recognized that knowledge is tied closely to the person who develops it, and hence what is developed are enhanced opportunities for sharing knowledge through direct person-to-person contact. The role of information and communication technology within this is to help people communicate knowledge, not to store it.

Individual learning

Social psychology has long been concerned with understanding the process by which individuals learn. Behaviouralists have studied the effects of different stimuli in conditioning learning, while cognitive psychologists have sought to understand the learning processes which occur within the 'black box' between the stimulus and the response. Models of the process of learning include Kolb's learning cycle (Kolb, 1983), with its emphasis on promoting better understanding of different individual learning styles. Organizational psychologists have enhanced our understanding of the factors that help or hinder individual learning within organizations. Recent concerns have focused on how to promote lifelong learning and the benefits of self-directed and problem-based professional education regimes in achieving this.

Organizational learning

Organizational learning is concerned with the way organizations build and organize knowledge and routines, and use the broad skills of their workforce to improve organizational performance. Factors that seem to affect ongoing learning include: the importance of appropriate organizational structures, processes and cultures; the characteristics of individuals who bring new information into the organization; and the role of research and development departments. Analyses of the learning routines deployed by organizations have distinguished between adaptive and generative learning. Adaptive learning routines may be thought of as those mechanisms which help organizations to follow pre-set pathways. Generative learning, in contrast, involves forging new paths. Both sorts of learning are said to be essential for organizational fitness, but by far the most common are those associated with adaptive learning.

our conclusion is that we need to work with inclusive definitions of both evidence and research and to emphasize a 'horses for courses' approach, adapting our evidence-gathering approaches to specific policy and practice issues.

Research evidence must, of course, compete with other forms of knowledge and experience, and the passive dissemination of research evidence is unlikely to impact significantly on policy development or service delivery. Existing evidence on the effectiveness of evidence-based strategies suggests the critical need for better ongoing interaction between researchers and research users, in long-term partnerships, which span the entire research process, from the definition of the problem to the application of findings.

Overall, the emerging lesson is that there are many challenges facing the development of evidence-based policy and practice. There are many good reasons why policy makers and practitioners should rise to this challenge but evidence will and should remain just one of the influences which shape policy development and service delivery.

QUESTIONS FOR REVIEW AND DISCUSSION

1 Why is evidence a useful resource for policy makers?
2 What are the key features of systematic reviews and how might they be used to improve public services?
3 What are the main obstacles to evidence-based policy and practice?
4 How might the concept of organizational learning be used to inform thinking about how to change service delivery practice so that it is more evidence based?

READER EXERCISES

1 Read Chapters 11–14 of Davies *et al.* (2000) and write a short essay on whether some forms of evidence are more valid and reliable than others.
2 Identify a policy and practice initiative that has been labelled as being based on good evidence (such as 'Sure Start'). Search for information on this initiative (via websites and journal articles) and write a report which describes and appraises the use of evidence within the initiative.
3 Scan recent newspapers for a high-profile report of a research project. Consider how the research has been presented and how it might be used by different stakeholders (e.g. policy makers, researchers, journalists, professional bodies and other interest groups).

CLASS EXERCISES

1 You are a cross-government group of people brought together to take a fresh look at policy development in relation to smoking. You have been asked to consider how smoking should be framed as a policy problem. For example, it might be viewed as a health problem, a fiscal matter or as an environmental/ regulatory issue.

235

- If seen as a health problem, then the focus is likely to be on the relationship between smoking and ill-health.
- If viewed as a fiscal issue, then the focus might be on ensuring that tobacco taxes cover the social and health costs of smoking, or interest might lie in addressing issues such as smuggling and duty avoidance.
- If seen as an environmental/regulatory problem then the focus might be on passive smoking and the regulation of smoking at work and in public places.

Discuss in class what sorts of evidence you would need to help you determine the most appropriate ways of framing smoking as a policy problem.

2 You are a group of staff within a government education department with responsibility for primary school education policy. A recent review of the evidence on how to teach maths at primary-school level has concluded strongly that one particular approach is more effective than others. Discuss how you go about trying to change teaching practice so that it is in line with the recommended approach to maths teaching. Reflect upon your initial thoughts by considering how they fit with the ideas of knowledge management, individual learning and organizational learning.

FURTHER READING

Huw T.O. Davies, Sandra M. Nutley and Peter C. Smith (2000), *What works? Evidence-based policy and practice in public services.* University of Bristol, Bristol: The Policy Press.

Public Money and Management. Theme issue on 'Getting Research into Practice', Vol. 20, No. 4, pp. 3–50.

Further information and suggested reading is also available from two key websites:

1 *The ESRC UK Centre for Evidence Based Policy and Practice* (together with an associated network of university centres of excellence) is intended to foster the exchange of social science research between policy, researchers and practitioners. For more information visit http://www.evidencenetwork.org.

2 *The Strategy Unit* (part of the Cabinet Office) has been given the task of promoting practical strategies for evidence-based policy making. It supports a 'policy hub' website providing access to knowledge pools, training programmes and government departments' research programmes. For more information visit http://www.strategy.gov.uk.

References

Richard Allen and Daniel Tommasi (eds) (2001), *Managing public expenditures: a reference book for transition countries*. Paris: OECD.

Graham T. Allison (1997), 'Public and private management: are they fundamentally alike in all unimportant respects?', in Jay M. Shafritz and Albert C. Hyde (eds), *Classics of public administration* (4th edn). Belmont, CA: Wadsworth, pp. 457–475.

Alan Andreason and Philip Kotler (2002), *Strategic marketing for nonprofit organizations*, (6th edn). Upper Saddle River, NJ: Prentice Hall.

Sherry Arnstein (1971), 'The ladder of citizen participation', *Journal of the Royal Town Planning Institute*, Vol. 57, No. 1, pp. 176–182.

Paul Atkinson and Paul van den Noord (2001), 'Managing public expenditure', *OECD Economics Working Paper No 285*. Paris: OECD.

Audit Commission (2000), *Aiming to improve: the principles of performance measurement*. London: Audit Commission.

Audit Commission (2002a), *Quality of life: using quality of life indicators*. London: Audit Commission.

Audit Commission (2002b), *The corporate performance assessment*. Consultation draft. London: Audit Commission.

Audit Commission (2002c), *Equality and diversity*. London: The Audit Commission.

Gerhard Banner (2002), 'Zehn Jahre kommunale Verwaltungsmodernisierung – was wurde erreicht und was kommt danach?', in Erik Meurer and Günther Stephan (eds), *Rechnungswesen und Controlling* (Vol. 4). Freiburg: Haufe Verlag, pp. 7/313–7/342.

Chester I. Barnard (1968, originally 1938), *The functions of the executive*. Cambridge, MA: Harvard University Press.

Marian Barnes, Steve Harrison, Maggie Mort, Polly Shardflow and Gerald Wistow (1999). 'The new management of community care: user groups, citizenship and co-production', in Gerry Stoker (ed.), *The new managemenr of British local governance*. Houndmills: Macmillan.

Michael Barzelay (2001), *The new public management: improving research and policy dialogue*. Berkeley: University of California Press.

Francis M. Bator (1960), *The question of government spending: public needs and private wants*. New York: Harper.

Robert D. Behn (2001), *Rethinking democratic accountability*. Washington, DC: The Brookings Institutions.

Christine Bellamy and John A. Taylor (1998), *Governing in the information age*. Milton Keynes: Open University Press.

Carolyn Bennett, Donald G. Lenihan, John Williams and William Young (2001), *Measuring quality of life: the use of societal outcome by parliamentarians*. Office of the Auditor General of Canada.

David Billis and Howard Glennester (1998), 'Human services and the voluntary sector: towards a theory of comparative advantage', *Journal of Social Policy*, Vol. 27, No. 1, pp 79–98.

Peter Bogason (2000), *Public policy and local governance: institutions in postmodern society*. Cheltenham: Edward Elgar.

Geert Bouckaert (1992), 'Productivity analysis in the public sector: the case of fire service', *International Review of Administrative Sciences*, Vol. 58, No. 2, pp. 175–200.

Geert Bouckaert (1995a), 'The history of the productivity movement', in Arie Halachmi and Marc Holzer (eds), *Competent government: theory and practice. The best of Public Productivity Review, 1985–1993*. Burke, VA: Chatelaine Press, pp. 361–398.

Geert Bouckaert (1995b), 'Improving performance measurement', in Arie Halachmi and Geert Bouckaert (eds), *The enduring challenges of public administration*. San Francisco, CA: Jossey-Bass, pp. 379–412.

Geert Bouckaert (1995c), 'Measuring quality', in Christopher Pollitt and Geert Bouckaert (eds), *Quality improvement in European public services. concepts, cases and commentary*. London: Sage, pp. 20–28.

Geert Bouckaert, Tom Auwers, Wouter Van Reeth and Koen Verhoest (1997), *Handboek Doelmatigheidsanalyse: prestaties begroten*. Brussel: Ministerie van de Vlaamse Gemeenschap.

Tony Bovaird (1996), 'Performance assessment of service quality: lessons from UK national Initiatives to influence local government', in Hermann Hill, Helmut Klages and Elke Löffler (eds), *Quality, innovation and measurement in the public sector*. Frankfurt am Main: Peter Lang Verlag, pp. 37–64.

Tony Bovaird (2002), 'Public administration: emerging trends and potential future directions', in Eran Vigoda (ed.), *Public administration: an interdisciplinary critical analysis*. New York: Marcel Dekker, pp. 345–376.

Tony Bovaird and Lucy Gaster (2002), *Civil service reform: evaluation case study* for Cabinet Office (unpublished).

Tony Bovaird and Arie Halachmi (1999), 'Community scorecards: the role of stakeholders in performance assessment', in Arie Halachmi (ed.), *Performance and quality measurement in government: issues and experiences*. Burke, VA: Chatelaine Press, pp. 145–155.

Tony Bovaird and Elke Löffler (2002), 'Moving from excellence models of local service delivery to benchmarking of "good local governance"', *International Review of Administrative Sciences*, Vol. 67, No. 1, pp. 9–24.

Tony Bovaird and Mike Owen (2002), 'Achieving citizen-led area regeneration through multiple stakeholders in the Beacon Housing Estate, Cornwall', in Tony Bovaird, Elke Löffler and Salvador Parrado Díez (eds), *Developing Local Governance Networks in Europe*. Baden-Baden: Nomos Verlag, pp. 57–73.

Tony Bovaird, Elke Löffler and Jeremy Martin (2003), 'From corporate governance to local governance: stakeholder-driven community score-cards for UK local agencies?', *International Journal of Public Administration*, Vol. 26, Nos 8/9, pp. 1–24.

Christopher Bovis (1997), 'The European public procurement rules and their interplay with international trade', *Journal of World Trade*, Vol. 31, No. 3, pp. 63–91.

George Boyne (1997), 'Comparing the performance of local authorities: an evaluation of the Audit Commission indicators', *Local Government Studies*, Vol. 23, No. 4, pp. 17–43.

Stratford C. Bromley and N. Rao (2000), *Revisiting public perceptions of local government.* London: DETR.

Michael Broussine and Pamela Fox (2002), 'Rethinking leadership in local government – the place of "feminine" styles in the modernised council', *Local Government Studies*, Vol. 28, No. 4, pp. 87–102.

Charles V. Brown and Peter M. Jackson (1990), *Public sector economics*, (4th edn). Oxford: Blackwell.

James M. Buchanan and Richard A. Musgrave (1999), *Public finance and public choice: two contrasting visions of the state.* Cambridge: The MIT Press.

Bernard Burnes (2000), *Managing change – a strategic approach to organizational dynamics.* Harlow: Pearson Education.

Sir Ian Byatt (2001), *Delivering Better Services for Citizens.* London: DTLR/LGA.

Cabinet Office (1999), *Report to the Prime Minister from Sir Richard Wilson, Head of Home Civil Service.* London: Cabinet Office.

Cabinet Office (2000), *Successful IT: modernising government in action.* (The McCartney Report). London: Cabinet Office.

Cabinet Office (2001), *Strengthening leadership in the public sector: a research study by the Performance and Innovation Unit.* London: The Cabinet Office.

CCMD (1998), *Citizen/client surveys: dispelling myths and redrawing maps.* Ottawa: Canadian Centre for Management Development.

Central IT Unit (2000), *E-government: a strategic framework for public services in the information age.* London: Cabinet Office, Central IT Unit.

James L. Chan (1981), 'Standards and issues in governmental accounting and financial reporting', *Public Budgeting & Finance*, Vol. 1, No. 1 (spring), pp. 55–65.

Chancellor of the Exchequer (1991), *Competing for quality: buying better public services.* London: HMSO.

Alfred Chandler (1962), *Strategy and structure.* Cambridge, MA: The MIT Press.

Martin Christopher, Adrian Payne and David Ballantyne (1991), *Relationship marketing: bringing quality, customer service and marketing together.* Oxford: Butterworth Heinemann.

John Clarke and Janet Newman (1997), *The managerial state: power, politics and ideology in the remaking of social welfare.* London: Sage.

John Clarke, Sharon Gewirtz, Gordon Hughes and Jill Humphrey (2000), 'Guarding the public interest: auditing public services', in John Clarke, Sharon Gewirtz and Eugene McLaughlin (eds), *New managerialism, new welfare?* London: Sage/Open University.

Elizabeth Coffey, Clare Huffington and Peninah Thomson (1999), *The changing culture of leadership – women leaders' voices.* London: The Change Partnership Ltd.

Commission of the European Communities (2001), *White Paper on European Governance.* Brussels: European Commission (http://europa.eu.int/comm/governance/white_paper/index_en.htm, as of 24 February 2003).

Committee on the Financial Aspects of Corporate Governance (1992), *Report of the committee on financial aspects of corporate governance.* London: Gee.

Committee on Standards in Public Life (1995), *First report,* Vol. 1. Cm 2850–1. London: HMSO.

Anna Coote (ed.) (2002), *Claiming the Health Dividend.* London: King's Fund.

Anna Coote and Jo Lenaghan (1997), *Citizen's juries: theory into practice.* London: IPPR.

Tony Cutler and Barbara Waine (1997), *Managing the welfare state.* Oxford: Berg.

Thomas H. Davenport (1993), *Process innovation: re-engineering work through information technology.* Boston, MA: Harvard Business School Press.

Thomas H. Davenport and Laurence Prusak (1998), *Working knowledge: how organizations manage what they know.* Boston, MA: Harvard Business School Press.

Huw T.O. Davies, Sandra M. Nutley and Peter C. Smith (2000), *What works? Evidence-based policy and practice in public services.* Bristol: The Policy Press.

Howard Davis and Bruce Walker (1997), 'Trust based relationships in local government contracting', *Public Money and Management,* Vol. 17, No. 4, pp. 47–54.

Howard Davis and Bruce Walker (1998), 'Trust and competition: blue collar services in local government', in Andrew Coulson (ed.), *Trust and contracts: relationships in local government, health and public services.* Bristol: The Policy Press, pp. 159–182.

Nicholas Deakin and Kieron Walsh (1996), 'The enabling state: the role of markets and contracts', *Public Administration,* Vol. 74, No. 1, pp. 33–48.

John Delafons (1995), 'Planning research and the policy process', *Town Planning Review,* Vol. 66, No. 1, pp. 41–59.

Department of the Taoiseach (2002), *Evaluation of the progress of the strategic management initiative/delivering better government modernisation programme.* Report prepared by PA Consulting (http://www.taoiseach.gov.ie/viewitem.asp?id=1150&lang=ENG, as of 24 February 2003).

Charles DesForges (2000), *Putting educational research to use through knowledge transformation.* Keynote lecture to the Further Education Research Network Conference. Coventry: Learning and Skills Development Agency.

DETR (1998a), *Modern local government: in touch with the people.* London: Department of Environment, Transport and the Regions.

DETR (1998b), *Modernising local government: local democracy and local leadership.* London: The Stationery Office.

DETR (1998c), *Modernising local government: improving services through Best Value.* London: The Stationery Office.

DETR (1998d), *Modernising local government: a new ethical framework.* Consultation paper. London: DETR.

DETR (1999a), *Local Government Act 1999: Part I. Best Value.* (Circular 10/99). London: Department of Environment, Transport and the Regions.

DETR (1999b), *Local leadership, local choice.* Cm 4298. London: Stationery Office.

DETR (2001a), *Allegations of misconduct in English local authorities.* London: DETR.

DTLR (2001b), *Strong local leadership – quality public services,* Cm. 5237. London: The Stationery Office.

Simon Domberger and Paul Jensen (1997), 'Contracting out by the public sector: theory, evidence and prospects', *Oxford Review of Economic Policy,* Vol. 13, No. 4, pp. 67–79.

John D. Donahue (1989), *The privatisation decision: public ends, private means*. New York: Basic Books.

Patrick Dunleavy (1991), *Democracy, bureaucracy and public choice*. London: Harvester Wheatsheaf.

Patrick Dunleavy (1994), 'The globalization of public services production: can government be "best in world"?', *Public Policy and Administration*, Vol. 9, No. 2, pp. 36–64.

Patrick Dunleavy and Helen Margetts (2002), *Government on the web 2*. London: National Audit Office.

Tom Entwistle, Steve Martin and Gareth Enticott (2002), *Making or buying? The value of internal service providers in local government*. Cardiff University: Local and Regional Government Research Unit, for the Public Services Network.

Andrew Erridge (2000), *UK central government civil procurement: summary report*. (ESRC personal research grant, No. 00237023.) Unpublished.

Andrew Erridge and Jonathan Greer (2002), 'Partnerships and public procurement: building social capital through supply relations', *Public Administration*, Vol. 80, No. 3, pp. 503–522.

J.M. Fernandez Martin (1996), *The EC public procurement rules: a critical analysis*. Oxford: Clarendon Press.

Norman Flynn (2000), 'Managerialism and public services: some international trends', in John Clarke, Sharon Gewirtz and Eugene McLaughlin (eds), *New managerialism, new welfare?* London: Sage/Open University.

Norman Flynn and Franz Strehl (1996), *Public sector management in Europe*. London: Prentice Hall Harvester Wheatsheaf.

Jonathan Freedland (1998), 'Britain's problem with corruption'. *Guardian*, 4 February.

Thomas Friedmann (2000), *The lexus and the olive tree: understanding globalisation*. London: HarperCollins.

Yiannis Gabriel (1999), *Organizations in depth*. London: Sage.

John Kenneth Galbraith (1958), *The affluent society*. Boston, MA: Houghton Mifflin.

Lucy Gaster (1995), *Quality in public services: manager's choices*. Buckingham, UK: Open University Press.

Lucy Gaster and Amanda Squires (2003), *Providing quality in the public sector: a practical approach to improving public services*. Buckingham: Open University Press.

Eleanor Glor (2001), 'Codes of conduct and generations of public servants', *International Review of Administrative Sciences*, Vol. 67, No. 3, pp. 524–541.

Sue Goss (2001), *Making local governance work: networks, relationships and the management of change*. Houndmills: Palgrave.

Barry N. Hague and Brian Loader (1999), *Digital democracy*. London: Routledge.

Declan Hall and J. Stewart (1997), *Citizen's juries in local government*. London: LGMB.

Gary Hamel and C.K. Prahalad (1994), *Competing for the future*. Boston, MA: Harvard Business School Press.

Martyn Hammersley (2001), 'On "systematic" reviews of research literatures: a "narrative" response to Evans and Benefield', *British Educational Research Journal*, Vol. 27, No. 5, pp. 543–554.

Charles Handy (1993), *Understanding organisations*, (4th edn). Harmondsworth: Penguin.

Morton T. Hansen, Nitin Nohria and Thomas Tierney (1999), 'What's your strategy for managing knowledge?', *Harvard Business Review*, Vol. 77 (March–April), pp. 106–116.

Jenny Harrow (2002), 'The new public management and social justice: just efficiency or equity as well?', in Kate McLaughlin, Stephen P. Osborne and Ewan Ferlie (eds), *New public management: current trends and future prospects*. London: Routledge, pp. 141–159.

Jean Hartley and Maria Allison (2000), 'The role of leadership in the modernization and improvement of public services', *Public Money & Management*, Vol. 20, No. 2, pp. 35–40.

Harry P. Hatry (1999), *Performance measurement: getting results*. Washington, DC: the Urban Institute Press.

HMSO (1991), *The citizen's charter*, Cm 1599. London: HMSO.

HM Treasury (1988), *Public purchasing policy: consolidated guidelines*. London: HM Treasury.

HM Treasury (1995), *Setting new standards: a strategy for government procurement*, Cm 2840. London: HMSO.

HM Treasury (1998), *Comprehensive spending review on efficiency in civil government procurement expenditure*. London: HMSO.

HM Treasury (2000a), *Government accounting 2000: a guide on accounting and financial procedures for use of government departments*. London: HM Treasury.

HM Treasury (2000b), *Improving police performance: a new approach to measuring police efficiency*. Public Services Productivity Panel Report No. 4. London: HM Treasury.

Home Office (2002), *Entitlement cards and identity fraud*. A consultation paper. London: Home Office.

Christopher Hood (1991), 'A public management for all seasons?', *Public Administration*, Vol. 69, No. 1, pp. 3–19.

Christopher Hood, Colin Scott, George Jones, Oliver James, and Tony Travers (1998), *Regulation inside government: waste-watchers, quality police and sleaze busters*. Oxford: Oxford University Press.

Melissa Horner (1997), 'Leadership theory: past, present and future', *Team Performance Management*, Vol. 3, Issue 4, pp. 270–287.

Gordon Hughes, R. Mears and C. Winch (1996), 'An inspector calls? Regulation and accountability in three public services', *Policy and Politics*, Vol. 25, No. 3, pp. 299–313.

Catherine Itzin and Janet Newman (eds) (1995), *Gender and organisational culture: linking theory and practice*. London: Routledge.

Peter M. Jackson (2001), 'Public sector added value: can bureaucracy deliver?', *Public Administration*, Vol. 79, No. 1, pp 5–28.

Peter M. Jackson and L. Stainsby (2000), 'Managing public sector networked organisations', *Public Money and Management*, Vol. 20, No.1, pp. 11–16.

Peter Joha (2001), *Local governance in western Europe*. London: Sage.

Gerry Johnson and Kevan Scholes (2001), *Exploring public sector strategy*. Harlow, Essex: Financial Times/Prentice Hall.

Gerry Johnson and Kevan Scholes (2002), *Exploring corporate strategy: text and cases*. Upper Saddle River, NJ: FT/Prentice Hall (Higher Ed.).

George Jones (1998), 'The leadership of organizations', *RSA Journal*, Vol. 3, No. 4, pp. 81–83.

Paul Joyce (1999), *Strategic management for the public services.* Buckingham: Open University Press.

Robert S Kaplan and David P. Norton (1996), *The balanced scorecard: translating strategy into action.* Boston, MA: Harvard Business School Press.

Walter J.M. Kickert and Joop F.M. Koopenjan (1997), 'Public management and network management: an overview', in Walter J. M. Kickert, Erick-Hans Klijn and Joop F. M. Koopenjan (eds), *Managing complex networks: strategies for the public sector.* London: Sage, pp. 35–61.

Walter J.M. Kickert, Erick-Hans Klijn and Joop F.M. Koopenjan (eds) (1997), *Managing complex networks: strategies for the public sector.* London: Sage.

Ian Kirkpatrick and Miguel Martinez-Lucio, M. (eds) (1995), *The politics of quality in the public sector.* London: Routledge.

Erik-Hans Klijn and G. R. Teisman (1997), 'Strategies and games in networks', in Walter J.M. Kickert, Erick-Hans Klijn and Joop F.M. Koopenjan (eds), *Managing complex networks: strategies for the public sector.* London: Sage, pp. 98–118.

Robert Klitgaard, Ronald MacLean-Abaroa and H. Lindsey Parris (2000), *Corrupt cities – a practical guide to cure and prevention.* Institute for Contemporary Studies, Oakland, CA: ICS Press.

Jan Kooiman (ed.), (1993), *Modern governance: new government – society interactions.* London: Sage.

Jan Kooiman (2003), *Governing as governance.* London: Sage.

David A. Kolb (1983), *Experiential learning.* New York: Prentice Hall.

John P. Kotter and James L. Heskett (1992), *Corporate culture and performance.* New York: Free Press.

Julian Le Grand (1982), *The strategy of equality: redistribution and the social services.* London: Allen & Unwin.

Gail Lewis (2000a), 'Introduction: expanding the social policy imaginary' in Gail Lewis, Sharon Gerwirtz and John Clarke (eds), *Rethinking social policy.* London: Open University in association with Sage Publications.

Gail Lewis (2000b), *Race, gender, social welfare: encounters in a postcolonial society.* Cambridge: Polity Press.

Local Government Association (1998), *Democratic practice: a guide.* London: LGA.

Elke Löffler (2001), 'Quality awards as a public sector benchmarking concept in OECD countries: some guidelines for quality award organisers', *Public Administration and Development*, Vol. 21, No. 1, pp. 25–47.

Vivien Lowdnes, Gerry Stoker, Lawrence Pratchett, David Wilson, Steve Leach and M. Wingfield (1998), *Enhancing public participation in local government.* London: DETR.

James J. Lynch (1992), *The psychology of customer care.* London: Macmillan.

David Lyon (1994), *The electronic eye: the rise of the surveillance society.* Cambridge: Polity Press.

Sir William Macpherson (1999), *The Stephen Lawrence enquiry.* London: The Stationery Office.

243

Shirley McIver (1997), *An evaluation of the King's Fund citizen's juries programme*. Birmingham: Health Services Management Centre.

David McKevitt (1998), *Managing core public services*. Oxford: Blackwell.

Michael Margolis and David Resnick (2000), *Politics as usual: the cybserspace 'revolution'*. Thousand Oaks, CA: Sage.

Brendan Martin (1993), *In the public interest? Privatisation and public sector reform*. London: Zed Books.

Steve J. Martin and Annette Boaz (2000), 'Public participation and citizen-centred local government', *Public Money and Management*, Vol. 20, No. 2, pp. 47–54.

Steve Martin, Howard Davis, Tony Bovaird, James Downe, Mike Geddes, Jean Hartley, Mike Lewis, Ian Sanderson and Phil Sapwell (2001), *Improving local public services: final evaluation of the Best Value pilot programme*. London: Stationery Office.

A. Mendelow (1991), *Proceedings of the second international conference on information systems*. Cambridge, MA.

J. Meyer and B. Rowan (1991),'Institutional organizations: formal structure as myth and ceremony', in Walter Powell and Paul J. DiMaggio (eds), *The new institutionalism in organizational analysis*. Chicago, IL: University of Chicago Press, pp. 41–62.

John L. Mikesell (1995), *Fiscal administration*. Belmont, CA: Wadsworth.

Ministers of State Services and Finance (2002), *Report of the advisory group on the review of the centre* (http://www.ssc.govt.nz/roc, as of 24 February 2003).

Henry Mintzberg (1987), 'The strategy concept 1: five Ps for strategy', *California Management Review*, Vol. 30, No. 1, pp. 11–24.

Henry Mintzberg (1992), 'Mintzberg on the rise and fall of strategic planning', *Long Range Planning*, Vol. 25, No. 4, pp. 99–104.

Elaine Morley, Scott P. Bryant and Harry P. Hatry (2001), *Comparative performance measurement*. Washington, DC: Urban Institute Press.

Frederick C. Mosher (1968), *Democracy and the public service*. New York: Oxford University Press.

Richard A. Musgrave (1959), *The theory of public finance*. New York: McGraw-Hill.

Richard A. Musgrave (1998), 'The role of the state in fiscal theory', in Peter Birch Sorensen (ed.), *Public finance in a changing world*. London: Macmillan Press, pp. 35–50.

Janet Newman (2001a), *Modernising governance: New Labour, policy and society*. London: Sage.

Janet Newman (2001b), 'What counts is what works'? Constructing evaluations of market mechanisms', *Public Administration*, Vol. 79, No. 1, pp. 89–103.

Janet Newman (2002a), 'Managerialism, modernisation and marginalisation: equal opportunities and institutional change', in Esther Breitenbach, Alice Brown, Fiona Mackay and Janette Webbs (eds), *The changing politics of gender equality in Britain*. Basingstoke: Macmillan, pp. 102–123.

Janet Newman (2002b), 'Changing governance, changing equality? New Labour, modernisation and public services', *Public Money and Management*, Vol. 22, No. 1, pp. 7–13.

Janet Newman (2003), 'New Labour and the politics of diversity', in J. Barry, M. Dent and M. O'Neill (eds), *Gender and the public sector: professions and managerial change*. London: Routledge, pp. 15–26.

NHS Executive (2000), *The vital connection: an equalities framework for the NHS*. London: The Stationery Office. (www.doh.gov.uk/nhsequality/nhsequalitiesframework.htm, as of 24 February 2003).

Sandra M. Nutley, I. Walter and Davies, Huw T.O. (2003), 'From knowing to doing: a framework for understanding the evidence-into-practice agenda', *Evaluation*, 9(2), forthcoming.

ODPM (2002), *Connecting with communities: improving communications in local government*. London: Office of the Deputy Prime Minister.

OECD (1993), *Public management developments: survey*. Paris: OECD.

OECD (1997), *In search for results: performance management practices*. Paris: OECD.

OECD (1999), *Public sector corruption: an international survey of prevention measures*. Paris: OECD.

OECD (2001a), *Engaging citizens in policy-making: information, consultation and public participation*, PUMA Policy Briefing No. 10. Paris: OECD.

OECD (2001b), *Public sector leadership for the 21st century*. Paris: OECD.

OECD (2002a), *Distributed public governance: agencies, authorities and other autonomous bodies*. Paris: OECD.

OECD (2002b), 'Overview of results-focused management and budgeting in OECD member countries', (http://www.olis.oecd.org/olis/2002doc.nsf/LinkTo/PUMA-SBO(2002)1, as of 24 February 2003).

Office of the E-Envoy (2000), *UK online action plan*. London: Cabinet Office.

OGC/Office of the E-Envoy (2002), *In the service of democracy. A consultation paper on a policy for electronic democracy*. London: Office of Government Commerce/Office of the E-Envoy.

Olov Olson, James Guthrie and Christopher Humphrey (1998), *Global warning: debating international developments in new public financial management*. Oslo: Cappelen Akademisk Forlag.

David Osborne and Ted Gaebler (1992), *Reinventing government. How the entrepreneurial spirit is transforming the public sector*. Reading, MA: Addison-Wesley.

Vance Packard (1957), *The hidden persuaders*. New York: D. McKay.

Ray Pawson and Nick Tilley (1997), *Realistic evaluation*. London: Sage.

Janie Percy-Smith (ed.) (2000), *Policy responses to social exclusion: towards inclusion?* Maidenhead: Open University Press.

Perri 6 (2002), 'Can policy be evidence based?', *MCC: Building Knowledge for Integrated Care*, Vol. 10, No. 1, pp. 3–8.

Perri 6, Diana Leet, Kimberley Seltzer and Gerry Stoker (2002), *Towards holistic governance: the new reform agenda*. Basingstoke: Palgrave.

Murray Petrie and David Webber (1999), 'Review of evidence on broad outcome of public sector management regime', *New Zealand Treasury Working Paper* 01/06.

Jon Pierre and B. Guy Peters (2000), *Governance, politics and the state*. New York: St Martin's Press.

PIU (2002), *Data sharing and privacy: the way forward for public services*. London: Cabinet Office (Performance and Innovation Unit).

Christopher Pollitt (1988), 'Bringing consumers into performance measurement: concepts, consequences and constraints', *Policy and Politics*, Vol. 16, No. 2, pp. 77–87.

245

Christopher Pollitt (1995), 'Justification by works or by faith? Evaluating the new public management', *Evaluation*, Vol. 1, No. 2, pp. 133–154.

Christopher Pollitt and Geert Bouckaert (eds) (1995), *Quality improvement in European public services: concepts, cases and commentary*. London: Sage.

Christopher Pollitt and Geert Bouckaert (2000), *Public management reform: a comparative analysis*. Oxford: Oxford University Press.

Christopher Pollitt, Xavier Girre, Jeremy Lonsdale, Robert Mul, Hilkka Summa and Marit Waerness (1999), *Performance or compliance? Performance audit and public management in five countries*. Oxford: Oxford University Press.

Michael Porter (1980), *Competitive strategy*. New York: Free Press.

Michael Power (1993) *The audit explosion*. London: Demos.

Michael Power (1997), *The audit society*. Oxford: Oxford University Press.

Pushkala Prasad, Albert J. Mills, Michael Elmes and Anshuman Prasad (eds) (1997), *Managing the organizational melting pot: dilemmas of workplace diversity*. London: Sage.

Lawrence Pratchett (2002), *The implementation of electronic voting in the UK*. London: Local Government Association.

Prime Minister and the Minister for the Cabinet Office (1999), *Modernising government*, Cm 413. London: The Stationery Office.

Robert Putnam (2001), *Bowling alone: the collapse and revival of American Community*. New York: Touchstone.

PUMA (2001) *Management of large public IT projects: case studies*. Paris: OECD Public Management Committee.

Aodh Quinlivan (2002), 'Community empowerment in Irish local government – strategic planning in Blarney', in Tony Bovaird, Elke Löffler and Salvador Parrado Díez (eds), *Developing local governance networks in Europe*. Baden-Baden: Nomos Verlag, pp. 107–122.

Charles Raab (2001), 'Electronic service delivery in the UK: proaction and privacy protection', in J.E.J. Prins (ed.), *Designing e-government: on the crossroads of technological innovation and institutional change*. The Hague: Kluwer International, pp. 41–62.

Stuart Ranson and John Stewart (1989), *Management for the public domain: enabling the learning society*. Basingstoke: Macmillan.

Christoph Reichard (1998), 'Ethics and accountability in the context of governance and new public management', in Annie Hondeghem (ed.), *EGPA Yearbook 1997*. Amsterdam: IOS Press, pp. 124–137.

Ortwin Renn, Thomas Webler and Peter Wiedemann (1995), *Fairness and competence in citizen participation*. Dordrecht: Kluwer Academic.

Rod Rhodes (1997), *Understanding governance: policy networks, governance, reflexivity and accountability*. Buckingham: Open University Press.

Stephen P. Robbins (1987), *Organization theory: concepts, controversies and applications*. Englewood Cliffs, NJ: Prentice-Hall.

Lester M. Salamon (2002), *The tools of government*. Oxford: Oxford University Press.

Ian Sanderson (2002), 'Evaluation, policy learning and evidence-based policy making', *Public Administration*, Vol. 80, No. 1, pp. 1–22.

Adrian Sargeant (1999), *Marketing management for nonprofit organizations.* Oxford: Oxford University Press.

Fritz W. Scharpf (1978), 'Interorganizational policy studies: issues, concepts and perspectives', in K.I. Hanf and Fritz W. Scharpf (eds), *Interorganizational policy making: limits to coordination and central control.* London: Sage, pp. 345–370.

Allen Schick (1996), *The spirit of reform: managing the New Zealand state sector in a time of change.* Report prepared for the State Services Commission and the Treasury, Wellington.

Allen Schick (1997), *Modern budgeting.* Paris: OECD.

Allen Schick (1998), 'Why most developing countries should not try New Zealand's reforms', *The World Bank Research Observer,* Vol. 13, No. 1, pp. 123–131.

Michael Scott Morton (ed.) (1991), *The corporation of the 90s: information technology and organizational transformation.* Oxford: Oxford University Press.

Willie Seal and Peter Vincent-Jones (1997), 'Accounting and trust in the enabling of long-term relations', *Accounting, Auditing and Accountability Journal,* Vol. 10, No. 3, pp. 406–431.

Peter Self (1993), *Government by the market?* London: Macmillan.

Peter M. Senge (1998), *The fifth discipline: the art and practice of the learning organization.* London: Century Business.

Rod Sheaff (1991), *Marketing for health services.* Buckingham: Open University Press.

Rod Scheaff (2002), *Responsive healthcare: marketing for a public service.* Buckingham: Open University Press.

Herbert A. Simon (1945), *Administrative behavior.* New York: The Free Press.

Robert Skidelsky (1992), *John Maynard Keynes: a biography. Vol 2: The economist as saviour, 1920–1937.* London: Macmillan.

Standards Board for England website (www.standardsboard.co.uk, as of 24 February 2003).

Gerry Stoker (1999), 'Introduction: the unintended costs and benefits of new management reform for British local government', in G. Stoker (ed.), *The new management of British local governance.* Houndmills: Macmillan.

Strategic Policy Making Team (SPMT) (1999), *Professional policy making for the twenty first century.* London: Cabinet Office (http://www.cabinet-office.gov.uk/moderngov/policy/index.htm, as of 24 February 2003).

Vito Tanzi and Ludger Schuknecht (2000), *Public spending in the 20th century.* Cambridge: Cambridge University Press.

Melissa A. Thomas (2001), 'Getting debt relief right', *Foreign Affairs,* Vol. 80, No. 5, pp. 36–45.

Gordon Tullock (1967), 'The welfare costs of tariffs, monopolies and theft', *Western Economic Journal* (June), pp. 224–232.

Peter B. Vaill (1999), *Spirited leading and learning: process wisdom for a new age.* Englewood Cliffs, NJ: Prentice-Hall.

Eran Vigoda (2002), *Public administration: an interdisciplinary critical analysis.* New York: Marcel Dekker.

Kieron Walsh (1991a), *Competitive tendering of local authority services: initial experience.* London: Department of the Environment.

Kieron Walsh (1991b), 'Quality and public services', *Public Administration,* Vol. 69, No. 4, pp. 503–514.

Kieron Walsh (1995), *Marketing in local government*. London: Financial Times Prentice Hall.

I. Walter, Sandra M. Nutley and Huw T.O. Davies (2003), *Models of research impact: a cross sector literature review*. Report for the Learning and Skills Development Agency. Research Unit for Research Utilization, University of St Andrews (http://www.st-and.ac.uk/~ruru, as of 24 February 2003).

Karl Weick (1979), *The social psychology of organizing*. Reading, MA: Addison-Wesley.

Carol H. Weiss (1998), 'Have we learned anything new about the use of evaluation?', *American Journal of Evaluation,* Vol. 19, No. 1, pp. 21–33.

O.E. Williamson and W.G. Ouchi (1983), 'The markets and hierarchies programme of research: origins, implications, prospects', in A. Francis *et al.* (eds), *Power, efficiency and institutions.* London: Heinemann.

Michael Woolcock (1998), 'Social capital and economic development: toward a theoretical synthesis and policy framework', *Theory and Society*, Vol. 27, No. 2, pp. 151–208.

World Bank (1989), *Sub-Sahara Africa: from crisis to sustainable growth. A long-term perspective study.* Washington, DC: World Bank.

Iris M. Young (1990), *Justice and the politics of difference.* Princeton, NJ: Princeton University Press.

Gary A. Yukl (2002), *Leadership in organizations.* Englewood Cliffs, NJ: Prentice-Hall.

Valarie A. Zeithaml, A. Parasuraman and Leonard L. Berry (1990), *Delivering service quality: balancing customer perceptions and expectations.* New York: The Free Press.

Index